AUTOMATIC
WEALTH

AUTOMATIC WEALTH

The Six Steps to
Financial Independence

MICHAEL MASTERSON

WILEY

John Wiley & Sons, Inc.

Published by John Wiley & Sons, Inc., Hoboken, New Jersey
Published simultaneously in Canada

For general information about our other products and services, please contact our Customer Care Department within the United States at 800-762-2974, outside the United States at 317-572-3993 or fax 317-572-4002.

Wiley also publishes its books in a variety of electronic formats. Some content that appears in print may not be available in electronic books. For more information about Wiley products, visit our web site at www.wiley.com.

ISBN 0-471-71027-X

Printed in the United States of America

10 9 8 7 6 5 4 3 2 1

CONTENTS

ACKNOWLEDGMENTS

I'd like to thank the following people for contributing to this book:

Bill Bonner
Lisa Bruette
Charlie Byrne
Maggie Crowell
Wayne Ellis
Debbie Englander
Justin Ford

Andy Gordon
Jon Herring
Susan Horwitz
Will Newman
Judy Strauss
Kammy Thurman
Mike Ward

PREFACE

WHO AM I? AND WHY ARE YOU READING THIS BOOK?

Who doesn't want to be rich . . . or at least more financially secure than they are now? As Gertrude Stein once famously said, "I've been rich and I've been poor. It's better to be rich."

And so have I. From dead broke to worse. And then from okay to affluent to more-than-enough.

I've done many jobs in my working life. My first job, drying rear windows in a car wash, paid me $1.75 an hour. Nowadays I can't be tempted to work for less than 500 times that amount. In this book you'll learn what I learned along the way: that it's not hard to become as wealthy as you want to be . . . as long as you are willing to follow six simple steps.

I've been a busboy, bartender, housepainter, carpenter, bouncer, aluminum siding salesman, soda fountain jockey, teacher, copywriter, and tinsmith.

I've also owned and run many businesses, including a pool installation service, a nutritional supplement company, a venture capital firm, at least a dozen publishing houses, a discount jewelry outlet, a dozen direct-marketing enterprises, two public relations practices, a career counseling service, at least a half dozen real estate development ventures, a fine art dealership, and a rare coin brokerage, just to name a few.

I have been a partner in two businesses that grew beyond $130 million and a dozen that surpassed the $10 million mark and have more recently mentored friends and colleagues in the successful start-ups of $6 or $8 million companies.

I've owned and run public and private companies, local and international, retail and wholesale, profit and not-for-profit.

I've done all that and other jobs I'm sure I can't remember (or don't want to think about).

What I haven't done is run a large (i.e., Fortune 1000) corporation. I don't think I've even worked for one. My expertise is in starting and developing small businesses, and I've had a good deal of success with start-up real estate ventures and investing in small business and real estate.

I'm not a stockbroker, insurance salesperson, or financial planner. I've never had any formal training in finance. Everything I know has come from the experience of my working life. That means you won't find much here that is conventional financial planning.

I'd like to think that what I lack in formal education I've made up for in a depth and range of business experience that spells practical, proven advice. So when you consider my credentials, take into account the sheer scope of my experience. Be assured that the advice I give you in this book comes from that experience. Also keep in mind my Rolodex—the contacts I've made and the people I've known. I am lucky to have worked with some true moneymaking and business-building geniuses. I've listened to them and observed their actions. I'll pass on everything I've learned from them to you.

And, finally, I must admit to a love of teaching. Before I began my business career, I taught a graduate course at Catholic University in Washington, D.C., and then was an assistant professor of English language and literature at the University of Chad. This teaching impulse has never left me. It erupts in product presentations, coaching sessions with protégés, and speeches, and I'm sure it's evident in the pages that follow. If I get a little preachy, please forgive me.

I'm also an avid student. Every experience I've had in my career has taught me something. And everything I've learned about making a good income and converting it into lasting wealth is detailed in this book.

INTRODUCTION

BOCA'S STORY: AN UNEXPECTED LESSON IN AUTOMATIC WEALTH

My jiujitsu instructor, Boca, taught me a new grappling technique. It took most of an hour to learn—drilling over and over again. Boca understands, as all good teachers do, the difference between comprehending a skill and possessing one. Until this technique becomes an automatic, effortless response, it is useless. So even after I told him, "I've got it," he made me repeat the move . . . 10 times to the right side, 10 times to the left side . . . back and forth and then in training.

I was dripping sweat, heart pounding, lungs heaving—mentally and physically spent. Boca, on the other hand, looked like he'd been lounging the whole hour—not a hair out of place. While I caught my breath, Boca leaned back against a wall mat, smiling at me. "Hey, Michael," he said, "what is a good work for me to make a lot of money?"

"Like how much money?" I asked.

"Like you, my friend. I want to be rich, like you!"

Boca's English isn't perfect, but he gets his point across perfectly well. He is 30 years old, he reminded me. He has only two or three years left to fight professionally. "Now is my time to look around," he said, cupping his hands around his eyes like binoculars, "to see what there is for later on."

Why Learning How to Build Wealth Is Like Learning Jiujitsu

I like Boca so much as a teacher and as a friend that I *want* to give him the secret of getting rich in a single one-hour lesson. But I can't. I can explain a few concepts. I can even tell him, in an abbreviated way, what I consider to be the most important things he must do. But an hour's worth of talk won't make him wealthy, any more than a single hour of jiujitsu with him will make me a black-belt grappler.

But what could I do? I told him a little bit about the six-step Automatic Wealth program I had developed and mentioned that I would give him a copy of the book I was writing—this book—as soon as it was published. Meanwhile, I challenged him to think about wealth building like jiujitsu.

"You are a great teacher," I told him. "In a single hour, you can teach me many things. You can teach me your best takedown technique, your favorite choke, the latest arm bar or footlock. You can do all that and probably even tell me some of your top 'secrets' about being successful at jiujitsu, too."

"But for that I must charge you a lot of money." (He was smiling.)

"Yes, you would. And you should. But if you gave me such a class, and I paid you whatever you asked for it, would you then give me a black belt?"

"Well, no, my friend. You get the black belt only when you can do."

"And to be able to do . . . to be able to defeat white belts and blue belts and purple belts and even brown belts . . . what must I do?"

"You must practice, my friend. For that, you must practice."

Becoming Wealthy Takes Time—but Not as Much Time as You Think

Boca had arrived at the point I was trying to make. Becoming wealthy is not about discovering some secret or stumbling upon a pot of gold. You won't get rich by playing the lotto or even searching for that thousand-to-one Internet stock. Becoming wealthy is a matter of planning and practice, of setting specific goals and pursuing those goals with specific actions. Changing into an *automatic* wealth builder is about changing habits . . . and changing habits takes time.

"But I don't have too much time," Boca protested. "My wife needs a home and my babies want one day to go to college."

"And so you'd like to be rich by next Tuesday," I answered.

He smiled again and nodded.

I told Boca I couldn't do that for him . . . but I could show him how to become wealthy before his children graduated from high school.

"All the other young parents you know right now will still be struggling to get their bills paid. And they'll be worried about paying for college. But you'll be financially independent. You'll have no debt, the college bills will have been prepaid, and you will be able to kick back and work less (or even retire) whenever you want."

His face brightened.

"How does that sound?" I asked. "Becoming financially independent in seven to fifteen years. Would you be happy with that kind of time frame?"

He grinned.

YOUR FAST TRACK TO FINANCIAL INDEPENDENCE

If, like Boca, you're willing to invest 7 to 15 years in the task of becoming financially independent, my six-step Automatic Wealth program is your answer.

This book contains everything I know about making money, saving it, starting a business, and achieving a life of moneyed leisure. And doing it fast enough to satisfy not just Boca but anyone who doesn't have the time or desire to do it *The Millionaire Next Door* way by saving a few thousand dollars a year for 30 or 40 years.

With my program, all you need to become wealthy—to have a steady stream of income *automatically* flowing into your pocket, even after you have chosen to retire—is 7 to 15 years . . . and the willingness to learn and put into practice the simple, step-by-step lessons that I am going to teach you in this book.

You can do it no matter what your financial situation is right now—no matter how little money you have in the bank. Even if you currently have a negative net worth.

If you have already acquired a reasonable nest egg—say, several hundred thousand dollars or more—so much the better. Your journey to automatic wealth will be smoother. Your arrival will come sooner.

Some of the ideas you'll encounter in these pages are refinements of ideas I've already discussed in *Early to Rise (ETR)*, my daily e-mail advisory service, or discoveries I've revealed in previous books, including *How to Create Abundance in Your Life, Confessions of a Multi-Millionaire,* and *How I Built My Wealth*. But I've revised and improved these ideas to relate to someone in Boca's shoes—someone who is starting from scratch and wants to get wealthy in a relatively short period of time.

Someone like you, perhaps.

Some of the ideas presented were the result of working with friends who have excelled in certain specific areas of wealth building:

- Steve Sjuggerud on stock investing
- Justin Ford on local real estate investing
- Bob Bly on direct marketing
- Paul Lawrence on starting a side business for less than $100
- Porter Stansberry on stock investing
- Bill Bonner on what it means to be wealthy
- Eddie Popkin on real estate limited partnerships
- Gary North on balancing wealth and wisdom
- Joel Nadel on alternative investing
- Sid Gershen on tax and financial planning

I know these people personally. I have worked with them, read their writings, discussed their ideas with them, sought them for advice on my own wealth-building goals—and I can vouch for their intelligence and integrity. With their help and mine, you will be able to achieve a significant level of wealth—enough to retire on, if you want to retire—in a relatively short period of time. Not overnight. But in much less than the 30 or 40 years that it would normally take you following conventional rules.

And you won't have to pinch pennies, either. I'll show you how to live like you're wealthy almost immediately, so you'll be able to have fun, enjoy your life—even blow a little money on some toys.

SIX STEPS TO AUTOMATIC WEALTH—IN A NUTSHELL

The program that I'm recommending to you—which incorporates nothing but strategies that have worked for me, for people I know, and for those I've mentored—is broken down into six steps:

- Step 1. *You're going to face some hard facts.* You are not going to get rich by saving 10 percent of your income every month. And you shouldn't be so foolish as to count on your company's pension plan or the government to take care of you when you get older. It's up to you.
- Step 2. *You're going to plan to be rich.* You can't wish yourself to wealth, you have to plan for it . . . one detail at a time. I'll show you not only how I did it but also what has worked for my friends and colleagues.
- Step 3. *You're going to develop wealthy habits.* The rich are different from ordinary people, and it's not just the money. There are specific behaviors that are likely to make you wealthier, just as there are specific behaviors that are likely to make you poorer.
- Step 4. *You're going to increase your income—radically.* Forget 3 percent or 4 percent raises. I'll show you how to boost your income 25 percent to 150 percent. And that's just for starters.
- Step 5. *You're going to get richer* automatically . . . *even while you sleep.* Getting rich is not just about increasing your income. The true secret to wealth is building equity. I'll show you how to do it . . . without quitting your day job.
- Step 6. *You're going to retire early (if you want to).* I don't believe in retiring. Not really. That's because I like my work and wouldn't enjoy life so much without it. But what you do in your retirement years, where you do it, and how many hours you work at it should be entirely up to you. I'll show you how to have that kind of control.

Although you should begin your journey by taking the first two steps in sequence, you can take the other four steps almost simultaneously.

THE ONLY REALISTIC WAY TO GENERATE SIGNIFICANT WEALTH IN A RELATIVELY SHORT PERIOD OF TIME

My approach to wealth building is to do a modest amount of everything that works, following a well-conceived plan that focuses on building income and equity simultaneously.

As you'll see, I have no bias toward one type of investment over another. I like real estate, but it's not the only thing I do. I invest in stocks and bonds—and have had considerable success in these areas (mostly by being conservative), but I'm hardly an expert. I am big on starting your own business, but I recognize that not everyone can do that. I like the fun of investing in high-income passive structures, but I recognize that many of these are not what they are cracked up to be.

The ultimate goal of my Automatic Wealth program is threefold:

1. To increase your net income dramatically and quickly
2. To develop your wealth-building skills and habits and turn yourself into an automatic wealth-building machine
3. To make it possible for you to retire early—if that's what you choose to do

I believe you can accomplish all of these goals in 7 to 15 years. You may accomplish them sooner. Many of the individuals I've personally mentored have set out with expectations of hitting their first million in 7 or 10 years, only to be surprised when they reached their goals in just 2 or 3.

That's what happened to Ron . . .

RON'S STORY: WHAT HAPPENED WHEN TWO OLD FRIENDS MET AFTER 25 YEARS

I hadn't spoken to Ron in 25 years. The last time I saw him, we were young men with no money and nothing but opportunity in front of us.

We were born in the same tenement building in Brooklyn. Our parents, writers and teachers, lived the lives that writers and teachers often do—rich in ideas but poor in funds. We lived upstairs; Ron's family was below us. The grammar school we attended was under the raised subway platform. The bar our dads drank at was around the corner.

We stayed best friends throughout our teens, even though my family had moved to Long Island when I was six. I'd spend weekends at Ron's apartment in the city, on 108th Street and Broadway. We ate pizza at the local greasy spoon and smoked pot with the Puerto Rican kids a few blocks away.

After high school, we lost touch. I buried myself in books, trying to make up for lost time. Ron moved here and there, ending up in California, where he studied martial arts and smoked more dope. Eventually, he got hooked on heroin and booze. And that, as I found out later, is how he spent most of those 25 years.

We might never have reunited had it not been for our older sisters, who continued to stay in touch. One day, I got a letter from my sister telling me that Ron had gotten clean and was working as a carpenter in upstate New York. She gave me his phone number and suggested that I call him.

I didn't—not for a year. But then, on the spur of the moment, I picked up the phone and invited him to join me on a weeklong trip to Key West.

It was a good week.

I Made Him an Offer He Couldn't Refuse

Ron was, indeed, clean and sober. And he was making a living building custom cabinetry somewhere north of Oneonta, New York. He was proud of what he'd accomplished, and I was proud of him, too. But he was working hard and wondering why he hadn't finished college. He was a better student and a better writer than I was when we were kids—and remembering that made me feel a little awkward about the success I had achieved and the amount of wealth I had made in the years since I'd last seen him.

So when Ron wrote me afterward, thanking me for the trip and complaining just a bit about his life, I jumped at the chance to offer him a position as an apprentice copywriter for a publishing business I was consulting with in Baltimore. He wouldn't make a lot of dough to begin with, I told him, but he could eventually become a well-paid freelancer. He could live in the apartment I used when I was there (I was commuting from South Florida), and I'd help him develop his copywriting skills.

Well, that's exactly what happened.

For about a year, Ron stayed at that apartment and worked on his copywriting assignments. When I was there, I reviewed his work and he endured my red marks, comments, and unsolicited advice about nearly everything.

Week by week, his skills improved. After about six months, he (i.e., we) had written his first big advertising promotion. It immediately broke all records. When his next promotion succeeded (and this one was 75 percent his work), he suddenly became the go-to guy in the marketing department.

He learned in leaps and bounds, absorbing ideas, tricks, and techniques from other experienced copy masters. And his compensation grew from $35,000 to $60,000.

Not bad.

But after having listened to my many lectures on what he could be and do, he wanted more. And he made the decision to become a freelance writer.

Ron Takes the Plunge

Frankly, I was worried. What if he wasn't ready? What if his first two copywriting successes were "too much me"? What if he was capable of writing, but unable to handle the other aspects of running a business?

I had a dozen reasons why he shouldn't quit his day job. But Ron wasn't interested in hearing them. He thanked me graciously for my help and set out on his own.

I'm happy to say that my fears were unwarranted. Ron applied himself to his new career as a self-employed copywriter with the same energy and intensity he had applied to mastering his skills. He began by negotiating a deal with his employer (my client) to make him a freelance consultant. He promised to do more work and make his employer more money, asking only for a fraction of the compensation more experienced freelance copywriters were getting for the same work. Then he contacted other people in the direct-mail industry to let them know what he'd done for my client and what he could do for them. He made phone calls, mailed self-promotional packages, and sent press releases about himself to trade magazines. He asked for referrals and actively pursued every lead.

His business took off like a rocket.

"I don't mind working 12 hours a day," he told me. "I love writing. And now I'm my own boss. Nobody is looking over my shoulder, telling me when to come and go or how to do my job. I listen to my clients and give them what they want and I get paid. I feel like I've died and gone to heaven."

Ron's skills continued to increase . . . and by the end of the following year, he was making a six-figure income. He moved to Florida and bought a beautiful little home by the water, a motorcycle, and a canoe that he paddled around in for exercise at lunchtime. Two years later, he was making more than $300,000 a year.

He Parlays His Expertise into a Side Business

Ron and I continued to stay in touch.

With his lucrative freelance copywriting business established, Ron was ready to branch out further. When he and his buddy Phil came up with an idea for a side business—a home-study program to teach other people how to start their own freelance copywriting careers—I hooked them up with a former protégé of mine who was a highly skilled direct marketer. And the three launched the American Writers & Artists Institute (AWAI).

AWAI started to provide its three founders with a second stream of income from the beginning. Although it paid them little or nothing during the first year, it gradually started throwing off dividends. And eventually, their passive income from this side venture was even more than they had been making in their professional marketing careers.

We All Start Dabbling in Real Estate

About six or seven years ago, Ron and I began dabbling in local real estate. Skeptical of putting too much of our hard-earned money in the seemingly overvalued stock market, we invested in the booming South Florida property market instead. Needless to say, it turned out to be a great move. This turned into a third stream of income for Ron and, a little later, for Phil, too.

Since then, Ron has added a fourth, a fifth, and a sixth stream of income. And one of them turned into a raging river. In fact, in the last six months, his income from this one side business has outpaced that of all the others. And the best part is that he doesn't even run it day to day. Other people do it for him.

Ron Helps Me Make a Transition of My Own

While Ron was making the transition from scraping by to financial independence, I was making another kind of change. In recent years my main business has been helping entrepreneurs start and grow their businesses by teaching them basic business-building and direct-marketing skills. This consulting practice provided a very good living for me, but it was taking a lot of my time and—having long ago achieved financial independence—I wanted to stop doing it full-time and devote the saved time to teaching and writing.

Ron helped me achieve that goal by getting me involved with his home-study business. He also encouraged me to start my e-zine, *Early to Rise,* which has became a vehicle for me to document my thoughts about achieving success in life and becoming wealthy, among other things.

It has taken me several years to change from being a full-time business consultant to a half-time writer and teacher, but it's a change that I'm very happy about. I feel like I'm semiretired—and I suppose I am, even though I still work 10 hours a day and continue to make more money than I need.

Ron's change is more remarkable because he started with less and in some ways achieved more. And my Automatic Wealth program is loosely based on the way he did it.

RON'S SIX-STEP WEALTH-BUILDING JOURNEY

1. *He faced facts.* He recognized that his financial situation was a disaster. He was brave enough to see that if things continued as they were going, he'd end up poor, unhappy, and unable to retire at any age.
2. *He planned to become wealthy.* He started by writing me a letter and asking for help. He knew that I could help him (a) get a job, (b) set achievable wealth-building goals, (c) learn

something about making money, and (d) get in touch with other people who could help him.

3. *He developed wealthy habits.* He earnestly studied marketing and salesmanship. He became my first copywriting protégé, the first person I taught everything I knew about advertising. And he worked long and hard to prove himself a worthy worker. He showed up early for work, left late, volunteered for extra assignments, and spent his spare time in the evenings improving his skills.

   Meanwhile, he didn't deprive himself. He prepared himself to live the lifestyle he was working toward—not by wasting money, but by making smart buys. He moved to Miami Beach, bought a beautiful Art Deco bachelor pad, and rewarded himself with a few things that he had always wanted.

4. *He radically increased his income.* Within 24 months, he was taking home double what his earnings had been as a carpenter. When his income stalled at about $60,000, he made the leap to go into business for himself—and within a few short years was making more than $300,000.

5. *He started to develop additional streams of income.* While Ron was still building his main business as a freelance copywriter, he formed a side business with two partners. Although he never invested a nickel and spent just a few hours a week at it, that asset continued to become more valuable—and today, his stake in the company is worth half a million dollars.

   But he didn't stop there. He began investing in local real estate. His first purchase was small. In time, he became more skilled at buying and selling properties, and his real estate portfolio grew.

   And he didn't stop there. He has since added three more streams of income to his rapidly increasing yearly earnings.

6. *He put himself on track to enjoy an early retirement.* Ever since the moment Ron decided to turn his life around, he has saved at least 10 percent of his gross income in a passive investment account. In the beginning, he made some foolish investments. He even got sucked into a few Internet stocks. But as his experience grew, he realized that chasing megaprofits—50 percent,

100 percent, and more—was a fool's game. He ratcheted down his investing goals to a modest 12 percent return on investment (ROI) and has seen his retirement nest egg fill up and then overflow.

IF RON COULD DO IT, YOU CAN DO IT

I'll show you how to follow in Ron's very successful footsteps in a time frame that meets your needs. Soon after you get started on my Automatic Wealth program, it will create a momentum of its own, and *it* will carry *you* to the level of financial security you desire. As your net worth compounds, you'll not only enjoy peace of mind, you'll also have earned the ability to make more choices . . . including the freedom to stop working.

To see that happen, though, you need to start *now.* You can always find reasons for waiting, but, to put it bluntly, time's a-wasting. You're holding a powerful tool in your hands that will allow you to start living richer immediately and gain financial independence in the next 7 to 15 years, but you have to put the program into action—starting with Step 1 on the next page.

STEP 1

RECOGNIZING REALITY

In this chapter, we're going to look at your personal financial situation—where you're at right now. We'll figure out what wealth means to you, look at some hard facts about the economy, and come to a realistic conclusion about what you need to do to put yourself on a path that will allow you to live well and retire comfortably.

But first, let me tell you how I got started on my own road to wealth . . .

THE DAY I DECIDED TO GET RICH

It doesn't take a genius to get rich. Nor are special talents required. You don't need to be lucky. And you certainly don't need to be privileged. You do, however, have to make getting rich a priority in your life—and be willing to focus the majority of your time and energy on doing what it takes to build real wealth.

I discovered this early on in my career.

It was 1982. I had just been hired as editorial director for a fledgling newsletter-publishing company in South Florida. Because I had to give the occasional speech, I enrolled myself in a Dale Carnegie course on public speaking. Somehow, though, I ended up in the Carnegie basic success course instead.

The How to Win Friends and Influence People program is a 14-week course in which you are asked to focus on a certain character-changing task each week and then report on your progress the following week.

I was the worst student in the class. Cynical and suspicious, I despised what I took to be the silly, do-goodish prattle of the teachers. But I'd paid good money to be there, so I grudgingly went along with the program—and I'm very glad I did.

The assignment for week 4 was to come up with a single goal that you would pursue for the remaining 10 weeks of the program. The idea was that by concentrating on only one goal, you could make much more progress than you would with a wider scope of objectives.

Sure enough, I had a hell of a time with that lesson. For me, it was by far the most difficult of the 14.

When I first started listing my goals, I could think of only two or three. But as I put more thought into it, the list began to expand . . . first to half a dozen . . . then to 10 . . . and then 20 . . . and on and on. Narrowing down the list was torture. Among other things, I wanted to be a great writer, a wise teacher, an admirable dad and husband, a linguist, a wine connoisseur, an athlete, and more. I was paralyzed. I simply couldn't tolerate the idea of giving up any one of those goals.

Finally, driving to the class at which I was to publicly announce my one main goal, I had a breakthrough. I realized that all my hard work and ambition had amounted to nothing because I had been spreading myself so thin.

Then I had an idea: "Why not make making money my number one goal?" I thought. "If I achieve that goal, I'll have all the money I need to pursue my other interests."

At the time, I knew nothing about making money. I had come from a family of teachers who didn't care much about money or the things it can buy. But I focused on that one goal and made it my priority. And it worked. Big time.

My income started to climb. I had been making $36,000 at the time, and it doubled in 12 months . . . and then tripled the year after . . . and then kept on multiplying. I developed an interest not only in how money is made, but also in how it is lost and what it can do for you.

I began reading about it, talking about it, asking about it—trying to unlock its secrets. At the same time, the publishing company I was working for was changing its focus from providing information about business and travel to financial planning and investing. And I was fortunate enough to get to know some very smart people who seemed to truly understand how money works and some very successful businesspeople who had demonstrated how wealth is actually made.

This experience completely changed my ideas about wealth. Before my conversion, I felt that money was, at best, a necessary evil. But after I took the time to learn about it, I decided that wealth is actually a pretty good thing—not the most important thing in life, but a good thing that can make it easier to find time for the other, more important things.

THE REAL MEANING OF WEALTH

I remember when my income first broke through the $150,000 mark. Louis, my accountant at the time, was amused by my innocent astonishment at making so much money.

"Welcome to the world of the rich," he told me.

"Come on, Louis," I said. "I'm making barely more than one and a half grand."

"Think of it this way," he told me. "When you have a family income of less than $50,000, it's a struggle. When you make between $50,000 and $150,000, you have everything you need and some of what you want. But when you make more than $150,000, life is good. You can live in a beautiful house in a safe neighborhood, drive nice cars, go out to dinner once or twice a week, and do some traveling."

"But what about the mansions, yachts, and private jets?" I asked. "I still can't afford those."

"Those are just toys," he said. "$150,000 per year is all you really need to live a full, rich life. And here's the interesting thing: This doesn't change in any meaningful way when your income passes $200,000, $300,000, or $400,000. In fact, it doesn't really change until you are making more than a million dollars."

Back then, I only half understood what Louis was trying to tell me. Now, I think I get it completely.

There are four basic income levels:

1. If you have a family income of less than $50,000, it's tough to make ends meet.
2. If you earn between $50,000 and $150,000, you are getting by. Your bills are paid and you can afford some small luxuries, but you have to be careful.
3. When your family income exceeds $150,000, you are living well and want for nothing (unless you have 10 children).
4. When your family income exceeds $1 million, you can spend money without much thinking. You don't need a budget. You can be extravagant.

But making a million dollars does not increase the quality of your life—and it does not, in itself, guarantee that you will have financial security till the end of your days. What it does do is make saving infinitely easier. Because unless you are completely out of control, you will be able to save most if not all of your after-tax income that exceeds the million. And saving is key to jump-starting the Automatic Wealth program.

So if you can get your income above a million, you can get rich, relatively quickly, merely by saving. And that may happen simply by following the advice I'll be giving you in Step 3.

But if your primary income doesn't grow so dramatically, don't despair. You can still achieve financial independence in a relatively short period of time (less than 15 years, certainly; probably less than 7) by developing additional streams of income. I'll tell you how to do that, too.

BEING RICH IS NOT JUST ABOUT HAVING MONEY IN THE BANK

One of the most active discussions that ever appeared on the online forum for *ETR,* my daily e-zine, was in response to the simple question "What is wealth?" This question prompted a deluge of interesting answers, from the mundane to the pragmatic to the philosophically problematic. Answers like these:

ARE YOU A SAVER OR A SPENDER?

As I see it, the wealth-seeking world is divided into two camps. In one, you have the wealth accumulators: men and women who are cautious about spending but eager to save and invest. The other camp is populated with spenders: men and women who are obsessed with things. They spend all their spare money, and often much more than that, buying things that say "rich" but actually impoverish them.

To become wealthy, first you need to build a small nest egg by spending less than you earn. Simple, huh? But not if you don't have the self-discipline to do it.

We'll be talking more about this in Step 3. Meanwhile, keep in mind that even though the material things you hunger for are indisputably of value, unless you have the financial capacity to keep them, to maintain them, and to replace them, you don't have wealth. You simply have its obligations.

- A million dollars in the bank
- Having everything you want
- The power to command results
- Being loved by your family and friends
- Having tangible assets sufficient to meet the physical needs of yourself and your loved ones
- Having a balanced life
- Inner peace and spiritual enlightenment
- Excellent health and immunity from disease

This is just a small sampling of what our readers had to say, but it gives you an idea about how varied and sometimes vague our thinking about wealth can be. And although I recognize the sense in many of these definitions, I find it impossible to talk to people about wealth unless I can get them to agree on some basic terms. So let's do that now.

I suggest that we start with this definition: *Wealth is a store of something valuable.*

I like that definition because it is simple and because, no matter what it is that you value, it emphasizes something essential about wealth: the idea of storage. Having the things you desire—say, a big house and fancy cars—does not make you materially wealthy if you don't have the wherewithal to keep those goods over a protracted period of time. Nor are you wealthy in friendship if the many friends you have now would abandon you if your fortune changed.

The point I'm making here may be too obvious to mention: that wealth is only sometimes about money. Understanding wealth in a broader sense, with implications that go beyond dollars and cents, is essential.

Yes, the main purpose of this book is to help you become financially independent. But you want financial independence for specific reasons:

- You want more freedom in your life. You want more choice about where you live, how you live, how much you work, and so on.
- You want more leisure in your life. You don't want to feel compelled to work 8 or 10 hours every day, or five and six days every week.
- You want more tranquility in your life. You would like an end to the stress that the lack of money sometimes causes. You want to be able to sleep easily at night and enjoy your days without worry.

These goals are wrapped up very tightly in your desire for wealth—and as a result, they are a fundamental part of every step in my Automatic Wealth program.

Let's push a little further along this path and delve a little deeper into the way you think about your life and the things you value.

INTERESTING FACT: Only about one-half of 1 percent of U.S. households have a net worth of $5 million or more, excluding primary residences, according to the Spectrem Group, a consulting firm specializing in affluent and retirement markets. And only 0.2 percent of U.S. households have a net worth of $15 million or more, including their homes, according to the Federal Reserve.

PLAN TO BE WEALTHY IN EVERY IMPORTANT WAY

I'm hoping that money is not the most important thing in your life.

Nevertheless, material wealth *does* matter. It gives you the ability to help your friends, provide for your family, pursue intellectual and artistic interests, and become an inspirational role model for members of your community.

Plus, if you don't have an income sufficient to meet your needs, you'll spend a good deal of time fretting about it—and when you spend time fretting about money, you can't enjoy the things you truly care about.

This is a truth that more and more baby boomers (including a few of my friends and family members) have recently discovered. Stumbling into middle age with lifetimes of educational, social, and recreational experiences, yesterday's hippies are hitting their 50s with the depressing realization that they are working harder than ever to maintain a lifestyle that is not much better than the one they had in college.

I've had the good fortune to be able to help dozens of such people work themselves out of this sort of bog, regain solid ground, and go on to achieve financial independence. It took some time and it wasn't always easy, but it always began with a revelation—a revelation that was especially bracing for some of the smartest of them—that becoming financially independent is a good thing, something all good people should aspire to.

Having enough money can liberate you from a thankless job, free you to follow dreams, and allow you to take care of your loved ones.

That's the reason you're reading this book.

But never forget that the desire for money can also corrupt you. If, in pursuing wealth, you begin to believe that the accumulation of money is an end in itself—well, that's a bad thing.

This book will help you make money. And if you follow my suggestions faithfully for a reasonable period of time, you'll some day—probably sooner than any of your friends or colleagues—discover that you are wealthy.

But when that day comes, I'm hoping the greed bug will not have infected you. I hope you won't have become addicted to the idea of making the money pile grow. I hope you won't have forgotten what you know now—that there are many things more important than money. (We'll talk much more about this in Step 3.)

FOLLOW POPULAR FINANCIAL GURUS AND STAY POOR

You won't find anything in this book that will give you instant wealth. I have no advice about making a fortune through buying hot stocks, day trading, or playing the lottery. But you don't want that kind of money anyway. Studies show that people who get rich rapidly blow it all quickly on things that have no lasting value.

My six-step wealth-building program is fast—realistically fast. Depending on your age, skills, and current income, I'll get you from where you are today to wealthy in 7 to 15 years. That's not tomorrow, but it's a lot better than you'll do by following most of the financial advice that's out there. Open a magazine or turn on the TV and you'll see that the majority of it falls into the category of financial planning, that is, ways to scrimp and save. Advisers who promote this concept assume you need to crawl toward retirement, clutching pennies until your fingers turn green.

But what about the quality of your life in the meantime? And when you're living paycheck to paycheck, how do you wring a nickel out of your budget for retirement, much less the $5 or $10 *per day* that these financial gurus recommend?

Getting wealthy is not a matter of scrimping and cutting corners. To make a lot of money, you must spend most of your working time doing the things I'm going to tell you about in this book—things that generate extra cash now that you can use to generate *automatic* streams of income in the near future. Yes, it is important to be careful about the way you spend your money—but if that's the main part of your wealth-building program, you probably won't get rich. And even if you do, you won't feel rich.

The problem is, most of those doing the preaching—those who would convince you that they understand wealth and can teach you how to get it—have never actually made significant money by following their own recommendations. Their great moneymaking skill is in selling people on buying their ideas.

During my years as an insider in the world of investment publishing, I saw

- Financial planning experts who were broke
- Stock gurus who never followed their own advice

- Brokers who talked about their clients with contempt
- Marketers who never checked their facts
- Business consultants whose businesses hardly worked
- Get–wealthy authors who made their money by talking about making money, not by actually earning it in business

Though it's true that some of my wealth has come from teaching others how to attain it, the vast majority is the result of my actual experience working in the trenches, learning from my mistakes, and capitalizing on my successes.

WHY THE POPULAR GET-RICH-SLOWLY-BY-SAVING IDEA (PROBABLY) WON'T WORK FOR YOU

There is good reason to be skeptical of the get-rich-slowly-by-saving doctrine—mainly that it is useful only for those with a lot of working years ahead of them. In *The Millionaire Next Door* (Longstreet, 1996), for example, most of the millionaires Thomas Stanley studied were ordinary working people who diligently saved for 35 or 40 years—a full lifetime of working.

Likewise, in *The Automatic Millionaire* (Broadway, 2003), David Bach often uses 35 and 40 years to calculate the power of compounded interest:

> Let's say that tomorrow you started having 10 percent of your gross in-come, before taxes, automatically taken out of your paycheck and put in a pretax retirement account. As a result of that simple, automatic process, you would eventually accumulate more wealth than 90 percent of the population. . . . Let's use the example of someone who makes $50,000 a year. If that's your annual salary and you took 10 percent out of each paycheck before the government got its bite, by the end of the year you'd have put aside $5,000. Now . . . [if you put that] in a retirement ac-count that earned an annual return of 10 percent, what would you have? The answer is that you would have more than 1 million dollars. Actually, a lot more. The exact figure is $1,678,293.

There is nothing inaccurate about Bach's calculation. In fact, the amazing power of compounding is even more startling when it is applied to

(continues)

people with more years ahead of them. I'm speaking about children here. In his Seeds of Wealth program, Justin Ford makes this point very powerfully:

> If your children average just over $1 a day in savings through the pre-teen years and a little more than $2 a day through the age of 21, they can end up with anywhere from $335,854 (at 13.2% returns) to $855,279 (at 18.8% returns) a generation from now.
>
> What's more, as they continue practicing those lifelong good money habits, it's very possible they can achieve a fortune in the millions of dollars during their 30s or 40s—even if they never make a great deal of money in their chosen careers. And while your child is quietly and methodically securing his or her financial future, he or she will be mastering life-long money skills that will enable them to further grow that nest egg into over a million by age 38 . . . and between $9 million and $10 million by the time they're ready to retire at 55!

When you have so much time to save, you can easily acquire great wealth by being frugal. Stanley's millionaires live in 40-year-old homes, have their shoes resoled, get their furniture reupholstered, use a shopping list when they buy groceries, and buy household supplies at bulk warehouses.

This sort of lifestyle—this commitment to saving—is exactly how David Bach believes wealth can and should be accumulated. He calls it the *latte factor:*

> One day . . . in an investment course I was teaching, a young woman . . . raised her hand and said, "Your ideas are good in theory . . . but in reality it's impossible . . . to save. . . . I'm living paycheck to paycheck. . . . How can I possibly save five to 10 dollars a day?" With just about everyone else in the class nodding in agreement, I threw out my lesson plan and decided to devote the rest of the time we had left to answering [her] question.

Bach questioned the young lady on her daily spending habits and discovered that she spent $3.50 a day for a nonfat latte, another $1.50 for a nonfat muffin, $4.45 for an afternoon protein drink, and $1.75 for a power bar. That gave her a total daily snack budget of $11.20.

> Let's say . . . that today . . . you started to save five dollars a day . . . in a retirement account . . . that equals $150 a month, or almost $2,000 a year.

Figuring, say, a 10 percent annual return, which is what the stock market has averaged over the last 50 years, how much do you think you could save by the time you're 65?

The answer was, again, over a million dollars. But the young lady with the question was 23 years old. That's 42 years of savings.

Again, there is nothing inaccurate about this argument. But, chances are, you're not 23 years old. My guess is that very few 23-year-olds will be reading this book. If you are one of them, and if you take my advice seriously, congratulate yourself. You'll be richer than Midas well before you are 65. But if, as is more likely, you can't (or don't want to) work full-time another 30 or 40 years, my Automatic Wealth program is a much more realistic approach for you to take.

HOW MUCH WEALTH DO YOU NEED?

Most books on the subject of wealth answer this important question in terms of a concept called *retirement*. And in today's world, you need a lot of money to retire well. Even people who had their retirement money safely tucked away in the stock market and thought they could look forward to a secure future are now in trouble.

Take Martha Parry, for example. The New York woman sold her insurance company and thought she had it made. According to a *Time* magazine cover story, she had $1 million in the stock market and was looking forward to a retirement of golf, travel, and good times.

Then the stock market crashed. And now, at 65, she has only $600,000 in her retirement account. And instead of playing golf and traveling, she's still at the office earning her living. And she's one of the *lucky* ones.

Another woman that I read about had to be put on medication for severe depression because a year after being downsized from her job, she learned her nest egg had plummeted from $1 million to $250,000.

And many victims of the stock market crash have been left in even worse shape.

Tim and Kay Plumlee saw their retirement fund plunge to a mere $60,000 after a broker recommended they put their life savings into a variable annuity—an investment that *seemed* like a profitable, risk-free opportunity at the time.

In a few year's time, people saw their life savings slashed by a quarter to a half—some lost much more. And despite the recent market rally, the fall of the dollar, the exportation of jobs to India and China, and the cost of the war on terrorism are likely to keep the 79 million Americans who call themselves baby boomers in jeopardy.

FINANCIAL SECURITY IS A BABY BOOMER PROBLEM . . . AND IT'S GOING TO GET WORSE FOR MOST

Like Martha Parry and the Plumlees, aging baby boomers all over America are realizing that there is very little chance that they will be able to retire at 55 or 65. A recent *USA Today* survey revealed that 35 percent of American workers over 55 admit that they are not financially prepared to do so.

How poorly prepared are they? Another study showed that 40 percent have an investable net worth of less than $50,000, 60 percent have less than $100,000, and 80 percent have less than $250,000.

If you figure on making 10 percent on your money, this means fewer than one out of five Americans who are nearing retirement age have the wherewithal to enjoy a passive retirement income of more than $25,000.

How well could you live on $25,000 a year?

Let's see. First we must deduct taxes (national, state, and local). Then we have to consider the erosive effect of inflation. What you end up with is a take-home income of less than $1,500 a month—barely enough to keep you in a cheap, two-bedroom apartment.

Most baby boomers are going to get poorer as they get older. Not only will their earning power decrease, taxes will likely go up. Add to that the probability of rising inflation, a significant stock market deflation, a flattening of real estate prices, and increased medical costs . . .

WHAT ABOUT SOCIAL SECURITY?

If you are thinking that Uncle Sam will step in to take care of you in your golden years, you're going to be bitterly disappointed. Uncle

Sam is trillions of dollars in debt, and Social Security and Medicare are going broke. Here's why . . .

Until now, the amount of money drawn into the Treasury from Social Security taxes (withheld from your pay as FICA and Medicare) has exceeded the outgoing payments made by the Social Security Administration (SSA) for these programs. But by 2017, the SSA will be paying out more in benefits than it collects.

In their 2003 Trustees Report, the SSA itself said, "If Social Security is not changed, payroll taxes will have to be increased or massive transfers from general revenues will be required."

Neither of these things is likely to happen. Young people won't allow their payroll taxes to be increased for the benefit of baby boomers who squandered the funds while they were running the government. Additionally, there are so many boomers retiring (as compared with the number of people who are working) that any tax increase would have to be enormous to have any real effect. And there are certainly no surpluses to be found in general revenues these days.

Something has to give.

The first cuts will be subtle. Cost of living adjustments (COLAs) will disappear. Then benefits will have to be cut. If not, the debt will become so large that the government will need to inflate our currency—which will result in a devalued dollar and diminished purchasing power. Either way, you'll end up with less.

And the outlook is even worse for Medicare. The *Annals of Internal Medicine* recently reported that older Americans with health problems are getting the care they need just 52 percent of the time. Can you imagine what will happen when Medicare starts paring back because of dwindling resources? In addition, we're living an average of 10 years longer than in the 1940s, and the costs of health care continue to increase with no real end in sight.

The future of Uncle Sam's retirement program looks grim. Very grim.

But your future doesn't have to be. You can separate yourself from the crowd of baby boomers who are following their Pied Piper financial leaders into the river of personal debt and misery. With my Automatic Wealth program, you can create your own retirement plan—a personal, financial reparation project that will take you from wherever you are now to relative wealth and comfort in 7 to 15 years.

You can live out the second half of your life in ease and comfort . . . but not if you are counting on the government. Take charge of your future now by following the recommendations in this book, and you'll never have to rely on anyone else, now or in the future, to take care of your needs.

WHERE DO YOU STAND RIGHT NOW?

Before I can help you lay out your wealth-building course of action—before we can come up with a plan to get you where you want to go—we need to know how much you are worth right now.

So let's figure it out.

Get a pad of paper and a pen and make a list of all your assets. By that I mean stocks, bonds, precious metals, money in individual retirement accounts (IRAs), certificates of deposit (CDs), savings accounts, and so on. You can also include the value (the true, current, salable value—don't fool yourself) of any valuable possessions you own, such as jewelry, art or antiques.

Now I'm going to give you an instruction that will contradict what you'll hear from just about every financial planner: In tallying your assets, do *not* include the value of your home, your car, or any possessions you know you'll never part with.

Although these are, indeed, valuable assets, they are assets you will almost certainly want to keep during your retirement years. This is especially true if you are able to achieve financial independence while you still have children at home. If you will be retiring after your children are grown and out on their own, you might very well choose to sell your house and get a less expensive one—but maybe you won't want to. And I believe in keeping what you have for as long as you wish. (If you follow my six steps to automatic wealth, you'll be able to do that.)

Okay, let's finish figuring out your net worth . . .

Now that you have a list of your assets, make another list of your liabilities, including credit card debt, personal loans, business debts, and so on.

Subtract your liabilities from your assets and you'll have your net worth.

If your personal net worth is less than $300,000, you probably don't have enough money to retire on. Pure and simple. Unless you intend to work till the day you die (which is something you might choose to do even if you don't have to—an idea that we'll explore later), you are going to need more than $300,000 tucked away in income-producing investments to live a decent lifestyle in retirement.

DO YOU HAVE ENOUGH TO RETIRE COMFORTABLY?

Your primary goal in terms of becoming financially independent is to accumulate enough capital to generate a passive income sufficient to pay for your basic bills—housing, food, utilities, education, and entertainment.

Passive income means income that you don't have to spend 40 hours a week generating. And you may already have some in the form of revenue generated by your investments in stocks, bonds, and so on. But in this book, you're going to learn how to generate far more passive income—enough to live on.

How much more do you need?

To get that answer, you have to know how many pretax dollars you will need to live comfortably—how much you'll need, per year, to cover housing, food, and utilities. So calculate that now (and be sure to add in the money you'll want to spend on travel, education, and leisure activities).

Once you've done that, the next step is pretty easy.

Simply multiply the pretax income that you're going to need by 10 (the average percentage of interest that you can reasonably expect to earn on your investments—the average that the stock market has historically returned is 10.4 percent, according to Ibbotson Associates) and then subtract that number from your current net worth. That will give you a quick estimate of how much more money you will need to add to your net worth before you can possibly retire.

"Social Security payments will probably exist in some form during retirement and you should include the benefits as a modest proportion of your retirement income. These are entitlements that will be available but the actual value is likely to diminish over time. Pension payments and Social Security are a realistic part of your income when you

VARIATIONS ON THE TAXABLE NATURE OF EARNED INCOME

The tax code provides for so many variations on the taxable nature of income, especially earned income, that we can only make an estimate of how much might be lost to the tax collector. Rules will change over the next 20 years. But remember, income from municipal bonds and distributions from Roth IRAs are tax free. Qualified stock dividends are now in a lower bracket.

A rough but easy way to estimate the required pretax income to support your lifestyle is to assume that your tax obligation will be approximately 20 percent to 25 percent of your income. That should still be true even if you are in a high-income-tax state. (If you think your taxable retirement income will be more than $200,000, then you could use an estimate of 25 percent to 28 percent.) To determine your expected gross income (pretax), take the estimate that you just made of what your lifestyle will cost and divide it by (100 – tax rate). For example, if you estimated your after-tax income needs to be $50,000, then $50,000 divided by .80 (100 – .20) would give you a ballpark estimate of a pretax income of $62,500.

qualify, but they cannot be the leverage which gives you financial freedom. If you have an average life span or longer, the actual purchasing power will be less than you will expect."

For example, let's say you've figured out that the lifestyle you envision for yourself in retirement will cost you $65,000 in post-tax dollars. That means you will need a pretax income of $90,000. And let's assume that your current net worth is $400,000. Ten times $90,000 is $900,000, and $900,000 less $400,000 leaves half a million dollars—which is the amount you'll need to sock away in investments generating 10 percent interest between now and the time you want to retire.

In this example, I'm assuming that you will spend, in retirement, only your interest income. If you manage to do this—and many wealthy people do—you'll end up with a significant estate to leave to a charity or your loved ones. You could figure out a way to spend part of your capital as well as the interest as you age. This is a more complicated calculation, but it does allow you to go into retirement mode with less money in the bank.

PROFILE OF THE TYPICAL AMERICAN MILLIONAIRE

Although there is considerable variation among the 4 million Americans who can call themselves millionaires, they are typically white, male, middle-aged, and . . .

- Made their money, rather than inherited it
- Have between $1 million and $5 million in net worth (with median net worth at $1.6 million)
- Made their money by running their own businesses
- Live frugally by clipping coupons, driving older cars, and so on
- Managed to save on surprisingly moderate, median-level incomes averaging $131,000 per year

Having a personal net worth of 10 times the amount you need to live on is, by almost any definition, comfortable. It means that if you live frugally and no emergencies come up, you can consider yourself to be pretty much financially independent. But that 10-times figure is based on the assumption that you put all your money in the stock market and that the stock market, as overvalued as it seems to be, continues to produce its historic ROI of about 10 percent.

If you are more conservative when it comes to personal economics and would like to see about half your money in bonds, you will need a net worth of at least 12 times the amount you need to live on. Again, that's assuming the stock market will produce an average return of 10 percent in the future and that bonds will give you their historic yields of 4 percent after taxes or 6 percent before.

If you are conservative and feel a bit gloomy about the future of the stock market, you'll have to raise that factor even more. If you think, for example, that you'll live another 30 years and believe that the market will average a mere 8 percent ROI, you'll need a multiple of 13 to consider yourself comfortably well off.

Let's look at another example.

Let's say you need only $40,000 to live a happy life in retirement. You've figured out that you would be comfortable with a posttax income of $35,000 and you know, from your Social Security files, that you can expect $1,500 a month from the government, which comes to $18,000 a year. Subtracted from $35,000, this gives you a requirement of just $22,000. At a multiple of 10, you would be financially independent when your net savings hit $220,000.

WHAT IS RICH?

From Jeanne Sahadi, *CNN/Money* Senior Writer:

1. To Blanche Lark Christerson, director of the Wealth Planning Group at Deutsche Bank, rich is a net worth of $15 million. Christerson figures that for married couples with two young kids, today's pricey lifestyle costs about $375,000 a year. If you are single with no dependents, Christensen says $10 million will do. (She's assuming that you'd have 45 years ahead of you and that you'd want to preserve capital and leave it to your heirs or charities. She's calculating a conservative 3.5 percent return on investments.)
2. To certified financial planner Jon Duncan, it's $7.5 million. Duncan is making the same assumptions as Christerson in terms of kids and lifespan, but he thinks it takes only about $200,000 a year to live rich. And because the stock market has historically yielded about 10 percent, he expects you'll get a much better return on your savings.

If you know you'll want your retirement funds in both stocks and bonds and accept my projection that such a portfolio would earn an average of 8 percent ROI, then the multiple you'd be using would be 12 and the amount you'd have to put into savings would be 12 times 22, or $264,000.

Again, this example assumes that you wouldn't spend any of the principal amount of your savings. If you did spend it—say, by spending $5,000 a year of your principal once you hit age 70—the amount you'd need to put aside would be significantly less.

HOW DO YOU PICTURE YOUR LIFE IN RETIREMENT?

Retirement, you may be surprised to learn, is a relatively recent idea. It was invented after World War II to keep the Silent Generation busily working away in the factories. The promise was: Work hard now, save your pennies, and retire in Florida.

It worked for some, but for most, retirement proved to be a cruel joke—enduring a meager life, living in a rented room, wearing old clothes, eating crummy food, and watching endless television.

Not only sordid, but boring.

Yes, you need money to retire comfortably—which is why the main point of *Automatic Wealth* is to help you formulate a plan to allow you to become financially independent and have the option to retire in luxury. But you need more than that. Even in retirement, you still need to fill your days with meaningful activity. And that's why, throughout this book, I'm going to argue that you should change the way you think about retirement. That instead of endless days of golf and tennis and hanging out, you may want to think of retirement as a time when you can achieve happiness by working at something you value.

Why You May Not Want to Stop Working . . . Even If You Can

I used to have very conventional views/feelings/ideas about work and retirement. I used to think of work as something dull and difficult that I needed to do to earn a living. I dreamed about the day I could stop.

And for at least the first 10 or 12 years of my working life, I worked like a dog and hated every minute of it. Then, one day, it occurred to me that my life was speeding up and would be gone before I knew it. The good parts of my life—time I had been spending with friends and family—were few and far between. The bad part of my life—working—was crowding everything out. I wanted to slow down and stop, but when I ran the numbers, I realized I couldn't. I needed to pay for the ongoing bills of a growing family and wanted, too, to save enough for the future.

I was stuck between a rock and a hard place.

But then the thought occurred to me: What if I learned to love my work? What if I actually enjoyed the 10 or 12 hours I was spending every day earning money? Wouldn't that be nice?

(continues)

I knew I had the capacity to enjoy work. I had passed so many hours as a kid working on all my hobbies—building things, planning events, inventing things. What if I could somehow change my job into something I liked?

It didn't happen overnight, but it did happen.

I'm going to be talking about that process—learning to love your job or finding a job you love—in this book. I'm also going to suggest that the sooner you do that, the sooner you'll realize that your ideal retirement will include not only plenty of leisure, but some very enjoyable work, too.

But for now, please consider this proposition: Happiness comes when you are busy doing something you care about. When you are doing something you care about, happiness surprises you.

If that statement seems reasonable to you, perhaps you'll agree that the secret to a great retirement is to figure out how to get paid for doing work you would gladly do for free and to be able to do that work when and where you want to.

Not because you *have to* work but because you *want to* work.

Name Your Dream . . . Pick Your Price

Somewhere in your past is a buried profession—something you long ago gave up on. What if you could reprise that dream?

- I know a man whose dream was to be a professional pilot. After working 30 years in a wallpaper business, he took my advice and got himself a job flying part-time for a small airline. A few years later, he became a part owner.
- My dad gave up a promising career in show business to become a teacher. Fifty years later, he went back into the acting business and became a professional actor.
- I met a guy who trades cigarette lighters online. This happens to be something he always planned to do once he stopped working. By taking advantage of eBay, he is already making more than $30,000 a year doing it just on weekends.
- You can become an Internet copywriter, an Internet editor, an Internet travel agent, or an Internet teacher, for example. You can make money giving marriage or dating advice on the Internet.

In Step 4 and Step 5 of this book, we'll look at many ways that you can convert your passions/hobbies/interests into solid, *automatic* streams of income.

For the moment, however, think about this. There is an old axiom in the success business that says that the secret to a good life is coming up with the right answers to the following three questions:

1. What do you want to do?
2. Where do you want to do it?
3. Whom do you want to do it with?

So ask yourself these questions about your retirement:

1. What work would I really enjoy doing for the rest of my life?
2. Where is my ideal retirement paradise? How can I live there and do what I want to do, too?
3. Do I want to work alone or with a partner? If with a partner, who?

If you follow the six steps recommended in this book, you will soon have several sources of *automatic* income. You will no longer be dependent on the job you have now. And you will see yourself becoming wealthier—and closer to financial independence—with each passing month.

As that process occurs, you'll be able to tune up your working life, running your own businesses, delegating all the tasks that you don't like and replacing them with work you enjoy. At some point in time—and it may happen very soon, but will certainly happen in 7 to 15 years—you'll realize that you pretty much can do whatever you want to do. Your days will be good days, filled with work that makes you feel good.

At that point, your new life of retirement will be a reality. But my guess is that though you'll have sufficient passive income to live on, you'll be reluctant to give up work entirely because it will be a major source of pleasure for you.

That will be a happy time. Your major challenge will be to decide how many hours of fun you want to get from working and how many hours of fun you want to get from your other activities. You may be surprised to find that you'll want to work more hours than you think you want to work right now.

But that will be a good thing, won't it?

NOW IS THE RIGHT TIME TO ACT

At the beginning of this chapter, I told you about the day I decided to get rich. Now it's your turn to do the same thing—and start to make it happen.

If you are not financially independent yet, I can put you on the right path—if you can commit yourself to the plan laid out in the pages that follow. Can you do that? Good.

Then I have one question for you: When are you going to start? Next month? Next week? When you get through reading this book?

The correct answer is "none of the above."

There is only one time to begin an important journey. And that is immediately. You don't have to invest in a stock today or buy a piece of property tomorrow, but you do have to do something that will get you going. And in Step 2, I'll tell you exactly what that is.

But before I do, let's talk about why it's so important to act immediately.

Because now is the best time ever to build wealth.

Why? Because now is always the best time.

Now is always the best time to start anything. Results take time, and time is a limited resource. The sooner you begin, the faster you'll get where you want to go.

This is universally true, but it's especially true when the goal is to build wealth. You can't control the economy. You can't predict the markets. You can't ultimately protect yourself from disaster. But you can make yourself richer tomorrow than you are today.

There's always something you can do. Work an extra hour in the morning. Work another extra hour before you go home at night. Sell an extra widget. Start a partnership. Cook up a moneymaking idea.

Remember, every dollar you earn today is more valuable than a dollar you earn tomorrow—because of the value of compound interest. And every financially valuable secret you learn today is more valuable than it would be if you learned it tomorrow—because of the value of compound knowledge.

Be cognizant of the times we live in—the slowing economy, the burgeoning debt—but be equally aware of the passing of time. Every day that passes is 24 hours of opportunity you won't have again. Why not put a bit of that time to work for you right now?

READY . . . FIRE . . . AIM

Ready . . . Fire . . . Aim. That's the way I've operated in my career.

Why not "ready, aim, fire"? Because if you're ready to make something happen and you spend too much time trying to get things right (aiming) before you take action (fire), you'll lose the momentum that is driving you. You can always go back and do some fine-tuning later.

In business, implementing a second-best idea now is often a better strategy than waiting a week or a month or a year to come up with the perfect idea. Because the right decision made too late is sometimes worse than no decision at all.

Almost all of the successful entrepreneurs I know have an instinct for moving quickly—and that includes the way they make decisions. Although they often understand the importance of consultation, study, and contemplation, their natural tendency is to make the decision quickly and move on it.

That is a good instinct to have.

Success comes from experience. You make some mistakes. You have some triumphs. You learn from all of them. The secret to advancing quickly—whether your goal is to implement a new business idea or build your personal wealth—is to accelerate the learning process. And that means Ready, Fire, Aim.

How Larry, Eddie, and I Became Entrepreneurs

I'll tell you a story that illustrates the Ready, Fire, Aim approach.

Before my freshman year of college, I got a job with a company in Brooklyn that installed aboveground pools. I worked 12 hours a day and was paid about $6 an hour for my labor, which was at the time a princely sum.

After that summer of hard work and big earnings, I began classes, working evenings and weekends at a minimum-wage job to pay my expenses. I was living on my own, paying my own way, and proud of it. When the next summer approached, I toyed with the idea of going back to work for the pool company, but I had this idea of starting my own business.

"If we could install pools on our own," I told my friends Larry and Eddie, "we could probably make ten bucks an hour apiece. We'd be rich in no time," I assured them.

I had this conversation with them about a half dozen times that spring. Practically every time we were together and beer was available to fuel the speculative mind, the subject occurred to me.

Had I been talking to almost any of my other friends, nothing would have come of it. I would have gone back to work for the pool company at $6 an hour, and Larry and Eddie would have continued flipping hamburgers down at Harry's on Park Avenue. But Larry and Eddie had a spark between them. The fairy tale I had conjured up for them lit a fire in their minds. They decided that they were tired of burgers and minimum wage.

"Who would we have to talk to about setting up our own company?" they asked me. I didn't have a clue.

"Maybe you should talk to your dad," I told Eddie. "He teaches business administration, doesn't he?"

And so Eddie talked to his dad. And his dad told him that we would need to form a corporation and have a partnership agreement and set up an office and all of that. "But the most important thing you need to do," he wisely counseled, "is get your first customer."

There is no smarter advice when it comes to starting a business. And so that is exactly what Larry and Eddie did. They looked up pool sales companies in the phone book and began calling them and asking them if they needed any new service companies to build their pools for them.

"We don't build our own pools," they were told by three of the companies they called. "We don't want to get involved in all the complaints and hassles. If you say you can build pools and you can prove that to us, we'll recommend you to our customers."

And those three responses were enough to get the process moving.

When Larry called to tell me we had an appointment with one of these companies to install a sample pool in the display lot, I was both impressed and frightened. Impressed that Larry and Eddie had the get-up-and-go to make the phone calls and persuade these guys to give us a chance. And frightened because I suddenly realized that although I had worked on a pool-building crew for three months, from dawn till dusk, I had never been the foreman.

"But I'm not sure I know everything there is to know about building pools," I sheepishly admitted to Larry one afternoon between racks at Bill's Cue Club.

"But I thought you said . . ."

"But I didn't say I was an expert. And this may be a different kind of pool. And I was working with experienced guys. You guys don't know squat."

"So what?" Larry said. "So we aren't exactly perfect. Let's give it a try and see what happens. What's the worst thing that could happen? The pool will cave in, they'll tell us to take a hike, and we'll be right back where we started."

Larry's simple logic was rock solid and irrefutable. I could do nothing but agree.

I remember our trial job like it happened yesterday. It was an 18-foot-round, a baby pool that we would eventually be able to throw up in less than an hour. We arrived at the pool company with our tool-boxes and smiles on our faces at 7 A.M. on a Saturday. By 6 P.M. we were still working.

Yes, the worst had happened. The pool collapsed not once but three times. Each time, we gathered around it like Kubrick's apes around the monolith in *2001: A Space Odyssey* and stared at it. What did we do wrong? What could we do differently next time? Luckily for us, the falling down didn't ruin the pool. Lucky, too, the owner of the company was gone most of the day at meetings.

By the time he finally returned, the sun had set and we were cleaning up the worksite. A perfectly constructed 18-foot-round pool was up and shining—and it had taken us only 12 times longer than it should have.

There was some fast talking to be done to keep him from ripping up our freshly printed business cards. He eyed us suspiciously, but told us he'd try us out on one customer to see if we could do a good job "in a real combat situation."

That's the phrase he used: "real combat situation."

Well, he was as good as his word, and we put up that second pool in a mere six hours . . . and the next one in three . . .

> **IT'S NEVER TOO LATE TO CHANGE YOUR LIFE**
>
> Henry Flagler was 70 when he fell in love with Florida. In the 15-year period of his retirement there, he built a railroad from Jacksonville to Key West, created three major cities, founded universities, and built world-class hotels.

and so it went. Eventually, we had a crew of 10 guys working for us, and we were each making not the $10 an hour I had predicted but $30 an hour, working nonstop for weeks at a time and raking in so much money we didn't know what to do with it.

I left the pool business the next year, but Eddie and Larry went forward with it. It became a lifetime business for Larry and his wife, giving them a very good living and providing their community with a very high quality of service for many years.

In the year I was a part of it, it paid for three years' worth of college tuition, a paint job for my parent's house, and a new pool cue and sneakers. Maybe there were other things. But those are the ones I remember.

Ready Yourself to Take Action Now . . . and Then Fire—
There Will Be Plenty of Time to Aim Later

Are you ready to fire away at a new life of wealth building and financial independence? Are you willing to start today?

Turn the page, and I'll tell you what to do next.

STEP 2

PLAN TO
BECOME WEALTHY

You are about to change your financial future.

You've thought about change before, but never before have you had the feeling that you're ready for it *now*.

You recognize that if you *don't* change now, the odds will begin to turn against you. With each passing hour, day, and week, your chances of changing the direction of your life from one of financial struggling to freedom will diminish.

Take a look around you. Think about your family, friends, and colleagues. They want what you want—a higher income, less stress, more fun, and enough money in the bank to quit working so hard and enjoy life.

You and they have the same basic wants, but the chances that they will achieve their dreams are small . . . and getting smaller every day. That is not true in your case. The difference: You've made a *commitment* to change.

But committing to change and changing are two different things. Unless you take action now, a year or two will pass by and you'll find yourself thinking, "What happened to that promise I made to myself? Why didn't I do it? How come I'm at the very same place, financially, that I was back then?"

WHY IT'S SO IMPORTANT TO SEIZE THE DAY

Let me tell you a story . . .

At an AWAI seminar, the publisher of a natural health newsletter business asked the participants if they wanted a shot at writing a professional promotion. Eight students raised their hands.

This was their big chance. All they had to do was follow up after the conference and they'd be on their way. Their long-held dreams of becoming professional freelance writers would become reality.

Here's what happened, according to the publisher:

> "They were all *very* eager to get started. I expected a rush of e-mails and packages with everything they had ever written, including grocery lists and letters to their mothers . . . but . . . only one person has ever contacted me."

Eight people had this gold-plated opportunity to realize their dreams, yet only one actually did anything about it.

It seems astounding when you think about it. Yet it happens all the time. (And, by the way, the one student who did reply is now making more than $100,000 per year as a full-time freelance writer.)

Don't make that mistake yourself.

THE TIME TO START IS RIGHT NOW

I spend a good deal of my time mentoring people. Over the years, I've developed a pretty good sense of whether those I coach will succeed.

One thing I look for—probably the most important thing—is their time frame.

I know from experience that virtually everyone who puts off change fails to make it. When I hear someone say "I'm going to start after Christmas" or "next month" or "on Tuesday," I think, "Like hell you are."

For when it comes to change, the sure sign of failure is procrastination.

Even setting a starting date of tomorrow is a bad sign. People who really, truly want to create a real and permanent change in their lives want to start *now.* That's how I feel every time I get on a new project, start a new business, or kick off a new exercise program. I know I've become tired with the status quo. I've figured out a way to make things better. That newness excites me. Why should I put it off?

When I catch myself saying that I'll begin at some later point in time, I know I'm in trouble.

Think about your own experience. Think about how many times you've decided to change before. How many of those times did you put off starting until some convenient point in the future? And when you did, how many times did you fail?

So, are you ready to begin building wealth now? Right now?

Good.

> Too many of us wait to do the perfect thing, with the result we do nothing . . . we discover that those who have gone fearlessly on before, have . . . traveled a considerable distance. If you start now, you will know a lot next year that you don't know now, and that you will not know next year, if you wait.
>
> —*The William Feather Magazine*

GETTING YOURSELF READY BY SETTING GOALS

This book is about wealth, but we are going to broaden the scope for a while and talk about what you want out of life generally. Do you have goals for your family? Social or charitable goals? Do you have personal, nonfinancial objectives? Do you daydream about becoming an actor, athlete, or magician? Would you like to work with children in your spare time? Or help the disabled?

If you have no goals other than becoming wealthy, your chances of success will be great—but the likelihood that you'll be dissatisfied will be great, too. There is no greater financial cliché than the poor man who builds a fortune only to discover that he lost everything that was really important to him.

I am not going to let that happen to you. You are going to become wealthy and wise and happy and healthy, too!

You begin the process by determining your core values.

WHAT DO YOU HOPE PEOPLE WILL SAY ABOUT YOU AT YOUR FUNERAL?

In Mark Twain's *Adventures of Tom Sawyer,* America's two favorite juvenile delinquents disappear from their small town for a boyish adventure and then return to find a funeral going on—for them. Hidden in the church's balcony overlooking the ceremony, Tom and Huck get to hear exactly what other people think of them. It is an eye-opening experience for the two young troublemakers—and imagining your own funeral can do the same thing for you.

So imagine being at your funeral. You are hiding up in the balcony. You can see your coffin. Standing behind the coffin are four people:

- Someone from your family or a close friend
- Someone you work with
- Someone whom you admire
- Someone who didn't know you

What do you hope each one of them would say about you? Go ahead. Write it down. Your wish list might include statements like these:

- "He always made me feel important, even when I felt like I had nothing to give."
- "He was the best father I could have ever hoped for. He taught me to be strong and independent and he showed me that I could be brave and loving at the same time."
- "He was a brilliant writer. For someone who spent so much of his life in the business world, I was astonished at how well written his stories were."
- "I would still be working as a security guard if it were not for him. To think of what I've become. I know how much of that I owe to his help and care."

These are the things that are really important to you—your *personal core values.* (And I'm guessing that "He was really rich" is *not* something that you'd put on this list.)

Now, let's apply what you just learned about yourself to your next task . . .

TRANSLATE YOUR CORE VALUES INTO FOUR LIFETIME GOALS

If you invited all the right people to your imaginary funeral, you can now figure out what your core values are in every important aspect of your life.

Your core values might look something like this:

- "As a worker, I want to be considered creative and helpful."
- "As a parent, I want to be thought of as supportive and kind."
- "As an individual, I want to be thought of as smart and interesting."

You are not going to publish this list. The point of making it is to help you know yourself in a way that matters. Which brings us to your next task: converting your core values to life goals. If you've done your work well so far—if you truly do know yourself—this will be surprisingly easy.

How many life goals should you have? Four is a good, achievable number. One of them, of course, will be to build wealth—not to accumulate money but because of what that money can help you accomplish in terms of your core values. As I said in Step 1, it gives you the ability to help other people, provide for your family, pursue your intellectual and artistic interests, and become an inspiration to members of your community.

What about your other three life goals? That's up to you. But I would recommend coming up with one that has something to do with your health, one that is concerned with your personal relationships, and one that targets your own growth and development.

Do that now—and put it in writing. Your list of four goals might look something like this:

1. *My long-term wealth-building goal:* To be financially independent. To be able to do whatever I want without worrying about money.
2. *My long-term health goal:* To be active, fully functioning, and pain free till age 90.
3. *My long-term personal-relationship goal:* To be remembered as a great dad, loving spouse, loyal friend, and charitable soul.

4. *My long-term personal growth and development goal:* To be a successful novelist, filmmaker, and linguist.

HOW MUCH OF THIS CAN YOU REALISTICALLY ACCOMPLISH, MEDIUM TERM— IN THE NEXT 7 TO 15 YEARS?

The purpose of this book is to help you achieve financial independence in 7 to 15 years—and to do that while still keeping you on track to achieve all of your long-term life goals.

BE SPECIFIC ABOUT LIFETIME GOALS

A good way to start is to add some specificity to your lifetime goal. Narrow it down in every way you can. For example, say your lifetime goal is "to become a great writer." Here are ways you can make it more specific.

TIME: Become a great writer by my 65th birthday.

TYPE: Become a great novelist by my 65th birthday.

DEFINITIONS: Become an award-winning novelist by my 65th birthday.

I've chosen this 7- to 15-year time frame somewhat arbitrarily, I admit, but with good reason. First, because I don't believe you are willing to wait 30 to 40 years to achieve financial independence. And second, because that seems to be a realistic length of time to achieve success in any type of business venture. Almost every one of the several dozen businesses I've started has hit its stride and become profitable in 7 years or less. Most do it more quickly than that—usually in 4 or 5 years. Some are winners from the start. Some fail, of course, but that's usually apparent early on. (Wise businesspeople recognize when this is happening and cut their losses short.) But I don't remember a single one that took longer than 6 or 7 years.

That's why I feel confident promising you results in 7 to 15 years (actually, more than confident . . . 99.9 percent sure).

Lifetime goals have the advantage of being long term and thus far away. Being so distant, it's possible to imagine yourself accomplishing practically anything. That's why, if you really want to achieve your goals, you need to work with a very specific medium-term time frame. I've defined medium term as 7 to 15 years. But you should narrow it down to an exact number.

And not only do you need to be specific, you also need to be realistic. For example, if your lifetime financial goal is to have a net worth of $5 million and you are currently 45 years old and broke, it might be realistic for you to set a medium-term goal of $1 million in 10 years. But if you already have half a million in the bank, it would perhaps be realistic for you to set a medium-term financial goal of $2.5 million in 7 years.

There are no absolute rules when it comes to this type of goal setting. You want your goals to be ambitious, but you also want them to be achievable. Spend some time now studying your list of lifetime goals, and figure out (and write down) specific medium-term goals for each one.

HOW MUCH CAN YOU ACCOMPLISH IN THE NEXT YEAR?

You are making good progress. You have a vision of what you must do in the next 7 to 15 years—and you are probably feeling pretty excited about it. Use this energy to break your goals down even further by setting 1-year objectives.

This is something many people do at the beginning of every new year. But you are not going to wait for January 1 to roll around. You understand the deathly danger of procrastination. You've already felt the power of taking action. So you take the next critically important step now.

Yearly goals should be specific and, if possible, measurable. A simple one-year plan might look like this:

My Wealth-Building Goals for the Year
- Get a $10,000 raise.
- Take a course in direct marketing.
- Start my own plumbing supply Internet business.
- Make friends with 12 powerful people in the plumbing industry.

My Health Goals for the Year
- Bench-press 250 pounds.
- Run six miles in 40 minutes.
- Get my HDL cholesterol to 80 or above.
- Master the lotus position.

My Personal Relationship Goals for the Year
- Host a monthly dinner party with friends.
- Raise $5,000 for my favorite charity.
- Repair my relationship with Aunt Pollie.
- Develop the habit of remembering people's names.

My Personal Growth and Development Goals for the Year
- Become a competent judge of good wine.
- Read 12 new books about science.
- Add 50 new stamps to my stamp collection.
- Learn to play something on the guitar.

A little later in this chapter, I'll show you how to break down your yearly goals into monthly, weekly, and daily objectives. (The focus will be on your wealth-building objectives, your lifetime goal of enjoying financial independence.) Plus, I'll share with you some techniques I've developed that will give you an 80 percent or better chance of actually accomplishing the goals you set for yourself.

But right now, let's discuss something you can start doing tomorrow morning that will make it possible for all of this to happen.

THE EARLY BIRD CATCHES THE GOLDEN WORM

Walk into your bedroom right now and set your alarm clock one hour earlier. If you are accustomed to getting up at eight, set it for seven. If your normal wake-up time is seven, set it for six.

From now on, you are going to wake up and get to work an hour earlier.

Getting to work early is such a common virtue of successful people that I'm tempted to call it the single most important thing you can do to change your life.

I wasn't always an early riser. For most of my 20s, if I saw the sun rise, it was before going to bed. And even in my 30s, I'd struggle to get in to the office by nine. I wasn't afraid of the work. Most days, I'd put in 12 to 14 hours. But since I had accustomed myself to late hours in college and graduate school, I saw no reason to change my waking and sleeping habits. "I do my best work after midnight," I used to say. And for a while, I even believed it.

My conversion happened in my early 40s, after I'd already become financially independent and retired for the first time (if ever so briefly). That being the case, I can't argue that it's impossible to become successful unless you get up early. I did it. And plenty of others did, too.

But I can say that the success I've had since then has been more dramatic . . . and has come a lot easier.

> We are all given an equal number of hours to spend each day. How we use them makes the difference between success and failure. I had learned, pretty early, the importance of working long and hard. What I never knew—until my conversion—was the immense benefit of getting to work early.

HOW I TAUGHT MYSELF THE VIRTUOUS EARLY-TO-RISE HABIT

At the time of my conversion, I was working about 65 hours a week, beginning each workday at 9 A.M. and working until about 8 P.M. Five days at 11 hours and at least half a day on Saturday and Sunday allowed me to reach that 65-hour average. (Needless to say, I wasn't seeing much of my family.)

My partner at the time was getting to work at 7:30 or 8:00 (I can't be sure, of course, since I was never there to greet him!) and leaving at about 6:30 or 7:00. He was working about the same number of hours as I was during the week but didn't work at all on weekends.

I was jealous of his weekends (he'd tell me stories of chopping wood on the farm, taking hikes along the river) and promised myself repeatedly that I'd not work weekends, either. But when Friday night came to a close, I never felt my work had been done. There were always several very important matters needing attention. Therefore, one weekend after the next became filled with catch-up work.

My family didn't like it. I didn't like it. But the really frustrating thing was that nobody at work seemed to notice all the extra time I was putting in. In fact, I was getting ribbed about coming in late.

After working especially late one night, I stopped for gas at about two o'clock in the morning. As I handed my credit card to the lady in the glass booth, she said, "Man, you look beat!"

"I've been working almost twelve hours a day," I told her. "And half-days on weekends."

She looked at me, unimpressed. "You talk about it like it's a virtue," she said.

"Well if working long hours isn't a virtue," I shot back, "what is?"

"Being the first one at work," she said.

It was a very bizarre moment: being lectured about virtue by a gas jockey at 2 A.M. But somehow I knew she was right. For all the extra hours I put in, my partner—who had his weekends free—had cornered the market as far as the Puritan work ethic was concerned. He seemed more virtuous not only to our employees but also, I suddenly realized, to me!

There is something about getting in earlier that seems wiser, nobler, smarter, or just plain more industrious than working late. Getting to work earlier says something about being energetic, organized, and in control. Staying late leaves the opposite impression: You are diligent but disorganized, earnest but erratic, hardworking but a drudge.

In *How to Become CEO* (Hyperion, 1998), Jeffrey J. Fox puts it this way:

> If you are going to be first in your corporation, start practicing by being first on the job. People who arrive at work late don't like their jobs—at least that's what senior management thinks. . . . And don't stay at the office until 10 o'clock every night. You are sending a signal that you can't keep up or your personal life is poor.

This lady in the glass booth was right. Getting to work first was better than working until dawn. From that moment on, I resolved to come to work earlier.

And I did. At first, it was difficult and my success was sporadic. But then I came upon a plan that worked. I resolved to set my alarm clock to wake me a minute earlier each day. A single minute would feel like nothing, I figured, yet in the course of two months I would have moved the start of my day back by an hour.

I used this minute-per-day program to move my at-work time from 9:00 to 8:30 and then to 8:00 and then to 7:30, and so on. Today, I typically wake up at 5:30 and arrive at my desk (or my workout) at 6:30.

WHAT YOU WILL GAIN BY GETTING TO WORK EARLIER

This change gave me the right to feel as virtuous as my early-to-rise partner. But the benefits were more than psychological. I began to notice all of the following physical and material benefits almost immediately:

- More energy
- More energetic focus throughout the day
- A chance to review my various in-boxes before planning and prioritizing my day
- Quiet time, without distractions, to concentrate on important tasks
- A feeling of being ahead of everyone else

"Early to bed and early to rise, makes a man healthy, wealthy, and wise," Ben Franklin advised almost 300 years ago—and taking that path really did make a big difference in my life. And I'm not the only one. There are several studies showing that successful entrepreneurs typically get to work at least an hour before their employees. So do most CEOs. Most of the wealthiest people I know get up early. In fact, this is such a universal trait of successful people that I'm tempted to say it's their number one secret.

YOUR WEALTH-BUILDING PLAN FOR THE NEXT 12 MONTHS

Most people don't marry into money or fall into an unexpected inheritance. Wealth usually arrives bit by bit as the result of carefully setting long-term, medium-term, and short-term goals and

> If you get up and get in to the office one hour earlier, you will immediately start to join the ranks of top management . . . the people who are always in the office first, sometimes by 6:00 or 7:00 A.M.

planning out what you need to do every month, week, and day to achieve them.

You've set your lifetime, medium-term, and yearly goals. You've made a commitment to "rise early and catch the golden worm" each morning. Good so far.

Now let me show you how to break down your goals for this year into concrete, achievable steps for this month, this week, and this very day. Since financial independence is one of your primary goals, let's take a look at how you might create and prioritize your objectives in terms of some of the wealth-building techniques I'll be teaching you later in this book.

I'm going to assume that your lifetime wealth-building goal is to be financially independent. But since I don't know what you've established for yourself so far in terms of your medium-term wealth-building goals, let's go with a hypothetical scenario.

So let's assume that your medium-term goal is to have $120,000 a year in pretax passive income and that your target for achieving that goal is seven years.

There are many ways to get to that $120,000 number. Let's say you're planning to do it this way:

Medium-Term (Seven-Year) Goal: $120,000 per Year in Pretax Passive Income
- Own, free and clear, $300,000 worth of rental real estate, yielding $45,000 a year
- Own $200,000 in bonds, yielding (pretax) $15,000 a year
- Have $200,000 in stocks, averaging $25,000 a year
- Own equity in a business distributing $35,000 a year

Now what? Now you have to figure out what you have to achieve this year in order to reach those seven-year goals. Your one-year goal might look something like this:

One-Year Goal
- Buy $60,000 worth of real estate at 20 percent down
- Buy $10,000 worth of bonds
- Buy $8,000 worth of stocks
- Get a business started

SETTING MONTHLY, WEEKLY, AND DAILY OBJECTIVES

The next step is to break your yearly goals down into manageable, bite-sized monthly objectives.

One of the yearly objectives in our example is to get a business started. So you would break that down into 12 monthly goals—what you need to do each month to get your business up and running, from doing the initial research to the grand opening.

Then you break each of those 12 monthly goals into 4 weekly goals. For instance, if your first monthly goal in getting a new business started is to identify a good business opportunity, perhaps each of your 4 weekly goals will be to research at least 10 possibilities.

Finally, you work your way down to the action you will take each day to fulfill your weekly objective. If you have made a commitment to research 10 business opportunities each week, that means one of the top priorities on your daily to-do list will be to research two possibilities.

Expect to spend one full day planning out your year. Once a month, you'll sit down for two or three hours to map out your goals for the next four weeks. Once a week, you'll spend one hour establishing your goals for the next seven days. And you'll spend about 10 or 15 minutes each morning organizing your day.

I know that sounds like a lot, but taken all together you're really spending no more than three days a year to map out your strategy for achieving financial independence in the next 7 to 15 years.

This is how I establish my goals, focus my objectives, and set daily tasks. It's not, by any means, an entirely original system. It's a patchwork of systems that have been developed by others and added to by me. But there is something about this particular system that seems to work.

It works so well, in fact, that I encourage everyone who works for me to use it. Those who do find that it works very well. I think you will, too.

DAILY PLANNING: GETTING THE MOST FROM EVERY MINUTE

There is no better time to collect your thoughts, review your goals, examine your current responsibilities, and plan your day than early in

HOW ANDY DID IT

Andy, a senior staff writer for *Early to Rise* (*ETR*), had been struggling to keep up with all the work I'd been giving him. I knew he could do everything I had asked him to do and much more, but he was swamped. When we talked about it, he explained that he was interrupted frequently, that oftentimes the research he did took much longer than he expected, and so on. I asked him if he followed my goal-setting program. He admitted that he didn't.

"I know I should start," he said, "but I've been so busy."

I encouraged him to give it a try, and he agreed to put together a weekly and a daily to-do list right away.

A half hour later, he came back—but with two almost identical lists. His weekly schedule had eight items on it. His daily list had almost all the same ones.

Looking at these lists, it was clear to me why Andy wasn't making the progress he was capable of:

- His daily task list wasn't balanced. (A balanced list is one that ensures that every day you spend a certain amount of time on each important long-term goal.)
- His tasks were not prioritized. He was feeling pressured to get a certain big job done because it was overdue, so he was spending most of his time on that job and neglecting tasks that were actually more crucial.
- Instead of taking a little extra time to follow my goal-setting program, Andy was organizing his work by writing down lists of chores that others had asked him to do—not according to what he knew he needed to do to advance his personal objectives. That made him a slave to those people instead of a master of his own time.

We went over the basics of my goal-setting program, and Andy agreed to get started on it over the weekend by coming up with his list of four life goals.

And he did.

His long-term wealth-building goal was (no surprise) financial free-dom—a life without debt. He had broken that down to the annual income he hoped to be generating at the seven-year milestone and had targeted a significant accomplishment for year one: to increase his income by 100 percent.

That may seem unrealistic, but he had already figured out that he could achieve that very aggressive goal by writing two winning promotional packages (what direct marketers call *controls*) for *Early to Rise*.

Here's where his impressive start began to fizzle. "I'm not sure how to get that done," he admitted.

"By identifying that goal and making it a priority, you've already done the most important thing," I told him. "Now you need to figure out how many promotions you'll need to write to give yourself a better than even chance of coming up with two winners."

He asked several experienced copywriters who have done it and found out that, on the average, you have to write six promotions in order to come up with two controls.

"Okay," I said. "You are on to something. To come up with two controls in one year, you're going to have to write a new promotion every two months. Now you need to break down the steps that it takes to write a promotion." And so he did:

1. Get the assignment.
2. Research the product.
3. Research past promotions.
4. Hold a brainstorming session.
5. Create two or three proposals.
6. Get them approved.
7. Write the promotion.
8. Get it critiqued.
9. Rewrite it.
10. Get it mailed.

By breaking the goal down into individual tasks, Andy could clearly see that he had to get started right away if he intended to achieve it by the end of the year. He'll have to go through this 10-step process six times—and that will keep his monthly, weekly, and even daily schedule very full.

the morning when the office is quiet and still. Here's the early morning routine that works best for me:

Get Your Inputs (5 to 10 minutes)

I start the day by scanning my daily task list, which I have written the night before. If for some reason I haven't prepared a task list, I do it then, based on my weekly list of objectives. I then scan my e-mail, not responding to anything but noting responses that will need to be made and putting some of them down on my daily task list. I do the same with the in-box that sits on my desk. Finally, I retrieve any phone messages and if one of them requires action, make note of it on my daily task list.

I make it a point to *not* do any work now (send out a quick e-mail response or return phone messages) because I know if I do I'll get caught up in a lot of small stuff that will bog me down and drain my energy. Instead, I devote this input time to polishing off my daily task list. As soon as that's done, I move on to the next step.

Sort and Prioritize (5 to 10 minutes)

> Effective people plan their time in tight time segments. They think in terms of 10- and 15-minute blocks. They plan every day in detail, in advance. They make every minute count. As a result, they accomplish vastly more than the average person, and they feel much better about themselves.
>
> —Focal Point *by Brian Tracy*
> *(American Management Association, 2001)*

Now comes the fun part. Assuming my daily to-do list has already been completed, I indicate for each task the approximate amount of time I expect it will take to complete it. I always try to be realistic in my estimations of time required. Over the years, I've trained myself to be very conservative.

As a general rule, I break up tasks into 15-, 30-, 45-minute, and 1-hour increments. But every once in a while (such as right now, while I'm writing this book), I allow myself 2 or 2½ hours for a single task.

I generally like to prioritize my tasks in terms of their importance and urgency. This idea is based on the quadrant developed by Steven Covey in his popular *7 Habits* books. He identifies tasks as being either (1) Important and Urgent, (2) Important but not Urgent, (3) Unimportant but Urgent, or (4) Unimportant and not Urgent.

If we work with this idea, your daily schedule should be focused mainly on (1) and (2) tasks, because these require immediate attention or will advance you toward your ultimate goals. Your schedule should contain a diminishing number of (3) tasks (since they indicate that you are not in control of your schedule), and no (4) tasks at all.

You could also assign priorities based on a well-known organizational technique known as the *ABCDE method*. It goes like this:

- An A task is something that is important, something you must do.
- A B task is something you should do, yet it's not an A.
- A C task is something that would be nice to do, but it won't change your life in a radical way.
- A D task is something that should be delegated.
- And, finally, an E task is something that shouldn't be done at all. It should be eliminated from your task list.

Another way to set priorities is to think in terms of the old 80/20 rule. As applied to productivity, the rule says that 80 percent of the things you do every day contribute to only 20 percent of the progress you make. But that means 20 percent of what you do is responsible for 80 percent of your success. For our purposes, the way to use the 80/20 rule is to scan the tasks on your to-do list and highlight the 20 percent (the 2 out of 10 or 4 out of 20) that will make a giant difference in your life. If you are thinking right, the tasks you highlight will be the ones that support your life goals.

Start with Something Really Important (15 to 60 minutes)

The third and most important part of my get-into-the-office-early time is devoted to accomplishing one Important-but-not-Urgent task.

I like to start out the day with a nonurgent task because these are usually the tasks that make the biggest, long-term differences in your life—and because they are not urgent, tend to be overlooked. In terms of wealth building, your Important-but-not-Urgent tasks might include

- Learning or improving a financially valuable skill
- Expanding your support network

- Pushing forward a major project that has stalled
- Writing a memo that will advance your career
- Brainstorming a new project

Doing an important task right off the bat gives me an immediate sense of accomplishment that fills me with energy that fuels my work for the rest of the day.

This is one of the reasons I don't allow myself to solve or even answer any of the problems I run into during my early-morning review of e-mails and my in-box. I understand the productivity concept of not looking at anything twice, but my early morning hours are just too important to spend on anything other than organizing, prioritizing, and attacking my Important-but-not-Urgent tasks.

I answer e-mails only once or twice a day, but not first thing. If I do that, I find myself quickly sucked into issues and situations that (1) aren't that important, (2) can often be handled just as well by someone else, (3) don't advance my long-term goals, and (4) sap me of mental and emotional energy that could be put to better use elsewhere.

HOW TO MAKE SURE THE IMPORTANT WORK GETS DONE

As you're mapping out your day, make sure you put at least one task on your to-do list that will get you closer to achieving your ultimate wealth-building goal. And make sure it is something significant. This will almost automatically make it more difficult in some way. More nervy. More stressful. But write it down anyway.

Then, when you are going over your list and highlighting your priorities, mark this one in a different color. (I use yellow for my normal, *business-maintenance* priorities and pink for *new-growth* activities.)

Highlight it in a different color, in any case, and don't—under any circumstances—fail to do it. Don't skip it for an easier task. Don't put it off until tomorrow. Tackle it first thing in the morning if that's what you have to do to get it done.

MAKE GOOD HEALTH ONE OF YOUR LIFETIME GOALS

When you figure out your life goals, don't forget about the importance of good health. Staying healthy is not something younger people usually think about. But as time wears you down, it becomes clear what a critical component of success good health is.

If you've ever been seriously ill, you know what I mean. There is not enough fame, fortune, or power in the world to compensate for the loss of your health. Not nearly enough.

Five Things You Must Do to Stay Healthy

I've been involved in the start-up of a health clinic in Florida that will specialize in rejuvenation. The doctor who is heading up the clinic has spent most of the last 10 years studying aging and helping middle-aged and older people get younger.

When we went into business together, I asked him to put me on a rejuvenation program, and he did. I've lost weight, gained muscle, increased my flexibility, and I feel stronger and more positive than I ever did before. I attribute it to this five-point approach to good health:

1. Diet
2. Aerobic exercise
3. Strength training
4. Flexibility
5. Mental attitude

As a busy, achievement-oriented person, you may be thinking that you don't have enough time in your day to take care of all those things. But I would disagree. If you plan them into your regular work schedule, you'll be surprised at how much you can do for your health on even the busiest days.

The first thing you need to do is recognize that physical fitness is almost always an Important-but-not-Urgent task, and unless you make it a specific daily priority, you will neglect it. So that's the first thing I'd like you to do. Put all five of these items on your to-do list every day as high-lighted, priority items.

Here's how I get them into my daily routine.

(continues)

1. *Diet:* I eat four small, no-starch meals during the day and one balanced meal (with a little starch) in the evening. I try to never eat after dinner. All meals but dinner are eaten alone over work, but never over stressful work.

2. *Aerobic exercise:* I mix it up a bit, but my aerobic activity can include sprints, bike sprints, jiujitsu (intense training), or boxing. I do either one or two 10-minute routines every day. Since these are sweaty workouts, I do them before or after work.

3. *Strength training:* I have a little gym right outside my office. I work out intensely for five minutes three times during the morning, after each task I accomplish. I view these exercises as bonuses. (If you can't set up your own gym, a pair of barbells in your office will do.)

4. *Flexibility:* I do a quick, 5-minute stretch every morning and another 10-minute stretch sometime during the day.

5. *Mental attitude:* This doesn't cost you any serious time, just a few seconds every day to remind yourself to slow down and enjoy life.

My goal is to be in the best shape of my life and to exceed that in 10 years. (Jack LaLanne swam from Alcatraz Island to San Francisco, shackled and handcuffed and pulling a rowboat with 5,000 pounds of sand in it, on his 60th birthday.)

I take care of my health because it makes me feel better and because it helps me work harder. Those two reasons are good enough for me. But plenty of studies show that a good diet and regular exercise make us less vulnerable to a wide range of serious and annoying health problems, including heart disease, cancer (colon, rectal, and prostate), poor circulation, obesity, diabetes, and more.

You don't have to work out 45 minutes a day to start off. Try 15 minutes and build from there. But start today.

REACH YOUR GOALS FASTER: EIGHT SECRETS I'VE DISCOVERED FOR TURNING WASTED TIME INTO PRODUCTIVE TIME

Now your challenge is to find more free time—the time you need to accomplish your goals. By "free time" I mean wasted time. The

5 minutes here and 10 minutes there that slip by unnoticed, but swallow up hours of your life every day.

Here are eight productivity secrets that can save you a good two hours each day that you can put toward achieving your dream of financial independence.

Productivity Secret No. 1: Streamline Your E-mail

E-mail has become a way of life for most of us—especially in business—but it doesn't have to take a huge bite out of your work life. With just a few changes in the way you manage e-mail, you'll save yourself one or more hours every day that you can apply to constructive goals.

I mentioned earlier that I sift through my e-mail only once or twice a day (at most) to keep it from consuming hours of my time. A lot of the messages that I get are questions about problems that people are looking to me to resolve. Most of them I simply ignore. And I find that they are usually handled just fine without my interference.

If you don't micromanage every situation, your staff will eventually get the point that it's up to them to take care of most of the day-to-day problems that arise. That will make them (and your entire organization) stronger and thus more profitable. And should an e-mail message raise your ire, you'll have given yourself time to cool down and respond to it in a professional manner.

Here are a few other ideas to help you streamline the process even further.

- Keep your e-mail messages short and to the point—and ask the people who e-mail you to do the same. Very few messages need to be more than a screen-page long—and those that pose a problem should always be presented with multiple-choice solutions.
- If you find that you need more than one screen page to say what you have to say, the subject is probably too involved to be handled effectively through e-mail. You need to do it over the phone or face-to-face instead.
- This bit of advice may go completely against your grain, but I'll give it anyway: Make it a point to let e-mail messages wait unless they're real red-light emergencies. Here's why I tell you that. It is said that Napoleon Bonaparte waited a month before

answering letters. "If a response is still needed, I will write it then," he said. I feel pretty much the same way about responding to e-mail.

- In addition to letting e-mails wait, you can cut the time it takes to answer many of them by creating templates to reply to the questions you are asked most often. Not only will you save time, your responses will also all be well structured and well written.

- Give your correspondents the courtesy of knowing when they will hear from you. This can be done by creating an automessage that alerts senders when to expect a reply. It will help ease their minds and keep them from sending you multiple *follow-up* messages. This works especially well when you're out of the office, so you don't come back to a barrage of e-mails from testy clients or employees.

- As many as 50 percent of the messages you send could be reduced to a short statement in the subject line. For example:

Staff meeting moved to 1:30 P.M.
FedEx package just arrived.
Yes, I'll marry you. (I hope, however, you'll consider handling this one in person.)

No need to waste your precious time going into detail about why the meeting was changed, admonishing people to be on time, and a bunch of other stuff that nobody cares about. By distilling your message to its essence in the subject line, you also save time for the people you're sending it to. They won't feel compelled to respond to it—and you won't have to bother with reading and deleting multiple versions of "Okay, I'll be at the staff meeting. Looking forward to it." Just think how much time everyone in your office and all your friends could save if they used this tip. How can you get them to do it? Lead by example. Start doing it yourself. And forward this tip to everyone with whom you regularly communicate via e-mail.

- One last piece of advice about e-mails: *Forget instant messaging!* According to the *New York Times,* a quarter of American employees use instant messaging at work. "It's free and easy to download," proclaims the article. "The most productive thing I've ever seen," rejoices one executive interviewed by the paper. Instant messaging is great if your primary goal at work is to waste as much of your time as possible. By allowing your workday to be interrupted constantly by friends and colleagues out there on the Web, you can be assured you will never spend any great length of time focusing. "Clients appreciate receiving an instant reply to a question," the executive cited above said. Maybe. But they might not like it so much if the replies were honest, such as "I don't have an answer for you on that now since I'm too busy answering instant messages."

Productivity Secret No. 2: Attack Similar Tasks in Blocks

Whether you have to answer 25 e-mails, make nine phone calls, or write three memos, you'll easily save yourself an hour a day just by lumping like tasks together and blocking out time in your schedule to tackle them all at once.

Assembling common tasks makes you much more efficient. So group them into one category on your daily to-do list and allot them a specific amount of time in your schedule.

And while you're at it, block out some time for yourself as well. Full schedules without relaxation lead to burnout. So along with the various and sundry tasks you have to accomplish, you need to give yourself a few 5-minute, 10-minute, and 15-minute blocks of "me" time each day.

You might enjoy a walk in the sun. Or a crossword puzzle and a cup of coffee. I have three routines I like right now. When I'm a bit pressed, I retire to a table and chair outside my office and read correspondence and other business papers while I enjoy a nice Dominican robusto. When I need to have a casual conversation with someone, I do it over a rack of pool (with cigar smoke mandatory). When I'm not overwhelmed by work, I smoke a cigar and read a poem.

Productivity Secret No. 3: Take Control of Your
Schedule with This Simple Device

Do you start your day with the best of intentions—organize your schedule, block out your time, highlight important goals, and vow to *stick to it today*—only to find your good intentions shot to hell by noon?

It's hard to keep track of the time. You bury yourself in work and the next time you look up, three hours have passed and you don't have half the things done you'd planned.

I've solved that problem with an electric egg timer. It looks like the conventional, windup kind but runs on batteries. When I begin a project, I allot it a certain amount of time. When that time expires, the timer signals me with an ascending scale of louder and louder beeps.

I keep the timer at the far end of the office so that I can't just reach over and turn it off. I have to get out of my chair and cross the room. Then, instead of returning to my desk to start a new task, I leave the office to take a brief, one-minute walk or stretch. This gives me a breather and helps me switch tracks to the next project.

Another way your timer can help you control your schedule is when someone comes into your office and says, "I have a quick question. Got a minute?" Say "sure," and set your egg timer for a minute.

Productivity Secret No. 4:
Get Company Meetings under Control

I believe wholeheartedly in limiting company meetings. Too much time gets wasted in daily meetings that stretch on for an hour and two hours without accomplishing anything of significant value for anyone there.

Whether or not you're leading the meeting, you should always have a plan before attending. Your plan should include a specific personal agenda (e.g., "I will leave the meeting with an agreement from Jeff on the new product") as well as ideas about how to attain that goal (e.g., "I'll make him a quick, logical argument—and if he doesn't go for that, I'll remind him of the favor he owes me").

Obviously, you can't just stop having meetings altogether. You can, however, reduce both the number held each week and the time they take. That leaves an extra hour or more of productive work to advance your company's objectives as well as your own career and personal goals.

The biggest challenge with meetings is to start them on time and keep them short and on point. It's aggravating when people walk in 10 minutes late and disrupt the flow of ideas in order to be brought up to speed. It's even more aggravating when the meeting then drags on, chewing up an hour or more of your time without accomplishing the things it was meant to.

If you find that the usual weekly meetings are starting late and going too long, you may want to try this: Rather than meeting for an hour every week, meet for 10 minutes on Monday, Wednesday, and Thursday.

With only 10 minutes available, the meeting will have to start on time. You will find—as I have found—that more gets done because you're forced to focus on the most important issues right away. You will save a half hour per week (three full days a year). And latecomers will learn a valuable lesson about punctuality: There's no time to bring them up to speed in a 10-minute meeting, so they will have to catch up on their own time—and will likely show up when they're supposed to next time.

Productivity Secret No. 5: Limit Memos to One Page

Another way you can streamline your day is by changing the way you write simple business documents. Writing a memo can take 30 minutes or more. But you can cut that time in half and double the power and clarity of your message simply by shortening the length and stating your primary point earlier.

When business writing is bad, it's usually because of one of four problems:

1. It's too complicated.
2. It's too confusing.
3. It's too vague.
4. It's unconvincing.

All four of these common problems can be combated by a straightforward thesis stated very early in the copy.

Stating your main point early lets your readers know exactly what you are talking about and why they should keep reading. If your thesis is strong (i.e., the idea is useful to them), it will appeal to your readers right away and motivate them to read with attention the rest of what you have to say.

The shorter the copy, the sooner you need to use your thesis sentence. Here's a rough guideline:

- For copy that's 500 words or less (the length of most memos), make your first sentence the thesis sentence.
- For copy between 500 words and 1,500 words, state the thesis in the first paragraph.
- For copy over 1,500 words, state the thesis within the first page.

There is no copy, however long, that justifies a thesis statement made later than the first page.

For most memos, one page (under 500 words) works best. Mastering the one-page memo is an invaluable business skill that will not only make you a more powerful communicator but also sharpen your thinking. One way to do it is to use this simple, three-part structure: (1) Tell it, (2) explain it, and (3) retell it.

Before you type a single word, ask yourself, "What is my bottom-line thought on this subject?" If, for example, you are writing a memo about your company's new budget, the thought might be "Our revenue targets are overly optimistic."

If your idea can't be expressed in a simple declarative statement like that, you need to keep thinking until you have it.

Use that statement as your first sentence. Then spend most of the rest of the page explaining what you mean by it. Don't overexplain. And don't underexplain, either. Provide as much evidence as you need to prove your point. Finally, compose a concluding sentence that harkens back to your opening statement and also ties together any loose ends.

Productivity Secret No. 6: Learn How to Delegate

It's not easy to delegate responsibility when you know no one else can do the job the way you want it done, when you want it done, and how you want it done. You're the go-to person, the one who can answer questions, explain things, get problems solved. This is a good and a bad thing. Good because it gives you power. Good because it advances your goals. Bad because it can overwhelm you if you are not careful.

Unless you are the only person in your business, reluctance to share the workload will cripple your company. It is foolhardy to think you can do everything yourself. Beyond driving yourself crazy, you will collapse from exhaustion and your business will collapse along with you.

At some point you'll have to learn to delegate or you'll burn out. Here are some guidelines to help you pick the right person for the task and let it go with confidence.

- *Decide where you need help.* Look at your weekly to-do list. Note the jobs you really enjoy doing and gain satisfaction from. Those are the ones you probably won't want to give up. Then note the jobs that make the most of your abilities. Those are the ones you probably shouldn't give up. What's left are the jobs you don't like or are not particularly good at. And those are the ones that someone else may be able to fill.

- *Select candidates carefully.* You don't want just anyone helping you, because when you delegate work, the way it is done reflects directly on you. Look for people who have an interest in the work, have the skills to do it (or are willing to learn them), and have the time and initiative to accomplish it.

- *Make your case.* Be specific about the work you want the people to do, project goals, and any deadlines. Let them know why you chose them and how doing the job can make them more valuable to the organization. Show them that it will benefit them as well as you.

- *Seal the deal.* For some people, a handshake may be enough. But to be on the safe side and to make sure you both understand what will be done, put it in writing. Notify your coworkers that this person now has the authority to do the job.

- *Follow up.* Check to see that things are getting done in a timely way. Keep in mind that if the job is being done differently from the way you would have done it, that doesn't necessarily mean it's being done wrong. Keep an open mind. But if there is a problem, address it—without getting personal.

Productivity Secret No. 7: Hire Great People

A friend and colleague of mine is a master of good hiring. His first hire—an entry-level marketing assistant—bloomed into a world-class marketing pro who is already running his business for him. The two of them hired a second superstar who helped them double the business in one year. Now the staff consists of four people, and they are doing the business it would normally take eight people to do.

It's not easy to hire good people, but it's well worth the time and effort that it takes. Here are the four most important things I've learned about how to do it:

1. *Make the commitment.* Anything worth doing is worth doing well. You can't expect to hire great people if you spend just a few hours working on it. I don't like interviewing, and I'm always impatient to hire the first decent person who comes along. That's a deadly combination.

2. *Look for the right things.* Intelligence is important, but I'd put it third on my list of things to look for. I agree with Jeffrey J. Fox in his book *How to Become a Great Boss* (Hyperion, 2002) that the two most important things to look for are attitude and aptitude.

3. *Flee flaws.* Generally speaking, you'll see job candidates at their best when you interview them. If you notice something that seems *wrong,* don't ignore it—especially if it concerns qualities that are important for the job. When it comes to interviewing, I've found that personal quirks are like the tip of an iceberg—what you see on the surface is a very small part of what you will have to deal with later.

4. *Don't worry too much about specific experience.* Of all the qualities that are important to look for in finding a great employee, specific experience is not very high on my list. Yes, it's good to know that the person you hire can do the technical work from day one—but on day 7 or day 14, you'll wish you had opted for the better, though perhaps untried and unproven, prospect.

Productivity Secret No. 8: Fire Bad Employees

When you want to save a hammock of endangered hardwoods, you start by chopping down a lot of trees. You must get rid of the younger, faster-growing trees that threaten the good wood in order to let the sun come in and give the really valuable growth a chance to develop. That is how it works in nature. And I have found that the nature of a business is not too much different.

So how do you weed out the mediocre employees who are interfering with the growth of your business? A successful newsletter publisher I know did it this way . . .

With every new person he agreed to hire, he made himself a promise that he would fire his weakest employee. He reasoned that the caliber of his workforce would gradually improve, so long as each new hire was better than his worst existing employee. He found himself targeting employees with attitudinal problems (those who seemed always unhappy) and problem workers (those who spent too much time on the phone, on breaks, etc.).

"The only difficult thing," he told me, "was learning how to fire someone. I recognized it was the fear of doing so that allowed me to tolerate those mediocre people all along. The first few dismissals were difficult, but after that it became easier. Eventually, I came to feel I was doing something good for the company, good for me, and good for the hardworking, serious-minded employees who didn't want to be slowed down by mediocre people."

The program worked better than he expected. Not only did he get rid of the laggards and sour apples, but the energy of the entire workplace improved. More work was being done more quickly. Profits and revenues were way up. Best of all, he no longer had to spend a lot of his time prodding the underachievers—and that freed him up to do more of the work he really loved (writing, editing, and promoting his newsletter).

CAN GETTING RICH BE SIMPLE AND EASY?

In putting together this book, I've reduced what was for me a complex, sometimes contradictory, experience of moving from debt to wealth into six simple steps.

Are they really simple?

It wasn't simple for me when I started out. That's for sure. Everything seemed like a jumbled blur of false starts, restarts, and retrenchments. But now, looking back at what I did and having the time to analyze what worked and failed, the pattern of success does indeed look simple.

Okay, achieving financial independence is simple. But is it easy? Or does it require a lot of hard work?

We are all driven by desires—to work less, to enjoy more, to have more money, to feel secure. Achieving financial independence is a big part of achieving those desires. And if you one day acquire wealth, it will be due in no small part to the hard work you've invested.

But here's the catch: *You don't want the hard work!* I know that. And I know that if I stress the hard work, I'll probably scare you off. So I'm not going to focus on that and I don't want you to focus on that, either. I want you to think about the money, fun, and power. I want you to dream about the toys. And when you set your goals, they should reflect those dreams, not the reality of hard work.

In truth, we all begin our greatest accomplishments with some naïveté about how much time it will take . . . how many obstacles we will encounter . . . how much frustration we will feel. If I were to take the time to list all the things I've done with my life—the accomplishments I'm most proud of—in not one case could I honestly say, "I knew what I was getting into when I began."

But that's fine. The important thing is to begin, to create momentum. A basic class in physics will tell you that it takes a great deal of energy to get a stationary object moving—yet once it's moving it takes very little effort to make it change course, speed up, or slow down.

So to get you going on your path toward financial independence, I've endeavored to make things as simple as possible. And I've tried to make the work seem easy. The point is to get you in motion. Once you are up and running, I promise you that it really will feel that way.

So now, turn the page and let's get to work . . .

STEP 3

DEVELOP WEALTHY HABITS

"Think and grow rich." How many times have you heard that before?

It's the title of one of the most popular wealth-building books ever written. And it's the idea behind so many success books, courses, and seminars that people think of it as a truism. But is it true? Can you really think yourself to riches?

In *The Power of Positive Thinking* (Ballantine Books, 1996), Norman Vincent Peale says:

> Too many people are defeated by the everyday problems of life. They go struggling, perhaps even whining, through their days with a sense of dull resentment at what they consider the "bad breaks" life has given them. In a sense, there may be such a thing as "the breaks" in this life, but there is also a spirit and method by which we can control and even determine those breaks. It is a pity that people should let themselves be defeated by problems, cares, and difficulties of human existence, and it is also quite unnecessary. . . . *By learning how to cast (obstacles) from your mind, by refusing to become mentally subservient to them, and by channeling spiritual power through your thoughts, you can rise above obstacles which ordinarily might defeat you.*

The opening chapter of Napoleon Hill's *The Law of Success* (Wilshire Book Company, 2000) expresses the same sentiment:

> Success is very largely a matter of adjusting one's self to the ever-varying and changing environments of life, in a spirit of harmony and poise. Harmony is based upon an understanding of the forces constituting one's environment. The most successful men and women on earth have had to correct certain weak spots in their personalities before they began to succeed.

As someone who has always been interested in the potential of the mind, I find this sort of idea appealing. If, indeed, I could think myself rich, what else could I do with my mental machinery? Maybe I could think myself cured of this chest cold? (And, yes, there's a large field of healing based on just such a notion.) If I can use thoughts to get healthier, why not to get smarter, too? And better looking? And taller?

The possibilities are endless. And tantalizing.

IT'S NOT ABOUT THINKING . . . IT'S ABOUT DOING

But if getting rich and successful were simply a matter of replacing negative thoughts and feelings with positive ones, why are so many of the richest, most successful people that I know miserable, grouchy, and gloomy?

Not all the time. And not in all circumstances. But as a general rule, it seems to me that most of the people out there making the big bucks are more driven than dreamy, more testy than tranquil, and more hard-pushing than easygoing.

Don't you agree?

Think about the really positive, really happy people you know. Are they the industry captains? Are they the million-dollar earners? The happiest and most well-balanced person I know is my wife—and she hasn't made a nickel in 15 years. A list of the other most happy people that I know would include

- TG, a bartender and beer guzzler who hasn't had a steady job in 30 years

- JF, who gave up a lucrative CEO spot 12 years ago to teach tai chi
- CF, who makes a living watering indoor plants

I'm not knocking positive thinking. And I'm certainly not saying that having a good mental outlook is detrimental to growing rich. What I'm arguing is that there is no statistical evidence that equates positive thoughts with rising net worth. In fact, the little data that we have on the subject suggests a different story:

- It is how you *act,* not what you think, that will determine your *success.*
- It is how you *think,* not what you do, that will determine your *happiness.*

RICHER DOESN'T MEAN HAPPIER

- A survey by *Forbes* magazine—itself owned by a billionaire— revealed that 37 percent of the 400 richest Americans are unhappy.
- A British psychologist, Ronit Lami, has interviewed many affluent people who develop a bunker mentality to protect themselves from a world that "doesn't understand." She recently teamed up with the Allenbridge Group, a wealth management service, to give the firm's clients advice on how to deal with the psychological effects of being seriously well off.
- A 2001 study by American psychologists found that excessive wealth, particularly for people unaccustomed to it, can actually cause unhappiness.
- Camelot Group PLC, operator of the U.K. National Lottery, released the first ever major survey on the lives of lottery winners and found the following:

55 percent are happier after winning.
43 percent say winning had no effect on their happiness.
2 percent are less happy.

In other words, almost half of the people who won the lottery are no happier than they were before!

Here's my point. I don't believe that the secret to becoming wealthy is to fill your head with positive thoughts. In fact, I don't think it much matters what you fill your head with. Based on personal observations and studies I've read, it's my belief that the secret to growing rich is to follow certain behavior patterns. To do what wealth builders do—and not waste any time getting your mind fixed beforehand.

In fact, from a cynical point of view, I could argue that the fix-your-mind-first philosophy is just another way to forestall action. And action, as I've argued in the past few chapters, is the sine qua non of change.

DOES YOUR MENTAL ATTITUDE DETERMINE SUCCESS?

According to Martin Seligman, the author of *Learned Optimism: How to Change Your Mind and Your Life,* pessimists, though miserable, tend to have a more realistic view of the world than their optimistic counterparts. Many studies conducted to test this theory have all come to the same conclusion: More often than not, the gloomy outlook is justified.

But what is better in terms of success? Optimism or pessimism?

After a quick mental survey of the successful people I'm friendly with, I'd say that they fall equally into both camps. SJ, a million-dollar-a-year copywriter, is a die-hard pessimist. BL, who has struggled in the past and is now doing extremely well, is irrepressibly bubbly. FW, who started and grew at least four supersuccessful businesses, is buoyant and bullish 80 percent of the time.

I'd say this: Your overall view about how things will turn out—the trained or instinctual response you have to problems—has nothing to do with how successful you will be. Your success depends not on your mood or your emotions but on your actions—what you actually do.

Your mental outlook does matter, though. It has everything to do with how happy you are. When I think about SJ, BL, FW, and others, I can see clearly that optimists have much more fun in life.

The ideal personality can see reality for what it is, act according to what is best, and believe that things will work out fine.

In the course of this book, I'm going to try to put certain ideas into your head, change some others that you might now have, and buttress my own ideas with all sorts of facts, numbers, anecdotes, and data.

But I don't believe you have to adopt or change a single thought to become wealthy. Keep the thoughts you have. No problem. However, if you want to convert your investment in this book into a higher level of wealth for yourself, you must follow the specific behaviors I'm recommending.

JUST DO IT!

If you wanted to become a world-class tennis player and had Andre Agassi at your disposal as a personal coach and mentor, would you spend your time with him finding out what runs through his head during matches? Or would you find a way to emulate his serve, his movements, and his swings?

In jiujitsu, the sport I enjoy, my first master had a rule:

> Don't think about what you learned here today. Don't go home and run it through your mind. Don't take notes. Don't look at books. Just practice the movements I teach you and, sooner or later, your body will know them, even if your mind is somewhere else.

That's the ultimate objective of learning, isn't it? To acquire knowledge so deep that it becomes subconscious . . . and automatic?

In *Zen in the Art of Archery* (Vintage, 1999), Eugen Herrigel describes it this way:

> The archer ceases to be conscious of himself as the one who is engaged in hitting the bull's-eye which confronts him. This state of unconscious is realized only when, completely empty and rid of the self, he becomes one with the perfecting of his technical skill.

PRACTICE MAKES PERFECT

The idea is this: If you want to master the art of wealth building—so you can become financially independent and create wealth automatically whenever and wherever you want to—you need to learn wealth building the way any master learns his art: by repeating, as closely as possible, the actions of successful wealth builders.

And this leads to an important paradox: If you want to master a skill as quickly as possible, practice it slowly.

Howard Roberts, the legendary jazz guitarist, made this point years ago at a small seminar I attended. In response to a question posed by NR, a friend of mine, Roberts said that he believed the secret to his virtuosity was that he "never practiced a mistake."

"For me, practicing the guitar is like walking to the outhouse," he said. "I always walk the same path, because if I ever have to walk that path at night I want to know exactly where to place my feet."

Roberts believed in practicing every note perfectly, even if that meant playing extremely slowly at first. And I'm told that many studies have validated his theory. The biological process of creating a neural memory path really is much like walking to the outhouse. Every perfect repetition beats a good path—one that you can travel on later. Every incorrect repetition beats a parallel but incorrect path—one that you can easily slide onto if you aren't careful.

The more you practice the right moves, the deeper the memory path. The trick is to make the correct paths as deep as possible and to make the incorrect paths shallow or nonexistent.

The faster you perform a task, the more likely it is that you will make a mistake—unless, that is, you have cut only one path for it. A perfect one. Likewise, when you are performing a task under stress, it is easy to bungle it—unless you have no neurological way to screw it up.

The reason so many guitar students rush when they're practicing, Roberts said, is that they are fixated on completing a piece rather than on performing it well. They figure that the sooner they can pretty much get it right, the better they are doing. But the truth is quite different.

I used to make the same mistake with jiujitsu. Whenever I was learning a new move, I tried to do it quickly. I had the mistaken notion that speed was an indication of competence. Instead of practicing each part of the movement slowly and with precision, I rushed to complete the entire thing. I was able to do it, but sloppily.

AT—a fellow jiujitsu student who started learning at the same time

UNDERSTANDING THE FOUR LEVELS OF LEARNING

There are probably a dozen levels of learning. But these four—broadly defined—may help you discover problems in the way you learn (or teach) things now.

1. *Telling it.* Teachers convey their knowledge by explaining it. This method often provides the most ego gratification to the teachers and the most entertainment value to the students, but it is the teaching method that leaves the shallowest impression and is most easily forgotten.

2. *Showing it.* Teachers do more than talk in abstract terms. They demonstrate their knowledge. Sometimes they show pictures or diagrams of what they mean. These visual clues help reinforce what they say and clarify the little misunderstandings and confusion that easily arise when using only words. Both telling and showing students something make it much more likely that they will remember it.

3. *Involving students.* When teachers involve their students in the learning process by getting them to actually practice the skill, the learning deepens because all of their senses are involved. Students who have learned a skill by practicing it not only remember its principles and elements but also understand how it feels.

4. *Letting students teach.* The highest and final level of teaching is to supervise students in teaching others. We discover the limits of our knowledge—the gaps we need to fill in—only when we teach a skill.

Think of the learning (or teaching) you are doing now. Which of these methods are you using? Make a commitment to develop a program that involves all four levels: telling, showing, involving, and then letting the student teach.

Think of the learning you are doing now. Which of these methods are your teachers using? Make a commitment to get them to show you.

as I did but became much better much faster—always told me to slow down. Now I understand why. Most things worth learning are complex. That's why we learn them in pieces. Whether it's guitar playing, dancing, or building wealth, the ultimate performance is a complex combination of many simpler skills.

To make the performance perfect, you need to perfect each of those simpler skills. This is the basis of most effective learning systems.

The fundamental rule is this: Slow down . . . until you can practice the skill with perfect technique. Continue practicing perfectly and you will find that your speed will gradually increase without any effort on your part. Eventually, you will do it quickly and perfectly.

You will find that you can apply this rule to almost any skill and achieve the same good results. In your efforts to train yourself to become a wealth builder, you should keep this secret in mind. Becoming a master at wealth building is a little like becoming masterful at guitar playing or jiujitsu. Each requires knowledge and experience. Each involves learning skills. Each of these skills may be complex, but if you break them down into their basic elements—and practice each one slowly and perfectly—you will master them.

THE EIGHT HABITS OF HIGHLY
SUCCESSFUL WEALTH BUILDERS

Early in my career, the time I spent thinking about money was strictly pragmatic: how to get it.

But then I started to think about wealth more analytically: what it is, how it's created, and how it disappears. And so I've looked back at what I've done (both good and bad) and the lessons I've learned from others. And this is what I now believe: There is no one way to become rich. But there are a number of habits that some people develop that give them an almost supernatural ability to earn money and build wealth.

I'd say these people have the following characteristics in common:

1. They work hard.
2. They are good at what they do.
3. They have multiple streams of income.
4. They live in (relatively) inexpensive homes.
5. They are moderate in their spending.
6. They are extraordinary in their saving.
7. They pay themselves first.
8. They count their money.

This is not everything you'll need to know about wealth building. We will discuss other important secrets in later chapters. For the moment, though, we are talking about developing wealthy habits. These eight are my recommendations.

1. WEALTHY PEOPLE WORK HARD

The average multimillionaire works an average of 59 hours a week. And many of those hours are challenging.

But you don't want to hear that now. And I don't want you to think about it.

Think about this instead: If you follow the advice in this book about transforming the way you work, the job you do, and the way you think about work, those 59 hours will fly by.

And there's more good news. Many of those hours won't *feel* like work. You'll actually enjoy them.

And after you've hit your first million or two, you can kick back and work less . . . if you want to. But you may not want to!

2. WEALTHY PEOPLE ARE GOOD AT WHAT THEY DO

Some people get lucky and stumble into riches. But master wealth builders—people who can create wealth easily and repeatedly—don't rely on luck. They are good at what they do.

Being good at what they do gives them confidence and poise. In discussing business or money, they are relaxed but focused. Intolerant of fakers, they move quickly when opportunity knocks.

You can tell when you are in the presence of natural wealth builders. There is something palpable in the way they hold themselves and the way they speak. It's more relaxed than tense and more flexible than fixed. Natural wealth builders have the confidence to know that they know. They've done it and they can do it again.

It all comes down to mastering a financially valued skill. I'll explain what that means and how it should fit into your wealth-building goals in the next chapter.

3. WEALTHY PEOPLE HAVE MULTIPLE
STREAMS OF INCOME

Natural moneymakers make most of their money by practicing a single skill within the context of a single industry. Don't be fooled by financial gurus who tell you otherwise. But they eventually develop *many* streams of income. And I'm going to argue that you should do the same thing.

To get your financial fortune started, you have to radically boost your income. And doing that, as I'll explain in the first part of the next chapter, requires doing one thing extraordinarily well.

In the second part of Step Four, we will talk about many ways that you can supplement your primary income. I'll show you how to start small and develop extra little streams of cash that happily float into your bank account every month and build up your wealth reserve.

Many master wealth builders I know enjoy a dozen sources of income. Some are modest, some amazing. That's the great thing about creating cash flow. Although you never know what will happen with any individual income source, if you get enough of them started, one will turn into a river.

4. WEALTHY PEOPLE LIVE IN (RELATIVELY)
INEXPENSIVE HOMES

How much do you think the typical American worth $6.8 million typically pays for a house?

I put this question to the *Early to Rise* staff. Their guess was between $2 million and $3 million. Being older and wiser, my guess was closer to the truth. I figured the number was closer to $1 million.

But then we checked the IRS records. And the answer was an astonishing $545,000. That's not a lot of money for someone who's worth almost $7 million. So what's going on here?

Take a look at Table 3.1. Why would a guy who's worth $1.4 million live in a $220,000 house? Does he know something that you should find out about?

TABLE 3.1

NET WORTH (IN MILLIONS)	AVERAGE NET WORTH	AVERAGE HOUSE VALUE
$1 to under 2.5	$1,470,553	$220,796
2.5 to under 5	3,392,416	354,043
5 to under 10	6,809,409	545,499
10 to under 20	14,045,501	779,444
20 and more	58,229,024	1,073,980

Actually, he knows two things:

1. *The cost of your house determines the cost of your lifestyle.* Consider this: Property taxes on a $500,000 house are about $4,000 to $5,000 more per year than on a $250,000 house. Utility expenses are also proportionately greater. If you live in a more expensive house, you'll pay a lot more for maintenance costs. And not just because there is more house to keep. When many contractors see that you live in a nice house in a fancy neighborhood, their fees shoot up. Call it a wealth tax. They figure, "He can afford it. I need it. So why not?"

   But taxes, utilities, and maintenance form just the tip of the expense-rising iceberg. The major cost of owning an expensive house is beneath the surface. The number one reason expensive homes cost so much (much more than you'd think) is because they are inexorably attached to a more expensive lifestyle. By lifestyle, I include everything you pay more for now that you live in a nicer neighborhood—furniture and landscaping, automobiles and education, restaurants and vacations, just to name a few.

   It's not that you are consciously trying to keep up with the Joneses. It's just that you can't seem to find those inexpensive things (or places or service people) anymore.

2. *Home-spending decisions are not—or should not be—primarily about return on investment.* In buying, fixing up, and furnishing your home, you will spend a good deal of money on things that will have a lot of emotional value but little financial worth. If you want to put a new set of windows in the living room, repaint

a bedroom, or buy a bookshelf for your beer can collection, you don't have to do a financial analysis first.

In contrast, the investments you make for financial gain can and should be decided on such rational, bottom-line thinking.

I bought my first house 20 years ago for $175,000. I put down about $15,000—which was the sum total of my net worth. Ten years later, I was living in an $800,000 house, which represented about 25 percent of my net worth. Today, I live in a more expensive home, but one that accounts for only about 10 percent of my wealth. And that feels good.

What about the Tax Benefits of Stretching Yourself Financially When Buying a Home?

It's true that a more expensive home that has larger mortgage payments will also have larger tax-deductible interest payments. But you're better off spending less money in the first place. Remember, in order to save money with tax deductions, you have to spend more than you save. If you are in the 28 percent tax bracket, for example, every dollar you spend on mortgage interest is deductible, and that will save you 28¢ in taxes. But you'll have spent a dollar to get that 28¢ saving and will be 62¢ poorer. It's better to take that 62¢ and invest it elsewhere. Soon it will be worth $5.

The bottom line is this: Buy a house that accommodates all your needs comfortably, and invest time and care to make it beautiful. Then, take the money you didn't spend on a more expensive home and invest it in something that will earn money for you. (I'll give you my recommendations in the next chapter.) You'll get richer faster.

5. WEALTHY PEOPLE ARE MODERATE IN SPENDING

Carlos, one of my jiujitsu instructors, is living the American dream. He came to this country to compete in mixed martial arts and earn his fortune as a champion fighter. While building a stellar win-loss record, he lived on club sponsorship and fees for giving lessons. For the first three years of his time here, he managed to support himself and his wife on less than $15,000 a year. Recently, he captured three title belts and now fights at the top level in Japan. His typical payday has gone from $500 to $25,000.

HOW BIG A HOUSE DO YOU NEED?

I grew up in a family of 10 in a four-bedroom home the size of a Hummer. I was embarrassed about having to bunk with two or three siblings, and I was amazed and in awe of Tommy Harrington, a friend whose house contained not only a full bedroom just for him, but also two huge staircases and a billiard room.

As I made my way up the success ladder, I traded in one house after another for a larger one—each time hoping my happiness would increase accordingly and always anticipating the day that I'd have a house with two staircases and a billiard room.

I ended up with many houses like that . . . but I don't live in one now. The house where I finally found happiness is modest by my old standards. We have regular-sized rooms and nine-foot ceilings and no room for a billiard table (although I do have one in my office).

When I look back at the many houses I've occupied over my lifetime, I can find no correspondence between the size of the house—or its cost—and my enjoyment of it. In fact, aside from my current house, my next-most-favorite abode was a 900-square-foot mud hut in the middle of Africa. The garage I'm building right now is larger (and about 10 times more expensive) than that little dream house.

When you are starting out, your home may represent most or all of your wealth. But as you start saving and investing, you'll want to gradually decrease that percentage from most of your wealth to half of it, then a quarter of it, and eventually (if you get really rich—and I hope you do) to a mere 5 percent or 10 percent of it.

Why? Because your home isn't meant to be an investment. It's a sanctuary.

"The problem with making more money in America," he told me, "is that every time you make an extra dollar you spend two."

How true. The first couch I bought cost $400. I remember thinking, "It doesn't get any better than this." And it never did. The couches I buy today give me no more pleasure, comfort, or space. Yet they cost much more.

What happened? Did I miss out on some inflationary spiral? The truth is that my own success victimized me. In earning more, I allowed myself to spend more on things like couches. If I had gotten more out of it, that would have been fine. But I didn't.

Master wealth builders understand a secret that it took me years to learn: You have to keep your spending down while your income increases.

We'll talk more about that later. But now, let's talk about Mike Tyson.

The Sad Story of Mike Tyson: A Spending Fool

During the 20-year span of his career, Mike Tyson's income exceeded $400 million. Yet in 2004, before his 39th birthday, this amazing moneymaker was $38 million in debt. He had some assets—equity in some mansions, some cars, and some jewelry—but insiders speculated their total value at less than $3 million. For the sake of wishing him well, let's assume it was twice that much. That would have put his personal net worth at negative $32 million.

Think about that: minus $32 million!

That could make him the world's poorest man. With a negative net worth that large, Mike Tyson is 160,000 times poorer than the average wage earner from Sierra Leone, the poorest country in the world, with an average annual income of $200 per person.

"How can a man with a $4 million estate in New Jersey be poor?" a colleague asked me.

"He can still make millions every time he fights," my sister said. "Anyone who can make millions isn't poor."

Yet by every recognized standard of accounting, he is poor. Extremely poor.

But he doesn't think so. And that's part of the reason he got so poor in the first place. The faster money came in, the faster it went out. Stories about his profligacy are already legendary. Tyson employed as many as 200 people, including bodyguards, chauffeurs, chefs, and gardeners.

He spent:

• Nearly $4.5 million on cars and motorcycles
• $3.4 million on clothes and jewelry

- $7.8 million on "personal expenses"
- $140,000 on two white Bengal tigers and $125,000 a year for their trainer
- $2 million on a bathtub for his first wife, actress Robin Givens
- $410,000 on a birthday party
- $230,000 on cell phones and pagers during a three-year period from 1995 to 1997

The purpose of this is not to shake a finger at Mike Tyson, but to alert you to the dangerous temptation to spend more when you make more. As someone who grew up drinking powdered milk and wearing hand-me-downs, I understand the strength of that temptation.

Why Spending Feels So Good

Why do we do it? Why do we feel the need to spend more when we make more?

Here's what I think. When you are poor, you are surrounded by things you think you would like to own but cannot afford to buy. After a while, you equate the feeling of unsatisfied desire with poverty. And when *desiring* begins to feel *poor, having* seems like it will make you feel *rich.*

That's the heart's logic, at least.

MY FIRST ATTEMPT AT FASHION

When I was about 14 years old, I got my first legitimate job working at a car wash on weekends. I worked 12 hours every Saturday and got paid $1.75 an hour—about $28 (counting tips) a week more than I had ever earned from chores. I remember distinctly the first thing I bought with that money: a pair of pointy-toed, buckled boots. They cost $42, two weeks' pay. Worth every penny, I thought, because they gave me something I was yearning for—the feeling of being rich.

I wore them to a birthday party that weekend. I was smitten by the birthday girl and dressed to impress. The shoes were a big part of my getup. But no sooner had I stepped into the room when someone pointed to my shoes and started laughing. The laughter was of the contagious variety. Apparently something had happened in the world of fashion that I was unaware of. The shoes went into the closet that evening and never came out again.

If that's the way you feel now—if your idea of being wealthy is filled with images of mansions and sailboats and expensive watches—you are going to have a difficult time saving money. And saving money is another one of the common habits of people who know how to build wealth.

6. WEALTHY PEOPLE ARE EXTRAORDINARY AT SAVING

The rich save more than the average person. Relatively speaking, that is. I don't mean they save more because they have more money to save. I mean they save more in general, because they have a saver's mind-set.

According to Thomas Stanley, author of *The Millionaire Next Door*, the average millionaire is much more frugal than you or I would have believed. (By the way, Stanley gets most of his data from the IRS and other government sources.) For example, the average millionaire

- Drives an older car
- Buys inexpensive presents
- Eats at home and seldom dines out
- Takes a vacation every other year
- Wears clothes until they fray and resoles shoes when they wear thin

To develop a saver's mind-set—a wealth builder's mind-set—you must change the way you feel about spending. You must teach yourself to feel the truth: that every time you buy a depreciating asset, you become poorer.

Remind yourself repeatedly that most of the junk you buy (1) becomes unused after a few months and (2) doesn't provide you with that much value anyway. Remember that the best things in life—the picnics you have with your family, the walks you take with your lover, the time you spend with your friends—are free, or nearly so.

There are so many ways to save money. You can spend less on just about anything without giving up either the pleasure you take in buying or the quality you get from your purchases.

Instead of buying new clothes that will be out of style in a year, buy vintage clothing that looks great and distinguishes you.

Instead of signing a lease for an expensive car you can't afford, find something old but still good that has a personality.

Instead of going out to lunch every day, eat a can of tuna at your desk. (This is one of the things I did. By eating a can of tuna every day instead of going to lunch with my coworkers, I saved almost $2,500 in a single year. Plus, I went from staff editor to publisher by applying that extra lunch-hour time to improving the business.)

Don't worry—I'm not going to try to turn you into a miser. The purpose of spending less is to have more. I enjoy the luxuries that wealth can bring, but—as I'll explain later—I don't believe you have to spend a lot more to get them.

You'll have your cake and eat it, too. You'll spend less, waste less, save more, and have plenty left over to enjoy life.

7. WEALTHY PEOPLE PAY THEMSELVES FIRST

Many financial advisers recommend sticking to a budget. By categorizing expenses and limiting spending, they argue, you can have enough left over every month to save money and grow rich.

The trouble is that budgeting almost never works.

Budgeting is like dieting: It's enormously sensible but almost never effective. I've tried budgeting myself a dozen times. I've also made the mistake of encouraging others to keep a budget. I can't think of a single case where it worked.

The problem is that when you budget, you pay everyone else first. As best-selling author David Bach says:

> [You] pay the landlord, the credit card company, the telephone company, the government, and on and on. The reason [you] think [you] need a budget is to . . . figure out how much to pay everyone else so at the end of the month [you] will have something "left over" to pay [yourself.]

So at the end of the month, you have nothing left to put in the bank. You promise yourself you'll do better next time, but you never do. There are always unexpected bills to pay, unanticipated sales to take advantage of, and that impossible-to-figure-out $200 or $300 that seems to fall through the cracks.

Budgeting doesn't work. But there is something that does: putting some predetermined percentage of your income into a savings account each month *before* you pay any of your bills.

Think of yourself as a personal corporation and the money you save as your personal income. All the other money you spend on house and car payments and so forth are the expenses of your personal corporation. Only the portion that goes into a savings account is really yours.

Of course, it's not enough to simply think of your income this way. You must actually do something to effect a change. You might, for example, have a portion of your paycheck automatically deposited in your savings account each month—as soon as the check is deposited.

Paying yourself first in this sense (i.e., saving before you pay bills) is actually, as Bach points out, paying yourself second. He reminds us that withholding taxes are the government's way of paying itself first. Before your salary is deposited into your checking account, the government has already taken its piece.

You can put yourself ahead of the government by setting up a pre-tax retirement account. Among the best known are IRAs, SEPs, 401(k)s, and 403(b)s. Table 3.2 shows the differences among these plans.

TABLE 3.2

401(k) and 403(b) Plans

These plans are designed for employees of midsized to large companies. Contributions are deductible from current taxable income and sometimes the employer makes a matching contribution. Check your employee handbook to learn what your match percentage is and if there is a vesting period. There's no good reason not to contribute 100 percent of what your employer will match. It's like doubling your money for nothing. When you are retired, you'll appreciate that free money from your employer's contribution and the compounding it may have produced. The maximum pretax amounts you can add are as follows:

YEAR	LIMIT 401(k)	LIMIT 403(b)	OVER-50 CATCH-UP BONUS
2004	$13,000	$3,000	$500
2005	$14,000	$4,000	$1,000

Traditional IRA and Roth IRA

You may open one of these tax-qualified accounts at any bank or financial services company (e.g., a brokerage firm or an insurance company). There are income limits that may prevent higher income tax payers from taking a full deduction on their contribution. A key advantage in this type of plan is that you have a much broader selection of investments that you can choose to put the money in, including individual stocks, mutual funds, and other financial tools. You also have flexible withdrawal options without penalties that are not permitted for 401(k) plans. These include

- First-time home purchase
- Certain medical expenses
- Health insurance premiums while you're unemployed
- Certain higher-education expenses

If you have one or more 401(k) or 403(b) accounts sitting around, you may want to consolidate them in an IRA to ensure that your total portfolio is diversified in a broad range of categories. But because there are some tax advantages if you own company stock in your 401(k), you may not want to roll that portion over to an IRA.

The Roth IRA is a unique retirement plan. The contributions to a Roth are made after tax, so you receive no current deduction from taxable income. But eventually, when you are retired, you can take distributions from the Roth tax free. Depending on your time frame and the tax bracket that you expect to be in during retirement, this can be a significant advantage, giving you another way to control your tax liabilities without having to give up income.

The maximum contributions that you can make to either a traditional or a Roth IRA are as follows:

YEAR	LIMIT	OVER-50 CATCH-UP BONUS
2004	$3,000	$500
2005–2007	$4,000	$1,000

SEP IRA

A simplified employee pension (SEP) IRA has special rules that make it particularly attractive to self-employed taxpayers or businesses with a

(continues)

small staff of highly compensated partners and employees. The contributions to this retirement savings plan come from the business, not the paychecks of employees. If the owners have discretionary income and are motivated to put aside higher amounts than are allowed by the aforementioned plans, they can use the SEP IRA to contribute up to 25 percent of income or a maximum of $41,000. However, they can't discriminate in the percentage and must include all employees or partners.

SIMPLE IRA

This type of IRA is attractive for small businesses or self-employed individuals. It requires a minimum of paperwork and allows each person to determine the amount they want to contribute. It allows a match of up to 3 percent for all employees who participate.

YEAR	LIMIT	OVER-50 CATCH-UP BONUS
2004	$9,000	$1,500
2005	$10,000	$2,000

All tax-qualified plans described here have these characteristics:

- They defer the growth and dividends that are earned into the future so that your portfolio has greater potential for efficiency and return.
- They have penalties for distribution back to your current income if you ask for a redemption before age 59½.
- You can name a beneficiary to receive the assets at your death and thus bypass the probate process.
- Each one (except the Roth IRA) requires that you take a minimum distribution each year starting at age 70½.
- Since you have control of the types of securities and funds where your money is invested, you can customize a portfolio.

What Your Government Already Knows about Getting Paid First

The government understands the power of being first at the pay trough. That's why it invented withholding tax.

Before 1943, Americans got 100 percent of the money they earned. The income taxes levied on them each year weren't due until the following spring. But as the government budget grew, so did income taxes. The 1 and 2 percent that was levied in the beginning began to rise. Soon it was 3 and 4 percent. And then 5 and 6 percent.

The government quickly discovered that its citizens were not eager to send in their taxes every spring. Some people had already spent all their cash. Others just couldn't get themselves to part with it.

This wasn't working out well for the bureaucrats who wanted to build a big government. And it wouldn't do for the politicians who wanted to get us involved in World War II. So they came up with a way to guarantee that they would get the money. They passed a law requiring employers to withhold employee taxes and then turn them over to the government.

In other words, they came up with a way to get themselves paid first.

Do It Your Way

By contributing to a tax-deferred account—a 401(k), 403(b), IRA, or SEP—you pay yourself even before the government takes its cut. That's because, in most cases, the money you contribute is tax deductible.

Most conventional savings plans are worked out on a yearly basis. The usual recommendation is to figure out what your gross or net income will be for the year and then invest 10 percent of that in an IRA, SEP, or the like.

Since contributions to tax-favored plans are made on a yearly basis, people who follow such plans usually invest their savings once a year. This can be difficult if you have trouble sticking to your budget. It's more sensible to put money aside every time you get paid. Most investment accounts will let you do that. Some allow your bank to automatically transfer savings as soon as they are deposited.

That's what I do, and it's what I recommend to friends and colleagues. Pay yourself first, the government second, and everyone and everything else last.

I pay myself first by putting as much money as I'm allowed into a tax-deferred savings vehicle. I do this for me, my spouse, and my children. I pay the government next by creating a separate holding account into which I deposit a percentage of every fee that's paid to me—the money that I'm going to owe in taxes. Then I pay my bills.

Actually, I pay my bills fourth. Before I do that, I deposit additional money into various savings and investment accounts. Since I save much more than I can put into SEPs and IRAs, I am able to make these additional, pay-myself-third deposits.

I don't really need all those holding accounts. I could deposit everything in a single account, let it accumulate, and make savings and tax-payment decisions later. But I'm always afraid that unless I get the essentials (savings and taxes) taken care of first, some catastrophe will occur or I'll go nuts and spend money tabbed for essentials on something ephemeral.

There is something about the process of transferring money to special accounts that feels like it's going away from me, that I don't own it any more. I should be embarrassed to admit that I still play this psychological trick with myself, but I do . . . and it works!

In defense of this defensive habit, I could tell you countless stories of super-high-income people I know who come to me, desperate, at

A FEW WORDS ABOUT TAXES

I'll spend little time in this book talking about tax-saving strategies. The reason is twofold:

1. Despite what you may have been led to believe, there are no significant tax loopholes for wealthy people. Except for the regular benefits you get from having your own corporation (and this you probably should eventually do), high-income earners have to pay their 40 percent taxes or go to jail.
2. Even if there were any tax shelters left, they aren't worth the time and trouble required to get into them. Everyone I know who has been involved in a tax shelter or some tax-avoidance scheme eventually has regretted it. If you want to pay less tax, you'll have to earn less income. As long as they are leaving you enough money to become financially independent, it doesn't pay to work yourself up over taxes.

tax season asking for bridge loans because they somehow spent the money they were supposed to put away for taxes on who-knows-what. (I'm always afraid to ask.) Surprisingly, more than one of these fellows have been well-known investment experts.

Save More . . . Much More

These days, I save about 35 percent to 40 percent of my income. It wasn't always that way. When I first began making a good living, I was saving less than 10 percent. As I came to understand wealth and change how I felt about saving, that percentage grew.

When I was saving 10 percent, it always seemed like enough. I was wrong. You shouldn't make the same mistake.

John, age 30, walked into my office the other day and said, "I've realized I will never be able to save enough to get wealthy."

"Not at 10 percent of your current income," I concurred.

I'm not sure where this 10 percent figure comes from. Perhaps it comes from the Greek and biblical tradition of tithing. Certainly, it's a percentage that most people of ordinary means can handle. But unless you are earning a million-plus a year or have 40 years to wait, 10 percent isn't going to do it for you.

If you are smart, you'll set yourself a more ambitious saving goal. Here's my suggestion:

Your First Saving Goal:
Every year, I will save more than I saved last year.

You can't really make this a monthly goal. If you follow the other wealth-building recommendations I'm going to be making in this book, you'll have too many sources of income to keep such a promise. (With four or five separate sources of income, your monthly numbers will fluctuate too much.) But if you make it a yearly goal, you can do this with relative ease.

Once you are comfortable with that—and perhaps you are already—set another, related goal that's actually much more powerful:

Your Second Saving Goal:
Every year, I will increase the amount I save in terms
of a percentage of my income.

That may not seem earth-shattering, but it's actually a big, ambitious goal. It means that if you start out saving 10 percent of your gross income now, next year you'll increase it to 12 percent or 15 percent or 20 percent. And the next year, you'll make the percentage even higher.

Be cautioned that you can't do this too aggressively. Nor can you do it forever. But if you increase your income every year and hold your expenses down, your savings-to-income ratio will get higher.

Here are some suggested targets:

If you are making less than $50,000 a year:	10 percent
More than $50,000 but less than $200,000:	15 percent
More than $200,000 but less than $500,000:	25 percent
More than $1 million but less than $2 million:	35 percent
More than $2 million but less than $5 million:	40 percent
More than $5 million:	45 percent

Once your income exceeds $200,000, you're going to be paying between 40 percent and 50 percent of your income to state and federal taxes. So a savings rate of 20 percent is really 60 percent to 70 percent. And a savings rate of 40 percent is actually 80 percent to 90 percent.

Start Saving Today

Starting today—literally, *today*—begin the practice of saving.

Even if you are living from paycheck to paycheck, you must start your saving program today. You must get your hands on some amount of money and invest it immediately. Start with at least 10 percent of your gross income. If you don't have that much cash, put away as much as you possibly can.

The reason you want to start saving now, even if your income is small, is that you want to create the *habit* of saving. When saving becomes habitual, it becomes easier. And anything that you can do easily, you'll do better, more often, and longer term.

Now, there's one more habit of highly successful wealth builders that I want you to start cultivating . . .

8. WEALTHY PEOPLE COUNT THEIR MONEY

I have no statistical evidence that this last wealth-building habit is a widespread trait among self-made rich people, but I suspect that it is.

I believe that most successful moneymakers regularly count their money. I don't mean that they literally count bills. Rather, they regularly assess their fortunes.

I believe this is true especially in the early stages, when they are just beginning to grow their wealth. As their net income grows and they feel more comfortable with their wealth and more confident of their income, they count less.

When they get superwealthy—Warren Buffett wealthy—they don't have to count their money. *Fortune* magazine and countless other entities do it for them. But on their way up, they count. And that's what I recommend you do.

Specifically, I suggest that you do a personal balance sheet every month. Create a spreadsheet that lists all your assets and all your debits. Include valuable possessions, stocks, bonds, mutual funds, gold, real estate (aside from your home), and so forth. Accurately estimate the value of everything. If there is a question about how much something is worth, choose the lesser number. List all your indebtedness, too. And be completely candid.

Just going through the process will train your mind (and heart) to understand financial wealth as financial net worth. After you've done this six or seven months in a row, it will become automatic.

And while you are doing that monthly spreadsheet, remind yourself of the saving goals you've made—that you will save more money, in both absolute and relative terms, with each passing year.

You can make this exercise a bit more exciting by promising yourself this: That you will be richer each time you check. That you'll do everything necessary to ensure that when you add up your assets every month, the bottom line will be larger than it was the month before.

You'll be amazed at how much this simple commitment can affect the way you think and even the way you act. I remember how it changed me.

Louis, the accountant I hired when I started to earn a radically increased income, got me started doing it. (You remember Louis. In

Chapter 1, I told you a little bit about what I learned from him.) We began our relationship by creating my first personal balance sheet. It was good to see that after so many years of struggling, I was finally worth something. Six months later, we tallied my wealth for the second time. I was anticipating a huge number, because I'd enjoyed several extremely significant financial windfalls. I was also enjoying my new life, my new house, my new car, and so on. You can imagine how upset I was to discover that I was not, as expected, getting richer. Instead, I was getting poorer!

"I guess I'll have to make more money," I said.

"You're making plenty of money," Louis assured me. "The problem is you are spending too much."

To remedy my overspending habit, I expected Louis would put me on a budget. "Budget-shmudget," he said. "We'll start looking at your balance sheet every month."

And that's all we did. Once a month, he'd stop by my office and we'd add up the numbers. And it didn't take long for my financial trajectory to begin moving in the right direction.

Simply by counting my money once a month, my bad spending habits quickly halted.

- I stopped buying things on credit—even cars.
- I started paying off my mortgage, as fast as I could.
- I stopped investing in volatile stocks—unwilling to see them take a dive.
- I started asking myself before I bought something: "Will this make me richer or poorer?"

Practice the habit of counting your money, and the same thing will probably happen to you.

WHILE YOU ARE DEVELOPING WEALTH-BUILDING HABITS, DON'T DEPRIVE YOURSELF

You can easily learn the eight habits of wealthy people. And when you do, you'll find that the poverty mentality that once mistakenly urged you to spend yourself rich has been replaced with a new kind of thinking that rewards you for spending less.

This happened to LJ. A hard worker and a natural salesman, he was making a good income in the early 1980s. He bought and renovated a beautiful house on Long Island, leased a few luxury cars, and filled his life with brand-name toys and gadgets.

He was making plenty of money, spending plenty of money . . . and he felt good about it. He wasn't generating much wealth, but he didn't care. "I can always earn more money if I need it" was his philosophy.

Then disaster struck. In a three-month period, he lost his job, lost $50,000 on a stock tip, and got hit with an expensive lawsuit. He did everything he could to work himself out of this hole, but things went from bad to worse. By 1995, when I met him, he was bankrupt.

We plotted out his comeback plan. He set his goals, got a good job, and began to create additional little streams of income. His situation went from extremely bad to not-so-bad to better. But at the end of each month, he still had no savings.

After some discussion, he agreed to work with Louis, who guided him through the same monthly balance sheet program he'd taught me. Gradually at first, and then like a torrent, LJ broke his spending habit and became a saver.

"Too much of a saver," his wife complained one day. "The dishwasher has been broken for six months and he won't put a new muffler on the Volkswagen."

LJ had made a dramatic change. He'd gone from being a spendthrift to being a miser. "It doesn't make any sense to spend money on the dishwasher," he told me. "We are perfectly capable of washing the dishes by hand." By "we," he meant his wife and kids. He was too busy.

"Your intentions are laudable," I said with a straight face. "But being committed to getting wealthy doesn't mean you have to deprive yourself."

That's what I told him, though I wasn't entirely sure what I meant by it at the time. I knew that I had managed to get wealthier without scrimping—but I didn't know if that would work for everyone. Could I teach anyone to live rich without spending a fortune?

The more I thought about it, the more possible it seemed.

HOW TO LIVE LIKE A BILLIONAIRE
WITHOUT SPENDING LIKE ONE

If you could enjoy the best things money could buy—the most cherished material goods that even the world's billionaires can enjoy—yet spend little more for them than you spend now, would you do it?

There is a way. The trick is to separate the wheat from the chaff. To figure out what things in life can bring you pleasure, how much pleasure they offer, and what you have to pay for them.

Don't wait until you become wealthy and have this type of thinking forced on you after you have the supposed privilege of spending a fortune on objects that give you almost no pleasure. After you've bought the big house, the expensive cars, the ostentatious clothes and jewelry—and then realized how little genuine pleasure they were giving you. Think about the things you have now—the car you drive, the clothes you wear, and the toys you play with. Think about them and their value.

In fact, make this into a little game. Take a sheet of paper and draw a vertical line down the middle of it. On the left side of the page, under a column marked "Things I Enjoy," make a list:

- Time with family
- Time with friends
- Reading
- My hobbies (list them)
- My house
- My car
- My stereo
- My television
- My clothes
- and so on . . .

On the right side of the page, write down a number from one to five that indicates how much ongoing enjoyment you get from each thing. What you'll probably find out is that most of the best things in your own life, as the saying goes, are, indeed, free.

That's the way it is for you. That's the way it is for me. And that's the way it is for everyone else, including billionaires.

HOW MUCH MONEY DO YOU REALLY NEED?

By Bill Bonner

"Women," said my old friend, Michael Masterson. "That's the reason we earn money."

I misunderstood at first. Yes, a woman can cost a lot to maintain. She will need food, clothing, transportation, and shelter. Her children will need braces and tuition. But it is not need that underlies man's drive for wealth; it is desire.

People do not buy chateaux because they need a place to live. Nor do they invest in stocks because they need pocket money. They seek wealth and its trappings for other purposes.

Dorothy Parker said, "You can't be too rich or too thin." But when Howard Hughes died, it looked like he was both. Hughes had the kind of wealth that meant he could do what he wanted. He didn't have to listen to anyone. He was so rich he could eat Campbell's chicken noodle soup every day if he wanted and wander around with Kleenex boxes on his feet.

In the end, Howard's wealth may not have helped him much. It cushioned him from reality, protecting him from the things that might have brought sanity to his life.

He might as well have been on welfare. Those people, too, are cushioned from the reality of everyday life, so they never have to learn how to earn a living and get along in the real world. That is also often true of the children of rich people. They don't have to learn how to hustle, and many never do. In this sense, wealth is not merely a burden like the Chateau de Bourg Archambault, but a threat.

At Ouzilly, deep in the French countryside, you can live well on a little money. On a beautiful day, you can sit out on the terrace of a stone farmhouse . . . you can drink local wine . . . you can eat local food . . . you can putter in your garden and take day trips to visit medieval towns. Life can be quite good—even with little money.

But when you don't have money, you don't have the option of changing your lifestyle. As long as I am content to live in rural France—or rural Arkansas, for that matter—I can do that on little money. But what if I want to live in New York or Paris?

(continues)

I'm going to find out how much it costs to live in Paris in a couple of weeks. We're moving to an apartment near the Trocadero. The modest, 4-bedroom apartment rents for 17,000 francs per month—about $3,000. Not bad. And cheap by New York standards. Paris is actually one of the cheapest major cities in the world. Still, with school fees, meals, transportation, maintenance, furniture, utilities, and professional fees, we estimate that it will cost us about $100,000 a year to live there. But the tax rate in France is 60%, so I will have to earn $250,000 just to keep my head above water.

Hmmm . . . this won't be cheap. How much capital would I need to earn $250,000 per year? Well, if I could get a reasonably safe return of 6%, it would mean that I would need $4.3 million. This does not provide a luxurious lifestyle, by any means. In fact, it barely pays the bills of a bourgeois American family . . . with six children in school.

Most people think you need at least $10 million before you can be considered rich. That amount would provide you with about $600,000 in income. Most people could live comfortably on that much.

But wealth is not always forthcoming when, and in the amounts, we want it. So, in practice, people don't really calculate how much they "need" to live the way they want. Instead, they try to earn as much as they can and adjust their sights accordingly. They do not need to live in Manhattan—life in Omaha is good enough for Warren Buffett, after all. They do not need to go to the Tour d'Argent for dinner. The food at Madame Grammond's is just as nourishing. So why the pressure to earn ever more money?

Bunker Hunt said that money was "just a way of keeping score in life." But to what end? What's the prize, in other words? Once you have a comfortable place to live, and decent food to eat, does additional wealth really add to your quality of life?

Does it help your children . . . or does it hurt them? Does it make you happier? More secure?

The major thing it does is expand your field of choice. You can decide for yourself whether you want to live in Omaha or New York, for example. More choice leads to more thought about what living well really means. This, in turn, may have the effect of enriching your life in unforeseen ways. Or it may simply make life more complex and difficult, like having to choose a long-distance phone service or an insurance program.

"Women," repeated Michael. "Without women, money would mean nothing." At last, I grasped his meaning. He was reaching for the deeper truth. For all the practical advantages of having wealth, men strive for it for impractical reasons: Money is status. There is some reproductive imperative that causes men to seek status and women to prefer men who attain it.

To express it crudely, money is a way of scoring (metaphorically, of course) . . . not just keeping score.

The most valuable thing that money can buy you is the freedom to spend your time as you see fit. And when you reach the point where you can spend most of your time paying attention to those things that bring you the greatest pleasure, chances are you won't spend a great deal of money (unless, that is, you are unfathomably shallow). You'll probably choose to spend your time conversing with friends, reading good books, enjoying art and travel—living the kind of life you imagine wealthy English or French aristocrats did in centuries past.

To some extent, at least, you can do that right now.

LIVING RICH . . . STARTING RIGHT NOW

When you think about the rich—the really rich—you may find yourself marveling at their . . . well, their money.

Take Bill Gates, the world's richest man. If you think $10 million is a fortune, then consider this: He has 8,000 of them. If he put his money in $1,000 bills, he'd have 80 million of them! His wealth is so great that the interest on it makes him $60 million richer every month. Bill Gates makes more money every time he takes a nap than most Americans make in 10 years.

But how much better does he live? Sure, he's got a huge house. And a yacht. Probably he's got a jet, too. But who needs that crap? Really!

You can live as well as Bill Gates does right now. And I'll prove it to you.

Let's start by identifying some of the basics of life:

* Sleeping
* Working
* Dressing
* Eating and drinking
* Enjoying leisure time

Now, the purpose of becoming rich—you would think—is to make each of these experiences as rewarding as possible. The more money you have, the more choices you have.

Take sleeping. What does a billionaire want out of sleep time? I'd say the same thing you do: blissful, uninterrupted unconsciousness. And (aside from peace of mind, which you can't buy) what will give you that?

Answer: a great mattress.

And how much does the world's best mattress cost? Maybe $1,500. That means you can buy yourself a million-dollar sleep on a billion-dollar mattress for no more than $1,500.

So get rid of that lumpy thing you are sleeping on and find yourself the absolute best mattress you have ever sat on. Buy it and go to sleep content that Bill Gates can do no better.

You can pay almost any price for anything—but after a certain price point, you are paying for prestige rather than quality.

Take steak. Ask those who know about beef and they'll tell you that the quality of a steak depends entirely on the meat. Buy a New York sirloin at Ruth's Chris and, for around $30, you are eating the best steak money can buy. Eat the same piece of meat at Le Cirque and you'll pay $75. What's the difference?

Yes—just prestige.

The same thing is true when it comes to your clothing. Beautiful, comfortable clothes are not cheap, but they don't have to cost a fortune. You can buy the world's best pair of slacks for $150 or you can spend 10 times that amount. The difference is the label on the waistband.

Champagne, anyone? *Consumer Reports* had some wine experts test a variety of champagnes and found that out of the five best, four were less than $40. Dom Perignon, listed fifth, will set you back $115. But you can have a better champagne for only $28.

And so it goes on.

The point is this: The best material things in life are affordable. They are not cheap—quality never is—but if you buy them selectively and use them with care, you can enjoy a life as materially rich as Bill Gates on an income that wouldn't get him through lunch.

> There is no cure for birth and death save to enjoy the interval.
>
> —*George Santayana, 1863–1952*

Your Dream House

I've lived in a three-room mud hut in Africa and a 5,000-square-foot mansion, and I can tell you this: The quality of a home has little or nothing to do with its cost or size.

Think about the houses you most admire. They are probably *not* huge and flashy. One of my current favorites is a modest, three-bedroom house in Cleveland that its owner transformed into a lush, luxurious museum of her love of travel, dance, and learning. Every room is a gem. I am completely comfortable and endlessly amused in this rich and interesting house.

Its value? As great as Bill Gates's 40,000-square-foot monstrosity in Seattle—yet this one has a market value of about $150,000.

STEP 4

RADICALLY INCREASE YOUR PERSONAL INCOME

When I met Steve Paulson, he was working as a research assistant for a publishing company, putting in 12-hour days and making $17,680 a year. This was not, as you might guess, 20 years ago. It was in July of 1996.

Steve, 23 at the time, was giving up sports, forgoing girlfriends, and eating lunch at his desk for a paltry wage—not because he was unable to find a higher-paying job (he could have earned more managing a fast-food restaurant), but because he had a hunch that this job as a research assistant would give him an opportunity to do well in the future.

He was right. And it happened faster than you might think. A year after he began, he got his first raise—a substantial 20 percent increase to $21,216 a year. Since then, his income has increased dramatically. In fact, this year, Steve's compensation will exceed $1 million.

Steve's income history has been extraordinary, but he's not alone. Don O'Hara's income during the same period of time has had a trajectory almost as strong:

2000:   Around $185,000
2001:   Over $100,000 (divorce year)

2002:   Around $200,000
2003:   Around $300,000
2004:   Much, much more . . .

Phil Hammer's income went from $29,500 a year in 1996 to $50,000 in 1997 and then $215,000 in 2000—and since then has never dipped below $200,000. In fact, Phil broke into the $350,000 range last year.

Ted Johnson has had a similar experience, seeing his personal compensation rise from $31,000 in 1998 to $59,000 in 2000 to more than $400,000 today.

And that's not to mention Marion Oaks (from $50,000 to $240,000 in six years) . . . and dozens of other people I've known and worked with.

Let's talk about how these people boosted their incomes so dramatically and figure out how you can do the same in the near to medium-range future. Or, at the very least, radically better than you are doing now.

But first, let's talk about why you'll never get rich by increasing your income the old-fashioned way—by working hard and waiting a long, long time.

WHY ORDINARY PAY RAISES WILL MAKE YOU POORER INSTEAD OF RICHER

Most people go through their lives working for businesses they care nothing much about, dealing with problems they'd rather not face, and getting paid wages they'd very much like to change.

They dream of a better life and may envy those who make more money, but they are stumped when it comes to figuring out what to do about it. If career work is a path, theirs has a very modest tilt upward. Yes, they will get raises—but how many and how much?

In a survey of 1,276 companies nationwide, Hewitt Associates, a global human resources outsourcing and consulting firm, found that average salary increases for 2003 were 3.4 percent—the lowest number ever recorded in Hewitt's 27 years of gathering and analyzing this kind of data.

In fact, the trend has been downward since the survey began. In the beginning, average raises were about 6 percent. Then, during the 1980s, they dropped to just over 5 percent per year. In the first half of the 1990s, they dropped to about 4 percent to 4.25 percent and stayed there through 2001. They dropped to 3.7 percent in 2002—before hitting record lows in 2003.

It's highly unlikely that you'll get rich on that kind of wage increase. That's especially true if you consider the effects of inflation. While wages have risen over the past several decades, so has the cost of living. Some studies show that net income (after adjusting for inflation) has not increased since the early 1980s.

And the trend is going the wrong way. Between 2000 and 2002, for example, pretax median household income rose 0.6 percent to $42,409. But when adjusted for inflation, that gain became a 3.3 percent *decline*.

The dismal truth is that working people in America have been getting poorer, not richer, despite higher nominative wages.

To beat this dismal trend, you need to earn above-average pay increases. That, I'm happy to tell you, can easily be accomplished. Remember, these depressing statistics are measurements of the *average*. They include data on some workers who get no raises, many whose raises track inflation, and only a few employees who do better than that.

You want to get yourself into the third category. In fact, your goal should be to radically increase your income. How do you do that?

Although it may seem hard to believe, most businesses are more than willing to give you above-average increases. But they will do so willingly only if you give them above-average work.

I'm not suggesting that employers are benevolent. Some are and some are not. But most healthy businesses are profit-oriented. And when they find employees who can help them increase profits, they are usually willing to reward them by returning to them a small portion of what they helped generate.

This has always been the case—especially with small and growing businesses. Today it's becoming more commonplace among larger companies, as they move toward *performance-based* pay (determining bonuses or other compensation on how well employees, teams, and the company do), to boost profits.

THE SECRET TO GETTING ABOVE-AVERAGE RAISES

To earn more—and enjoy better-than-average pay increases—there are two things you must do.

First, you must become a better employee. And second, you must make sure that everyone who matters knows you are better.

To earn *radically* more than you do now, you must make yourself a *radically* better worker. I'll explain how you can do that a little later. For the moment, though, let's set our sights on more modest goals.

How to Become a Noticeably Better Employee

My early career as an employee was spotty. There were times when I came in early, worked hard, and never took a moment's break. Then there were times like these:

- At 14, working at a car wash, my buddy Brian suggested we go on a sort of work slowdown. Instead of jumping in and out of the cars to clean the interior windows, the only thing we did was dry the radio antennas. (At 5 P.M., we were handed our first little pink slips.)
- At 16, as a stock boy at a grocery warehouse, I was caught playing cards with "Fast Eddie" in a hideaway high up in the racks. (I got off with a warning that time.)
- At 18, hired to sell appliances door to door, I'd trash the sales brochures and spend my hours reading by the river. When challenged, I had no explanation for the fact that I hadn't sold a single thing. (Job duration: two weeks.)

It wasn't until I had a family to support that I made the transformation from a functionally bipolar employee to a dependable (and noticeably better) one.

The change happened the day after our first child was born. I realized that even with my wife's salary ($12,000) and mine ($13,000) combined, we weren't going to be able to raise children in any sort of comfort.

I was working at a small publishing company at the time. My yearly review was coming up, and I knew that to get an above-average increase (I was hoping for $2,000) I would have to do two things. First, I would have to get my immediate supervisor, Jeremy, to support me.

Next, I would have to get the company president, Jeremy's boss, Max, to notice me.

It wasn't hard to win Jeremy over. I began by working longer hours and doing everything he asked immediately and well. He remarked on the improvement in my productivity almost immediately. Within a month, he was favoring me over the other employees, ever so slightly, when it came time to delegate responsibilities.

But Max wasn't going to be so easy.

Max directed the company almost exclusively through Jeremy. Although he was open and friendly with everyone on the staff, he avoided any one-on-one business discussions with anyone else.

Knowing that Max was very concerned about expenses, I spent a week looking into ways we could reduce them. Although we were a small organization, we spent a good deal on typesetting and printing. By calling around town to other typeset shops and printers, I was able to come up with a plan to reduce our yearly costs by about $48,000.

I presented my plan to Jeremy by way of an interoffice memo, copied to Max. Even though he had nothing to do with my cost-cutting idea, I was careful to give Jeremy partial credit for it. ("Our recent conversations," I wrote, "made me realize how important it was to look for cost savings.") To win Max's attention, I wasn't going to risk losing Jeremy's approval.

It was the right thing to do. Max boosted my income to $16,000 several weeks later (a raise that was about five times the company average). It was a start—but it wasn't as much as I needed to pay for my family's growing expenses. So I redoubled my efforts to make myself a more valuable employee by learning everything I could about the publishing business from Jeremy.

In Jeremy's view, the road to success was paved with consistently better editorial. So to become more valuable to him, I focused on improving the editorial quality of our subscription-based products.

As a direct result of my efforts, our renewal rates improved. This brought in more revenues and higher profits.

By the end of the next year, I was making $21,000—an $8,000 (or 66 percent) increase.

Over a period of three years, Jeremy and I managed to increase company revenues and profits by about 50 percent—and our personal incomes increased accordingly.

My income went from $13,000 to $16,000 to $21,000 to $24,000. Not bad. It was a radical increase in terms of percentages, but having started out so low on the income scale, I was hardly getting rich.

But something had happened to me during that time that was going to help me get wealthy. In trying to do everything I could to win my boss's approval, I had changed the way I *acted* as an employee. I was no longer satisfied with doing my work competently. I had learned what it felt like to do an excellent job, and the feeling was good. I was developing self-expectations and a work habit that was going to serve me well for the rest of my wealth-building career.

Make Sure the Right People Know How Good You Are

Becoming a more valuable employee is the first and most important way to boost your income, but it's not enough. Corporate culture being what it is (in most places), you must also advertise your value.

Of course, you don't want to come off as a braggart. That will create unnecessary pockets of resentment. The secret to successful self-promotion in a business environment is threefold:

1. Promote only what is true.
2. Give some credit to others, even if it hasn't been earned.
3. Be persistently self-effacing. Or so it should seem.

If you don't promote yourself, you are leaving the fate of your salary in the hands of chance and circumstance. But while you want to make sure that the people in power hear of your accomplishments, you also don't want them to think of you as an ambitious blowhard.

Put It in Writing

A good course of action is to get into the habit of writing regular reports on all the important projects you are involved in. Focus the report on the business, not you. Make it brief—one page is enough. Praise everyone involved. Play down your own role. But make sure the subtext is clear: Here is yet another good thing you have brought to the table.

There is a good business purpose for writing such memos. Your boss (and maybe even your boss's boss) is interested in these projects. He or she doesn't want to know the details. And he or she especially

FIVE HABITS OF SUCCESSFUL EMPLOYEES

If you want to increase your income, your first objective should be to transform yourself into a more valuable employee. You can do that by

1. *Working longer hours.* There is no better way to demonstrate your commitment to your company than by getting to work earlier than everybody else and staying later.
2. *Understanding your responsibilities.* You may have received a job description when you were hired and it may do a pretty good job of telling you what you have to do. But until you figure out how the company works, how it makes its money, how it creates a profit, and what place it occupies in the marketplace, you won't understand what really matters.
3. *Working harder.* You want a higher income. You recognize that you can expect to get one only by becoming a more valuable employee. Working longer hours and understanding how your job affects the company's bottom line are critical components . . . but so is old-fashioned hard work.
4. *Working smarter.* Ask questions. Read memos. Take work-related courses. Do everything you can to make yourself smarter and more effective at what you do.
5. *Helping your boss do better.* Doing your own job well is good. But doing that *and* helping your boss do his or her job well is a whole lot better. In most businesses, most of the time, power is transferred from the boss to the best employee. If that's the way your business works, when you help your boss move up by making him or her look good, the boss will do the same for you.

As an employee, you have a distinct advantage over your boss, because you are probably, in some way or another, closer to the action. You may be closer to the customers or to the production process or to the fulfillment problems. You may be closer to what goes on internally—the strife and turmoil among employees. Whatever it is, you have an opportunity to help your boss succeed by coming up with perspectives, questions, and solutions he or she can't clearly see.

Do that, and the boss will be your strongest supporter when it comes time to upgrade your income.

doesn't want to know about all the hassles. But your boss does want to be kept informed with very brief updates on where each project is, what has been done, and what is left to do.

When you or your team is faced with an important problem or challenge, you can write a report on that, too. Again, make sure it is short and sweet. Again, give credit where it's due. And make sure that it is routed in such a way that you don't offend by going over anyone's head. Most important, never present a problem without also presenting at least three possible solutions. If you do, you'll get a reputation for being a good thinker.

By working harder and smarter to accomplish more and letting key people know what you are accomplishing, you'll find that everyone will be much more receptive to granting you above-average pay raises when your review comes around every year.

Let's take a look at how that could affect your earnings over an extended period of time.

If You Have 40 Years to Wait, You'll Get Rich
Just by Being Better

For the purposes of this illustration, I'm going to talk in the same terms that most financial planners and wealth experts usually use: the span of a 40-year career.

If you've read the introduction to this book, you are probably saying to yourself, "Why is he using a 40-year time frame? Didn't he say that this sort of calculating is fundamentally deceptive? Who has 40 years to get wealthy? Only the very young. And even among the young, who wants to wait that long?"

You're right. Still, I'm going to go forward with this illustration because what I really want to convince you to do in this chapter— *radically* increase your income—will appear that much more impressive by contrast.

Oscar Ordinary is 25 years old, makes $28,000 a year, and gets ordinary 3 percent to 4 percent yearly increases. Over a 40-year career, he makes approximately $2.3 million.

Elwood Exceptional is not satisfied with ordinary. He's ambitious and hardworking, and averages a 6 percent increase in wages over the same 40-year period. In other words, he earns more than his colleague Oscar. Not a lot more—at least in the beginning. But the difference becomes much more significant as time goes on, because the salary on which Elwood's raise is based gets consecutively higher. And over a 40-year period, Elwood earns about $4.3 million, almost twice as much as Oscar.

If Elwood and Oscar live in similar homes and spend approximately the same amount of money, Elwood will have a nest egg that is about $3 million to $4 million larger than Oscar's, assuming they both earn the long-term stock market average of 9 percent or 10 percent on their savings and that inflation averages 3 percent to 4 percent.

A $3 million retirement fund will provide a very good income for Elwood and his wife. Oscar's chance of a financially comfortable retirement, on the other hand, is very remote.

Getting better-than-average increases every year can make a substantial difference in the wealth you can acquire over the course of a lifetime. The reason for this, of course, lies in the enormous power of compounding interest, especially over an extended period of time.

Think about your own career and imagine what would happen if, like Elwood, you could earn 6 percent more each year than you've been earning so far.

By making yourself a more valuable employee and by promoting your value to key people in your business you'll get the extra salary increases you need to eventually retire rich at the end of your career. But that's your 40-year backup plan. Let's talk about something much more exciting: How to boost your income by 10 percent to 100 percent a year (or more) so you can get wealthy in 7 to 15 years.

Transitioning from "Better" to "Invaluable"

If getting better-than-average pay increases can be achieved by becoming a better-than-average worker, then it follows that extraordinary pay raises may come if you become an extraordinary employee.

Think of it this way: Good employees earn good salaries because they are valued. But great employees earn amazing salaries because they are considered *invaluable*.

Let's take a moment to define terms here, because words like *valuable* and *invaluable* are often too liberally used. For example, a boss may say that her personal assistant is invaluable when she simply means that the assistant takes care of all the boss's needs and makes her life a lot easier.

FIVE WAYS TO FIGHT BACK AND COME OUT ON TOP IF YOU ARE TURNED DOWN FOR A RAISE

Since I changed the way I worked at my job, I've never been turned down for a raise. But I've had the awkward duty of declining raises to dozens of employees. Most of them simply sulked and disappeared. But a few of them took the experience as a wake-up call and fought back. They didn't see themselves as losers, and they weren't going to let me view them that way, either.

If you get turned down for a raise, arguing with your boss won't do you any good. But if you can take advantage of the situation by following the suggestions listed here, you may be surprised at how dramatically you can improve your future income.

1. *Thank your boss.* Yes, thank him or her. If you didn't get the raise you wanted, there is a very good chance it's because you didn't deserve it. If you are like most people, this idea is going to be very hard to try on. But if you spend some time thinking very objectively about your performance (asking yourself questions such as "Was I always early?" and "Did I stay late?" and "Was I always eager and energetic and helpful?"), you will probably come to see your performance for what it was—less than stellar.

   If you thank your boss for making you see the light, you'll shock him or her into paying attention to you. If you follow that up with some kind of modest pledge to do better, your boss will be watching for you to do so.

2. *Come in earlier.* There is no more impressive way to show you are serious about your work than to get in earlier than you have been. A half hour is enough. If you can, get in before your boss does. Get in earlier, and make sure your boss knows it.

3. *Work harder.* However hard you've been working so far, it hasn't been enough to establish you as the number one worker in your department. Getting in earlier and then paying complete and serious attention to your work will demonstrate your intent. As time goes by, the extra time and energy you give to your job will show up in higher-level skills, better knowledge, and—most probably— more money.

4. *Get more training.* Take every chance you get to become better educated about your job. Take advantage of whatever programs your company offers. If something comes up and your company doesn't want to pay for it, pay for it yourself. (As with working harder, you don't want to let your extra training go unnoticed.)

5. *Help your boss plan your future.* After a few weeks of being the new you, ask for an appointment with your boss. He or she may be afraid that you are going to ask for a raise. Assure your boss that nothing is further from your mind. When you get the boss alone, reconfirm your gratitude for the wake-up call, brief him or her on the changes and improvements you've made, and then ask what else he or she thinks you can do to move forward even faster. Don't ask for anything in return. Make it seem as if job satisfaction is your only interest.

This is a radical approach. Ninety-five percent of the people who read this will never give it a try. You may be the exception. If you are, you will see dramatic results. Your income will improve in six months or less—and it will keep improving thereafter. Before you know it, you'll be at a whole new level. Just as important—or maybe more important—your job satisfaction will skyrocket. You'll like your job better because you'll be better at it—and everyone around you will take notice, including your boss.

But is the assistant invaluable in the sense of being worth an almost unlimited amount of money? Would the boss double her salary to keep her? Triple it?

You want to be considered invaluable, but not the kind of invaluable that gets you a pat on the head and an extra $20 a week in your bank account. To be truly invaluable, you have to be more or less irreplaceable. And how can you do that?

Well, the truth is, you can't do it absolutely. Everybody, including Donald Trump and Oprah Winfrey, is replaceable. But the closer you can get to seeming to be irreplaceable, the better your chances of radically increasing your income.

As I will show you, you will have to learn more about your

business. And you may also have to alter your job description (at least somewhat). You will almost certainly have to expand your circle of contacts to include more people who can help you achieve this goal.

But the most important thing you'll need to do is this: Master a financially valued skill.

What Is a Financially Valued Skill?

Let's start with this last concept and work our way backward.

A financially valued skill is one that plenty of other people are willing to pay good money for. How good? I'd like to begin the bidding at, say, $130,000 per year.

This is, admittedly, a somewhat arbitrary number. But it does have the advantage of giving you an after-tax income of about $90,000. That's enough to allow one or two people to enjoy a reasonably comfortable lifestyle *and* put at least $13,000 into savings. Invest $13,000 over a 15-year career at 12 percent and you'll have a net worth of more than a million dollars. (And I'm going to show you how to do *much* better than that by investing your time and money in ways that will create additional and *automatic* streams of income for you.)

Before we take a look at the sort of jobs that pay a $130,000 salary, let's say a few more obvious but important things about the term *financially valued*.

- We are talking, now, about monetary value only. We acknowledge, as I pointed out before, that there are other, more important values in life.
- I am using the word *valued*, rather than *valuable*, because I want to emphasize the idea that the perception of value that counts is in the marketplace. We are not concerned, for the moment, with what you may personally find valuable or fulfilling, but only with what other people value in terms of money.
- I am emphasizing the idea of skill rather than profession, because skills are transferable in a way that professions aren't. Also, it is possible to combine several valued skills within a given profession and thus multiply your income. I'll explain more about that later.
- Finally, note that I used the word *master.* That will become important later on.

So let's take a look at some popular professions in terms of their average incomes.

Figure 4.1 shows the average incomes of 14 U.S. professions. Those that fit my definition of financially valued (i.e., paying in excess of $130,000) are highlighted.

It may surprise you to learn that the median income for a dentist or lawyer is less than $130,000. But that's just median income. Median income includes all businesses, big or small, weak or strong, and in all sorts of industries.

Obviously, larger businesses often pay more than medium-sized ones. Small businesses pay practically nothing at first—but when they

Figure 4.1 Median U.S. salaries by profession.

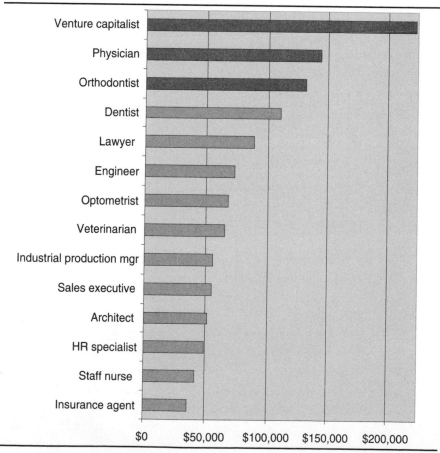

begin to grow, the money they pay their top people can meet or exceed even that of some Fortune 500 companies.

If you consider the top-paying jobs within these professions, the numbers get larger. (See Figure 4.2.)

So What Can You Do with This Information?

If you are already employed in a financially valued profession and are already making at least $130,000 (and assuming that you're happy with your career choice), you have three objectives.

Figure 4.2 Top U.S. salaries by profession.

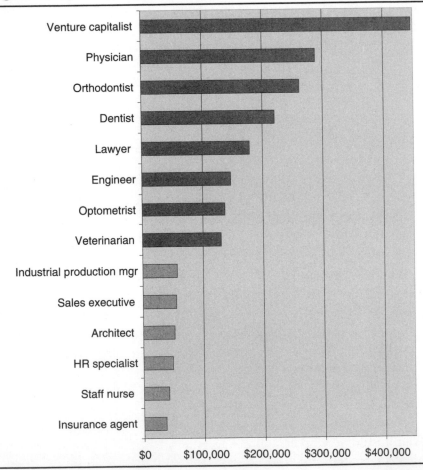

1. You must master the *essential* skill of your profession—the skill that brings in the most money for your business.
2. You must become adept at selling the idea to other people that you are masterful.
3. You must keep your spending in check so that as your income skyrockets (and it can easily rise to double or triple the standard for your profession), you will be able to invest a larger and larger portion of it into (a) creating additional streams of income and (b) building equity.

If you can boost your income to $130,000 a year, you should be able to create a million-dollar net worth (not counting your house and car) in 7 to 15 years, assuming you keep your expenses in check.

In the pages that follow I'll tell you several ways to do that. We'll begin by talking about how you can boost the income you get from work.

HOW TO BE A TOP EARNER IN YOUR BUSINESS

Basically, there are three kinds of jobs in the business world: technical, administrative, and profit-generating.

- *Technical jobs* include most positions in information technology and engineering, and some positions in legal, financial, and accounting fields.
- *Administrative jobs* include most positions in corporate management, product fulfillment, operations, and customer service, as well as some positions in finance and accounting.
- *Profit-generating jobs* are those that are directly involved in producing profits for the company. Profit generators include marketers, salespeople, copywriters, people who create new products, and the people who manage all of these employees. In most companies, the leading profit generator is the CEO, because the CEO's main job is to deliver a bottom line.

Administrative workers, on the average, are the poorest-paid group. Generalists by training, they compete against a large pool of other generalists in jobs that require no special skills or talents. If you are an administrator, and a very good one, you can expect to see your income rise as your performance improves. But more likely than not, it will be at the 4 percent or 6 percent level—probably not enough to meet your medium-term (7- to 15-year) wealth-building goal.

Technical workers are usually better paid than their administrative counterparts. This is especially true at the beginning of their careers, at which point even an entry-level position requires a high degree of specialized knowledge. Computer engineers, information technology people, and certified public accountants (CPAs) typically start at higher salaries than do fulfillment managers and customer service clerks, but the difference tends to diminish over time. Top engineers often make more than operational vice presidents, but not much more.

Profit generators are usually the highest-paid employees. More important, they have the greatest potential for income growth.

If you work for a small or medium-sized company and fall into one of the first two job categories, you'll reach the $130,000 level only by rising to the top of your division—and then only if the business you work for is profitable and growing. With larger companies, you might achieve a salary of more than $130,000 as a technical specialist or a manager of technicians and administrators.

But even if you can hit that kind of number, your upside potential will be limited. That's because regardless of how good you are at what you do, what you are doing is usually seen as a necessary expense, not a part of the secret process of making money.

I'll have much more to say about this in a little while. For now, you have to ask yourself a simple question: "If I work harder and better at what I am doing now, are the chances good that I can reach at least the $130,000 income level in the next two to three years?"

If the answer is yes, fine. If the answer is no, you must be prepared to make some radical changes.

So let's talk about that now: how to develop the skills and convert your job into one that merits the $130,000-plus level of compensation.

Imagine Yourself as a Bookkeeper . . .

Let's say you work as a bookkeeper for a new-car dealership and are not satisfied with your $30,000 salary. You could dream of owning the business, but that's not likely to happen anytime soon. You need

WHY PROFIT GENERATORS MAKE A LOT MORE MONEY

The first-year compensation for marketing majors is considerably lower than it is for techies. But their average salary increases are higher. Over a career of salary increases, this can add up to a lot of money.

Here's an example of what this meant for two employees at a company I consult with:

- The entry-level computer tech started with a salary of $25,000. Over the course of about 12 years, this person rose to become the top computer guru in the company—and now earns $175,000.
- The young marketing associate started with a salary of $20,000. Over the course of 12 years, this person rose to become a profit center manager—and now earns $400,000.

The curve to get to these numbers is about the same, but now the profit center manager will earn at least $225,000 more than the computer tech for 20 more years. More important, people in profit-generating positions generally have a better opportunity to work their way up to CEO.

money to own a car dealership. Money you don't have right now. For the immediate future, you have to set your sights on something that is attainable. So, look around.

Aside from the owner, who else is making good money? Well, the sales manager is bringing down a steady $70,000 a year. That's not bad. And then there's Joe, the number one salesperson, who is making even more than that.

You check it out and discover that you can't be the sales manager because the company has a firm policy of hiring only MBAs for that job. So that leaves you one option: becoming a salesperson and going on to claim Joe's spot as Numero Uno Salespro.

You could tell yourself, "Forget about it! I am not a natural, and God only knows it takes a natural schmoozer to sell cars." But if you are smart, you will recognize that selling cars, like almost everything else in life, is a process that involves no magic—just specific actions, each of which can be studied and then learned.

Let's say you become friendly with Joe and eventually gain his trust. You take him out for a drink one evening and get him to open up and reveal his secrets—the things he does to consistently outperform (and outearn) every other salesperson. I'm not an expert at selling cars, but I wouldn't be surprised if the conversation went something like this:

JOE: If I'm selling to a couple, I always shake hands with the man first. That way, he feels important. Something he needs to feel to make the decision I want him to make.

YOU: That's neat, Joe. What else?

JOE (*smiling*): One thing I never do is say, straight off, how much a car costs. If, before I'm ready to close, a customer pops the ugly question, this is what I say: "Let me ask you something, Mr. So-and-So, how important is it to you to drive a car that is safe and comfortable for your family?"

And then Joe would tell you a few more things he always does. Now, these things individually may not amount to all that much. But put together in a single presentation, they add up to this: how Joe manages to be the company's number one salesperson, month after month after month. Since that—becoming as good as Joe—is your goal, these specific things he does are the secrets you need to learn.

The great salesperson, you now understand, is not somebody with supernatural powers but an ordinary person with specific, valuable knowledge.

And so you learn the skills required to perform not the job you are currently doing but the one *that you aspire to.* By working above and beyond your work description, you get noticed. You also get good at what's important. And as you become more of an expert in the work you want to do, it will start to show. You will become more informed and more confident. You will speak with greater authority and more clarity. People will begin to treat you differently.

Then, one day, the job you want will open up for you. And when that happens you will not have to apply. It will be offered to you. Why? Because the word about you is already out. You have already demonstrated that you are perfect for the job, and so the decision to hire you is an easy one.

In this case, you would be hired as a car salesperson because you know the cars—cold—and you know their prices, and you know the selling protocols and procedures, the company requirements, the legal requirements, and so on.

Your next goal would be to outsell every other salesperson. And you would do that by, again, studying the specific actions of the company's best salespeople.

Before you knew it, you would be at the top of the heap—earning the kind of money you are right now only dreaming about. And then you could start making promises to yourself. First, to make a hundred grand. Then $130,000. Then a half a million. Then a million.

Yes, you could make a million a year by mastering the skills of a marketer, salesperson, product creator, or profit manager. Plenty of others have done so. Why not you?

This, by the way, is almost exactly what happened to a friend of mine. In less than three years, I saw his personal income rise from less than $30,000 to more than $175,000 by following these steps. That happened 10 years ago. I saw him just last month. He looked good, and he should have. He was working half-days three days a week and was worth several million.

Put Yourself into Your Company's Cash Flow

If you merely do a good job in a technical or administrative position, you can expect only modest pay increases. Become very good, and you'll get relatively very good raises. But if your objective is to sky-rocket your salary, you will have to become a key profit generator. It's as simple as that.

How big of a contribution must you make to the company?

A good rule of thumb is this: If you want to get a raise that's $1,000 more than ordinary, make sure you've been a major contributor to an idea that will generate at least $10,000 to $20,000 in additional net profits for your company.

This is an absolute minimum. For larger companies your impact will have to be much more than that—20 to 50 times.

If you want to increase your current income by, say, $25,000, you are going to have to find a way to increase business profits by $250,000

THE MIRACLE OF COMPOUND LEARNING

When you invest your time in mastering a financially valued skill, it will help you make good money almost immediately. Every year you continue to use it, you'll find that it is easier to get promotions and take jumps in income.

Over time, your income will be in an entirely different category. And not because you asked for it, but because you've made yourself into an entirely better and perhaps even an invaluable employee.

Like money, the value of financially valued skills *compounds* over time. Let me explain.

If you were to learn a particular marketing skill today—say, how to write great headlines—it would help you significantly if you were writing a direct-marketing package tomorrow. It might, for example, double your response rate to that package. That effect—the doubled response rate—might well be worth thousands, maybe even tens of thousands, of dollars to you.

And as you applied that same bit of knowledge over and over again, you'd get better at it. And that improvement would result in higher response rates and higher net dollars to you.

As you added more skills to your copywriting arsenal, your headline-writing skill would achieve a more powerful response, because it would be operating together with other tricks and techniques.

And that's not the only way investing in learning a financially valued skill is like investing money. Because once you learn a financially valued skill, the amount of money you earn from it is mostly about *leverage*—about knowing how to apply that knowledge to increasingly lucrative opportunities. In other words, the same skill that can earn you $130,000 when your business is relatively small might earn you $260,000 or even $560,000 (or even 10 times that much) if you moved to a larger business or your business grew. Your knowledge compounds over time and so can the opportunities toward which you apply it.

This is what you want—to be able to earn a great deal more money in the future for the same amount of work you are doing now. That can best be ensured by learning how to make your business grow and then enjoying the salary raises as it does.

or more. And your idea can't be a one-time deal. The $250,000 extra your work has to contribute must be generated again and again in the future.

To maintain a much-higher-than-average salary, you need to have a very substantial effect on your company's growth in income.

This rule of thumb is true for most growing companies. It may not be true for a business that is large and static. Large businesses, as a rule, offer stability of employment and predictability of income in place of high salary curves. It stands to reason if you think about it. Big companies attract smart, hardworking but sometimes conservative people. There is sometimes more good talent than is needed.

In general, you'll have the best chance of radically increasing your income if you work for a business that has

- Significant sales (in the millions or, preferably, tens of millions of dollars)
- Reasonable profits (what "reasonable" means depends on the industry)
- A recent history of growth (both in sales and profits)
- A vision of further growth

And, as I suggested, a small number of employees (so your contributions will stand out).

If the business that you are working for meets none or few of these criteria, start looking elsewhere. Unless you can single-handedly turn such a business around, there won't be enough financial resources available to meet your financial objectives.

Your ideal situation would be to position yourself as an invaluable profit producer in a small, fast-growing, and highly profitable company. If you can do that, great. If not, don't worry. There are plenty of other ways to dramatically boost your income.

Changing Yourself into a Profit Producer
So . . .

If you want to make a superhigh income, you have to become a supersignificant contributor to your company's bottom line. That means being an influential force in product creation, marketing, sales, or profit management.

WEALTH PRODUCERS VERSUS WEALTH WASTERS

In the simplest terms, there are only two things that you can do with your money:

1. You can save it.
2. Or you can spend it.

Saving your money increases your wealth. Spending it makes you poorer.

By the same token, there are only two basic roles that you can play as a worker:

1. You can produce profits.
2. Or you can reduce profits.

A profit producer is someone who creates a product, markets it, sells it, or manages the bottom line. A profit reducer—like it or not—is everybody else.

Yes, this is an oversimplification. Individual workers, at any given time, might be engaged in either or both kinds of activity. But when it comes time to reduce or expand the workforce and award raises, that binary perspective is in the back of every business owner's mind.

The key to long-term job security and big-time pay raises is to get your boss to think of you as a major profit producer. The only way you will be able to get your boss to do that is by actually doing it.

Want a big, $130,000-plus salary? Start generating big, million-dollar-plus profits for your business.

If your current job is outside any of these areas, you must either switch roles or expand your position so that it is directly involved in one of them.

This is not as far-fetched as it might seem. Let me give you two examples of people I know who have done that.

When I met Ted Johnson in 1998, he was employed as a midlevel manager for a direct-mail business I consulted with. I was impressed with him right away, because he had the courage to disagree with me at our first meeting. I had advised his boss to take a certain course of action regarding an advertising campaign. And although Ted was hardly a marketing expert at the time, he said, "That doesn't make sense to me." And so we discussed it.

Ted wasn't right. But his reasoning was sound and his instinct for marketing was apparent. I told his boss that she should groom Ted for a marketing position. Within a year, he was in charge of one of the products.

After that, there wasn't a week that went by when I didn't hear from Ted. He was constantly bombarding me and his boss with all sorts of ideas about how to sell more product, increase customer satisfaction, and so on. Not all of his suggestions had merit. But those that did were implemented.

Meanwhile, his enthusiasm and activity never wavered. With each month that passed, he learned more and his intuition improved. That made his suggestions more valuable. And the next time a marketing management position opened up, he was given the opportunity.

Ted's transition took less than two years. And his salary almost doubled: from $31,000 to $59,000. Once he was in a position to create his own products and run his own advertising program, his learning curve accelerated even faster. In the four years that have elapsed since then, his portion of the business grew from $1 million to $16 million (with more than a 20 percent profit margin). He was clearly the key person in this expansion. And so it was easy for his boss to justify Ted's phenomenal rise in income: from $59,000 to more than $400,000 in 2004.

Another example is Marion Oaks. She was working as an editorial assistant for another publishing business that I consulted with, also about 1998. After listening to a seminar her boss and I gave about why copywriting was such an important element of their bottom line, Marion switched from editorial to copywriting.

For almost two full years, her income stagnated. Then she wrote her first breakthrough promotion. That success inspired her to work even harder. Within the next 12 months, she was generating millions every quarter in additional sales for the business. And her income soared—from about $50,000 to $240,000 in 2004.

Are These Numbers Realistic?

Not if you aren't going to transform yourself and make a difference. But if you do become a critical part of the growth of a business, it is reasonable to expect very large increases year to year. Table 4.1 shows some examples based on the records of people who have worked for one of my clients:

TABLE 4.1

	HIRE DATE	STARTING SALARY	PERCENT INCREASE	CURRENT SALARY
a	7/24/1996	$25,000	500	$150,000
b	3/6/2000	$24,000	233	$80,025
c	6/20/1989	$65,000	131	$150,000
d	12/14/1993	$75,000	47	$110,000
e	6/4/2001	$16,640	291	$65,000
f	2/1/1999	$26,000	150	$65,000
g	9/2/1998	$20,800	142	$50,400
h	9/3/1997	$28,000	168	$75,000
i	5/17/1999	$23,000	139	$55,000
j	2/9/1998	$32,000	196	$94,600
k	8/28/2000	$55,000	82	$100,000
l	9/6/1994	$37,000	157	$95,000
m	11/4/1996	$48,000	213	$150,000
n	4/10/2000	$45,000	52	$68,500
o	1/17/1995	$80,000	119	$175,000
p	8/8/2000	$50,000	48	$74,000
q	5/24/1999	$62,500	84	$115,000
r	2/4/2002	$33,000	67	$55,000

If you would like to experience a radical salary increase like this in your own career, here's what you have to do:

- Figure out how your business creates profits.
- Understand how your job contributes to that process.
- Modify your job so that more profits are produced as a result of what you do.
- Make sure the people who are in charge of giving raises know how much more money you are making for the company.

Learning How Your Business Makes Profits

Most employees know little or nothing about how the companies they work for earn profits. They may know what the company sells (i.e., they can identify its products), where it does its marketing (television, direct mail, the Internet, etc.), who it caters to in general terms (seniors, young girls, etc.)—but they go mute if you ask them how and why sales are made.

How much do you know about your company's core profit strategies? Answer these questions:

- Can you name five *primary* benefits of your company's top-selling product/service?
- Can you name the chief *secondary* (psychological) benefit of this product/service?
- Can you name one unique selling proposition for each of your company's top-selling products/services?
- What is your company's primary competitive advantage?
- How is that advantage employed in (1) product creation, (2) marketing, and (3) sales?

If you know your business the way you should, you will have quick and confident answers to all of these questions. If they leave you guessing, you have work to do.

Here's something to keep in mind: Every business has, at its core, some unique way of developing and selling its products/services that is invisible to outsiders—even, in most cases, to competitors.

Only by understanding the business in a very deep way (and especially understanding how its products are created, developed, and sold) can you hope to become a major part of the company's profit-making inner circle.

You can acquire a good deal of this invisible knowledge simply by speaking to people who are in the know. Make an appointment to speak to your boss and surprise him or her by asking, "What makes the business work?"

Talk to every friendly face in the sales and marketing departments. Ask them how they do their jobs. Speak with customer service people. Find out what the customers are asking for. If you know people who have responsible positions in marketing, product creation, or profit management in other companies, give them a call.

As these conversations take place, you'll begin to get how the business operates, what sort of things matter, and what sort of things are simply time wasters. Your goal is to have that invisible profile of the company gradually come into focus for you. It will.

Figuring Out How Your Job Contributes to the Bottom Line

Once you've learned the core profit strategies of your business, it will be relatively easy to figure out how to make the work you do essential to its financial success.

You can get a good idea by asking yourself this: "In the eyes of upper management, is the job I do considered (1) nice but unnecessary, (2) necessary but not of much interest to them, or (3) essential to the growth and profitability of the business?"

Be honest. If, for example, your job is in corporate communications, you are in the first category. If you work for the accounting or legal department, you are in category one or two, depending on what you actually do. And even if you are in the marketing, sales, or product development area, you can't be sure that the work you do is considered essential.

Know this: If what you do is beneficial to your business but unnecessary, you have no job security, regardless of how well you do it. Even if the work you do is critical to the operations of the business, if you yourself don't create profits, you are at risk.

So long as the business is thriving and you work hard and well, your salary will go up. But the moment things turn bad or you can be replaced with someone else who can do the same job as well for less money, you will be out the door.

As I've said, this is *not* true for someone who *demonstrably* generates growth and income for a business.

Growth and income producers are viewed as not just good but necessary and desirable. By making yourself one of the few people in your company who know how to bring in the bacon, you give yourself the greatest chance of getting big raises, big promotions—and, eventually, earning a six-figure income.

Here's a simple test to determine how essential you are to your company. Answer the following questions:

- Have you created a successful new product/service in the past year?
- Do you have bottom-line responsibility over a product, group of products, or division? If so, was it profitable last year? And will it be as or more profitable this year?
- Are you directly responsible for sales or a team of salespeople? If

so, did your department meet or exceed your boss's expectations last year? Will you do it again this year?
- Have you come up with several new sales-boosting ideas lately?
- Do you personally generate sales of more than 10 times your salary?
- Are you in charge of an important marketing or advertising function? If so, did you meet or exceed your boss's expectations last year? Will you do it again this year?
- Have you made at least one suggestion this past month about improving the company's marketing or sales strategies?

If you answered yes to at least several of these questions, you are where you should be—in the profit stream of your business. If you couldn't answer yes to any of them but still feel that you are capable of making a major contribution to your company's bottom line, you're going to have to make some changes.

Modifying Your Job to Become a Critical Factor
Your plan is to gradually shift your work activities so that you are gradually doing more and more of one or several of the core, invaluable jobs:

- Making sales
- Creating products
- Managing profits

The idea is to keep your present job while you make the shift. *And you're going to do this with the full knowledge and support of your current boss.*
If you leave your boss in the dark, you risk making an enemy of him or her. And that would be damaging to your plans. So in everything you do from this point on, consider how it will affect your boss.
If the boss is a reasonable person you will be able to explain what you are doing and why. If he or she understands that you will continue to offer support and do a good job, the boss shouldn't be threatened by your ambitions. Most important, be sure your boss understands that your future success will make him or her look good. The boss was, after all, your mentor and inspired you to make a career with the company. Because of your boss, you will help the company make more

money. The boss will get a lot of credit from the people responsible for *his or her* raises.

But before you have that conversation—if you have it at all, you need to identify a job in your company that you want to do.

Identify which people in your company make the most money. Then find out exactly what they do and what skills they need to do a good job. It may seem like a stretch at the moment, but it's entirely possible that you could one day do the same job. After all, all of the most highly valued skills—marketing, sales, product creation, and profit management—are not particularly specialized. Yes, they require knowledge, but it's the kind of technical knowledge that any bright, ambitious person can acquire.

Starting today, try to learn something about that job every week. Find out what it takes in terms of hours and days. Discover what it typically pays and when it pays more and why. Identify the daily routine, the common problems, the biggest challenges, and the best rewards. Ask. Observe. Read.

Keep it up, week after week, until you start to feel as if you get it. When you feel ready, talk to your boss about your plans.

Then approach key people in the department you're interested in. Tell them (honestly) that you think their field is something you'd be good at. Say you've been learning about it in your free time and you'd like to volunteer to help them out whenever you can so you can learn even more.

In volunteering to help out, you have three objectives:

1. To demonstrate your commitment to the business
2. To develop relationships with essential employees in your organization
3. To learn an essential (i.e., financially valued) skill

Your first objective will be realized almost immediately. Most people will be impressed by your willingness to dive in and give them a hand. If your intentions are sincere and your follow-up is diligent, you'll soon enjoy a reputation for being an up-and-comer (no matter how old you are).

Your second objective will be achieved over a period of months, as you demonstrate what you can do. Remember, the key to establishing good relationships with these people is to focus on *helping them*. If your efforts are transparently self-serving, it will have a neutral or negative impact.

Your third objective—learning a financially valued skill—will take some time. But the benefit you'll get when you achieve it will be enormous. Mastery of a financially valued skill will virtually guarantee you a high income for the rest of your life.

IF YOU'RE NOT SURE WHICH SKILL TO MASTER, TRY THIS ONE FIRST

Of all the skills you can have—the ability to speak like Winston Churchill, to paint like Rembrandt, to calculate like Albert Einstein—none will help you achieve wealth as well as knowing how to sell things.

So if you're not sure which financially valued skill to target, I recommend becoming an expert in the kind of sales that make your company profitable. And I'm going to give you a minicourse in selling right now to help you decide if this is for you.

Every private enterprise—every school, restaurant, law office, hospital, building supplier, hardware store, and entertainment complex—survives and prospers by virtue of its commercial activity.

In my own life, this lesson was hard to learn. Coming from a non-business background, I looked at the commercial world from the outside in. An art gallery, to me, was a place where intelligent people gathered to talk about the latest trends and connect with like-minded art lovers. When I fantasized about owning my own gallery, that's the way I saw it. Until I actually bought one. The reality was very different.

A successful local dealer I knew told me in passing one day that he was planning on retiring in a few years. I immediately suggested that he allow me to buy into his business. He declined at first, but we kept talking. A month later, we had a deal. I paid him a sizable chunk of cash for a 50 percent interest in his thriving business. I was entitled to acquire the remaining shares over a three-year period, during which time he'd teach me what he knew and phase himself out.

The first thing he had me do was invite every friend and family member within 100 miles to come to a new opening of the gallery.

"When we get them in the door," he explained, "we'll get to work on them."

I had no interest in "getting to work" on my friends and family members. But he was adamant. "These are prime prospects," he told me. "They like and admire you. And they know you collect art. The seed has already been planted!"

I didn't know exactly what he meant, and I didn't feel good about it. Nevertheless, I dutifully sent out the invitations. When opening night came, I followed him around as he worked the room. I was shocked and embarrassed by how hard he was selling.

The evening was a disappointment for both of us. For him, because we didn't sell nearly as much art as he felt we should have. For me, because I suddenly realized that the dream I'd bought into was, in fact, a business based on hard-core selling.

I shouldn't have been that naïve. After all, having been in the marketing business for years, I knew a lot about how to make a sale. But I had mastered the skill of selling through the written word. I never actually saw my prospects face-to-face. Now I was involved in this wonderful world of art, but I had discovered that it survived on selling, too. A very direct, person-to-person kind of selling—a skill I hadn't learned at all and had no desire to learn, especially at the expense of my friends and family.

A month later, I bought myself out of his business. It was a very expensive lesson. But it taught me a great deal about business and life that has been enormously helpful to me since then.

For example:

The reason this art dealer was so successful (he was making a very high income even during periods when other art dealers were going out of business) was because he was an expert at selling art. His knowledge of art history was limited. He wasn't ignorant, by any means. He knew the important, inside stuff—what type of paintings a particular artist was admired for, what periods of production were considered the most valuable, and so on. But his main skills were in (1) getting people to come into his shop and then (2) getting those who bought to keep buying, year after year.

I began to see that virtually every private enterprise functions that way. To keep doing what you want to do (and to make a profit from it), you have to (1) attract customers at a reasonable cost and (2) convert them into repeat buyers.

Let's call the first task the *front-end* sale and the second task the *back-end* sale. In the years that have passed since, I've learned to look at virtually every moneymaking enterprise in terms of these two selling skills.

This perspective has allowed me to quickly understand how many businesses operate, even ones of which I have only outside knowledge. It's no longer a mystery to me why, for example, so many restaurants and small hotels go out of business, why people in the travel and leisure business make so little money, why you shouldn't even try (as I explained to a conference attendee just the other day) to make a business out of a llama farm—and why most good small businesses fail when they attempt to get bigger.

This fundamental perspective on sales has allowed me to provide helpful advice to all sorts of different businesses in almost every conceivable industry. I can see now how every successful start-up business is one that has quickly and correctly answered two very simple questions:

1. What is the most cost-effective way of attracting customers?
2. What is the best way to keep those customers buying?

If you can learn to see your business that way and can one day discover the correct answer to these two questions, you will quickly become recognized as an invaluable employee. That will happen because you will understand your business from the inside out. You will know it better than 90 percent of your fellow workers.

When problems arise—no matter what they are—the solutions must address one or both of two objectives:

1. Lowering the cost of acquiring new customers
2. Increasing the lifetime value of each existing customer

Even the stickiest problems in business—which are always people problems—can be analyzed effectively by considering possible outcomes against these two objectives.

BETTER YET, TURN YOURSELF
INTO A MARKETING GENIUS

Skilled marketers are consistently among the highest-paid individuals in any industry. They earn high salaries, extraordinary bonuses, and the respect and admiration of colleagues and competitors. Marketers who master their trades are all but guaranteed a life of wealth, security, respect, and satisfaction.

Anyone of average intelligence can become a skilled marketer. You don't need a quick wit, a flair for the dramatic, or a degree from a top business school. What's required is an understanding of why people buy things.

Basically, the best marketers know how to apply three fundamental principles. I'll give you a brief overview of them here to help you decide whether this is something that interests you.

The First Principle: The Difference between Wants and Needs

In today's consumer-driven economy, it's easy to mistake a want for a need. How many times have you heard one of the following statements:

- "Sally needs a new wardrobe. The clothes she's wearing make her look silly."
- "John hates the way his hair looks. He says he needs a better barber."
- "I simply have to have that new handbag!"
- "We need a bigger house."
- "We need a nicer car."
- "We need a bigger lawn."

None of those things are needs—as in something you can't live without. Our needs are really few and simple: air, water, food, shelter, transportation (sometimes), and clothing (usually). Everything else we buy is based on our wants. And even when it comes time to purchase needs, such as food and clothing, our buying decisions are usually based on wants. (We want a certain type of bread, a specific brand of clothes, a house in a particular style, etc.)

When you realize that your customers don't need your product or service, you recognize that the way to convince them to buy it is to stimulate their desire for it. The most effective way to do that in your advertising is to

- Promise your prospective customer (usually implicitly) that taking a certain action (buying your product) will result in the satisfaction of a desire (want)
- Create a picture in your prospect's mind of the way he or she will feel when that desire is satisfied
- Make specific claims about the benefits of your product and then prove those claims to your prospect
- Equate the feeling your prospect desires (the satisfaction of a want) with the purchase of your product

The medium doesn't matter. Wherever you find your customers—on television or radio, in magazines or newspapers, at home reading the mail or on the Internet—the basic process is the same. The moment you forget this first principle—that you are selling to wants rather than needs—your marketing will fail.

The Second Principle: The Difference between
Features and Benefits

A pencil has certain features:

- It is made of wood.
- It has a specific diameter.
- It contains a lead-composite filler of a certain type.
- It usually has an eraser at the end.

And so on.

These features describe the objective qualities of the pencil. So if buying were a rational process, selling would be a matter of identifying the features of your product.

But as you just learned, buying is an emotional process. And that means you must express the features of your product in some way that will stimulate desire. You do that by converting features into benefits.

For example, the features of the pencil might be converted into the following benefits:

- It is easy to sharpen.
- It is comfortable to hold.
- It creates an impressive line.
- It makes correcting easy.

The Third Principle: The Difference between Benefits and Deeper Benefits

The reason some marketers do a better job than others is because they understand the difference between benefits and deeper benefits.

In our example, for instance, what might be the deeper benefit of having a pencil that sharpens easily?

To figure that out, master marketers ask themselves, "Who is my target customer? And why, exactly, does this customer want little things (like sharpening pencils) to be easy?"

Of course, there's no single answer to such a question. It depends entirely on who that target customer is. If he's a busy executive, his deeper reasons are going to be different than if she's a busy housewife.

Perhaps the executive wants more ease because he's buried in minutiae. Perhaps he senses that if he could just get a little more spare time in his day he could catch up with his work. And if he could finally get his in-box conquered and his e-mail cleaned up, perhaps he could write that memo or make that phone call that would boost his career.

Master marketers who understand these deeper motives—the desire to be more successful at work, for example—can create stronger advertising copy because they will be appealing to emotions that are closer to their customers' core desires.

The example I'm using is, admittedly, far-fetched. But I'll continue to push it to make the point. Our master marketers have dug a bit below the surface now. They recognize a deeper desire than mere ease, and they are going to appeal to it. But before they do, they stop and deconstruct the deeper benefit. They ask themselves more questions: "Why does my customer, this busy executive, want more success? Is it because he wants a better salary? And if so, why is that? Is it because he wants a nicer home? And if he wants a nicer home, why? To please

WHERE TO GO TO LEARN FINANCIALLY VALUED SKILLS

There are many ways to learn financially valued skills. You can learn pretty much everything there is to know about sales and marketing, for example, by reading

- *Scientific Advertising,* by Claude Hopkins (Chelsea House, 1980)
- *Ogilvy on Advertising,* by David Ogilvy (Crown, 1983)
- *Tested Advertising Methods,* by John Caples (5th edition, Prentice-Hall, 1997)
- *The Copywriter's Handbook,* by Bob Bly (Owl Books, 1990)
- *Influence: The Psychology of Persuasion,* by Dr. Robert Cialdini (Perennial Currents, 1998)
- *The Tipping Point,* by Malcolm Gladwell (Little, Brown, 2000)
- *Selling the Invisible,* by Harry Beckwith (Oxmoor House, 2000)

But most people don't like to learn from books. And with good reason. Books are designed to communicate ideas, to excite, to inspire. But they are usually not written to guide you along a path of knowledge. For the sort of learning we're talking about here—acquiring skills—you are better off taking actual courses.

The Agora Learning Institute (agoralearninginstitute.com) specializes in teaching people financially valued skills through home-study programs and seminars. Other groups that do the same thing include Nightingale-Conant (nightingale.com) and the American Management Association (www.amanet.org).

It takes a long time (in my experience, as much as 5,000 hours of study and practice) to master *any* complex skill. That's true of financially valued skills as well. But you don't have to be a master of selling, marketing, product creation, or profit management to start making good money. Achieving a level of competence (which takes only about 1,000 hours) is enough.

Since you probably already have some skills in these areas, you will need to spend that much less time. And if you combine a good program with the help of a good mentor, you can accelerate your learning very significantly.

his family? To impress his friends? And why does he want to please his family and impress his friends?"

Marketers who can figure out the answers to questions like these hold their prospects' hearts in their hands.

NOW IT'S TIME TO GET GOING

If you do everything I've recommended so far, you'll be in a position to demand a much higher salary:

- You will be operating in the profit-making vortex of your company.
- You will be doing work that is most important to the top boss.
- You will be better than anybody else in a similar position.
- And you will begin to seem—and eventually be—invaluable and irreplaceable.

You will also be—in case you happen to be in the very rare situation of working for a business whose decision makers are so dense they don't recognize your full value—in a position to take your skills elsewhere—or sell them to your business as a freelance consultant.

HOW TO BECOME A CONSULTANT
TO YOUR OWN COMPANY

The single biggest complaint I've received since I started writing *Early to Rise* has come from my clients. "Stop telling our best employees to become freelance consultants!"

What happens is this: Some enterprising young person takes my advice to heart and transforms himself into a bona fide marketing genius in (usually) three or four years. Then he either demands a huge salary increase or offers to provide future services on a freelance basis.

The complaint is about compensation. "He was making $40,000 a year before he started reading *ETR*. Now he's given us a proposal that will cost more than three times that much."

I am not happy this is happening. Well, maybe I am. But I am a little bit embarrassed to have to point out the following:

If your employee transforms himself from a good, hard worker who is worth $40,000 into a marketing genius worth three times that much, that means he is making your business worth that much more. Since his compensation is, and always will be (even as a consultant), a fraction of what he gets paid, the more he makes, the better his boss should like it.

In the businesses I've owned, I've always been thrilled to see my employees make this kind of transition. That's because I knew how valuable they were to me. For every dollar extra they earned, my business gained 10. Who could resent that?

And I'm not the only one who likes to see his employees get rich. Most of the best businesspeople I know are thrilled to award high incomes to employees who earn them. So don't worry. You'll almost certainly get the salary you are seeking if you do what I told you to do:

- Put yourself into your company's profit stream.
- Help make your business more profitable.
- Internally publicize your value.
- Expect to be properly compensated.

If you work for a small to medium-sized growing business, you shouldn't have any trouble getting the money you deserve. But with larger, older organizations, fair compensation is sometimes a problem. That's because some corporate leaders forget their focus and create agendas that are about politics (power) rather than business (profits).

If you get stuck in such a situation, you need to gradually reposition yourself as a self-employed consultant. There are plenty of books and programs on the subject of setting up your own consultancy, including one from the American Consultants League (americancon sultantsleague.com). Basically, here's how to do it.

Plan A: Try to Stay on the Payroll

The moment you made the decision to become a consultant, the relationship you had with your employer changed—even if he or she didn't realize it. In this new context, your employer is a prospective client, and as such, must be treated with all the coddling and cuddling any future client would merit.

In the months and weeks prior to your changeover, make sure that your reputation goes from good to unimpeachable. Meanwhile . . . develop a secret plan.

Don't announce your intentions—at least, not immediately. Focus on doing a great job, increasing your financially valued skill, and building profits for your company. In the meantime, create yearly, monthly, and weekly objectives for your new career.

Plan to make at least twice as much per hour as you do now. Remember, as a freelance consultant, you'll have some additional expenses. Plan for these expenses, too. Your initial goal will be to net 110 percent of your current salary in your first full-time year. But you should expect your income to go up somewhat substantially after that. I have mentored at least a dozen people who have made this transition—and I can't think of one who didn't end up making at least double the salary he left by the end of his third year as a consultant.

After you have perfected your skill and established your goals, it's time to make your pitch. If you adhere to the following guidelines, your risk of failure will be almost nil:

1. *Don't be resentful.* You tried to persuade your boss to pay you the big bucks you deserved, and he or she didn't. That's water under the bridge. You won't win any points by bringing up the subject again.

2. *Make the message positive.* Even if you have banished resentment from your feelings entirely, it's not advisable to tell your boss that the reason you want to stop working at the company is to go into business yourself and make more money. Your making money is not the boss's top priority. (If that wasn't clear to you when you failed to get the raise you wanted, it should be obvious now.)

    It's better to state the facts and then sell your boss on the benefits. Make him or her understand that the work you'll be doing will benefit the business and that if he or she has your support, the feather will be in his or her cap. Focus on your good ideas—not the position change. Those ideas, if they are really good, will change your role from employee to consultant. But don't say that to your boss directly. He or she will figure it out in the long run—especially a few years down the road when he or she realizes how much cheaper it would have been just to pay you $130,000 in the first place.

3. *Don't talk about the money—not at first.* Your primary objective in having this first, transitional conversation with your boss is to convince him or her to hire you on a part-time basis. Since you know you can improve the company's profits, you don't need to worry too much about how much you will eventually get paid—so long as you tie your compensation to the bottom line. There are dozens of ways to do that. The main thing right now is to get the deal. You will be able to ratchet up your fees as time goes by and your client becomes comfortable with the new arrangement.

4. *Stress the benefits.* Virtually everything you say after that should emphasize the benefits you will bring to your boss and the business. The most important thing is to convey the idea that you want what's best for the boss and the company.

When constructing a list of benefits (and you should do this formally and put it in writing), consider

- How much time it will save your boss
- How much stress it will eliminate (now that you'll be taking charge of one of the boss's biggest headaches)
- How much more focused the boss can be now that he or she can pay attention to core tasks and not worry about managing you
- How much better your boss will look to his or her boss (now that this part of the business will be working almost automatically)

If your boss doesn't go for your proposal, back off and thank him or her for the time. Don't be resentful. And whatever you do, don't threaten to quit. If you weren't able to convince your boss of the value in your going freelance, then you need to get back to the drawing board and create more value. Keep at it until what you are offering is simply too good to refuse. Now you go to Plan B.

Plan B: Sell Your Expertise to Someone Else

In my experience, great employees who wanted to go freelance never failed. That may be because most of the businesses I have worked with have been growing enterprises and thus eager to retain good relationships even on a freelance basis. It may also be because most of the freelancers I mentored were very good at what they did.

If your boss won't or can't hire you on a freelance basis, there will be others who will.

So get to work on your network. Send out notes. Make phone calls. Make visits. Don't shortchange your boss while you are doing this (respect for your current paycheck is paramount), but don't feel bad about selling yourself, either.

You are, in effect, looking for another job. The only difference is that instead of asking for a salaried position, you're going to be selling yourself as a freelancer—someone with the skills to help the business grow. (If you have an employment agreement with restrictive convenants concerning working for competitors, you'll have to respect that.)

In marketing yourself as a freelance consultant, make your proposal irresistible by stressing benefits like these:

- You don't have to keep me unless you like my work.
- You don't have to pay my overhead.
- You don't have to train me, manage me, or keep me busy. All you have to do is assign me your most challenging jobs and let me take care of them for you.

If you do your homework by studying each prospective employer before you make a pitch, you'll have a good idea of just what that employer needs. Prepare for your presentation by finding out the following:

- What does the employer consider the company's unique selling proposition?
- How are the products sold?
- What are the company's most successful customer acquisition methods?
- What are its most profitable back-end products?
- What's working best for them right now? What's not working?

A SIMPLE TECHNIQUE THAT WILL GUARANTEE YOUR SUCCESS AS A FREELANCER

Before you launch into your self-promotional campaign, create a grid of 500 boxes—10 squares across and 50 squares down. Label it "Hours to Go Till My New Life Begins," and tack it up on the wall. Now start your countdown.

Scratch out a box for every hour that you work on selling your freelance services. Don't count commuting time. Don't count thinking time. And don't count time you spend worrying. Do count the hours you spend making up your contact lists, writing and sending letters, traveling to and conducting interviews.

Count, too, the time you spend reviewing your presentations and making improvements. Make it a specific goal to get better at selling yourself each time you do it. Selling yourself, like selling anything else, is a specific skill that can be mastered.

Follow up after every presentation you make, successful or not. Stay cheerful. Be thankful. Ask for referrals . . . and keep on trying.

I've recommended this technique to several people I've worked with and, based on their experience, I can guarantee you this: Long before you ever reach that 500th box, you'll have all the freelance work you are looking for.

You can get answers to most of these questions simply by doing a little research.

DEVELOPING YOUR SECOND (AND THIRD AND FOURTH) INCOMES

By mastering a financially valued skill and marketing yourself properly, you will soon be on track to making *at least* $130,000 a year. But there are many other ways you can boost your income.

The simplest way is to use the skills you've developed to start a side business that can feed you a steady, healthy, second stream of income.

Not everyone has the time or energy to do this. But if you can find a way to give it a try, the results may surprise you. I know more than a few people who have created side jobs for a little extra income.

Before they knew it, they were earning more money on weekends than they were making during the week.

A couple I know decided to supplement their income by creating a temp service that placed nurses with hospitals. The idea came from a casual conversation with another couple. Both of the wives worked as nurses and both were saying that they made more money when they worked by the hour than they could ever make working full-time. (There were and are various good reasons for that. Temporary nurses are direly needed, for one thing—and they are accounted for as off-budget expenses.)

For a while, the four friends had to reinvest all their profits into building their part-time business. But by the end of the second year, they were making thousands of extra dollars. By the end of year three, the business had graduated to full-time status. By year four, all four of them were working full-time in a business that eventually made millions. The year after I met them, they had just sold a half-interest in the business for $25 million.

That's an exceptional example. But it shows you what can happen when you start a side business.

The Difference between an Income-Generating and an Equity Business

In this chapter we are talking about ways to boost your income. Starting a side business can do that. But it can also make you rich through the appreciation of your equity in it.

The difference is very simple but very important.

An equity business is one that you can sell for a profit. Most small businesses, interestingly enough, aren't of that sort.

If you have a one-person law practice that pays you $300,000 a year, that's a good business, but it may not be a business you can sell. Yes, your clients are valuable—but are they valuable to someone else? Will someone else feel confident that these clients will continue doing business there?

When you are choosing a side business, figure out what your purpose is: equity or income. The advantage of an income-oriented business is that the income can be produced relatively quickly. The advantage of an equity-oriented business is what it becomes worth over time.

In this chapter, we'll talk about businesses from an income point of view. In Chapter 5, we'll look at the other side of the coin.

Shooting for an Extra $25,000 a Year Is a Good—
and Reasonable—Place to Start

There are all sorts of ways to supplement your income by $25,000 a year. There are as many ways as there are businesses. We've talked about increasing your income by selling your services to the business you work for—going freelance. You can also add a second stream of income by selling your services to other firms while you're still working for your current employer (noncompetitive firms—you don't want to do anything you could get fired for).

If you have a financially valued skill, you can expect to earn between $100 and $500 an hour for your services. At $100 an hour, you would have to work 250 hours—an extra five hours a week—to make $25,000. At $500 an hour, it would take you only about an hour a week to earn $25,000.

Consider Branching Out into the Direct-Mail Industry

If you would rather supplement your income by trying out a different financially valued skill, consider becoming a salesperson, advertising copywriter, list consultant, marketing manager, or graphic artist in the direct-marketing industry.

Why direct marketing? Three reasons:

1. Direct marketing is (if you include direct marketing on the Internet) by far the largest single form of advertising. It is larger than television, larger than cable, larger than magazines, and larger than newspapers.
2. Not only is it immense, but it's also growing. This is especially true since e-mail advertising has become such a large part of Internet commerce. It's fair to say that no other form of advertising is growing as quickly as direct marketing.
3. Finally, and most important, direct marketing is a business that measures results in terms of dollars and cents added to the bottom line. Freelance professionals who help direct-marketing companies make money are capable of demanding large incomes. That's

because it's easy for everyone to see the positive effect they have on sales.

That may need some explanation.

Conventional advertising measures its results with consumer surveys and broad-based studies of product sales. When Pepsi-Cola spends several million dollars on a television campaign, it can't measure its effectiveness directly. Yes, it can poll TV watchers to find out how many remember seeing the commercial. And it can track sales in regions where the advertising appeared. But it can rarely, if ever, know for sure whether any particular ad brought in more net dollars than it cost to produce.

In fact, the very idea of general advertising is indirect: Create an image or idea in the prospects' minds and sooner or later they will come. Brand recognition is the mantra. And brand recognition does matter when you are selling commodities. But that doesn't mean that any particular ad meant to increase brand awareness will do it. Nor does it mean that if it does indeed increase brand recognition, it will increase sufficiently to cover (or more properly, exceed) the cost of the advertisement.

I've said this many times in *Early to Rise:* When it comes to general advertising, the real selling goes on between the advertising company and the manufacturer, not between the manufacturer and the end user.

With direct-response advertising you don't have to worry about wasting your money on marketing campaigns that don't work. You can control all the critical factors that affect sales. And you can measure results.

A typical direct-response marketing campaign measures exactly how many dollars were spent and how many dollars were received. Let's say, for example, that a manufacturer of health products hired a direct-response copywriter to create a catalog, which the manufacturer then sent to 50,000 potential customers. Assuming the cost of the catalog was $25,000 (or 50¢ per catalog) and the resulting sales totaled $50,000, the gross profit would be $25,000.

Now, let's say that the same manufacturer hired a second copywriter, who produced a second catalog that also cost 50¢ to put in the mail. But this one achieved a return of $100,000, or a gross profit of $75,000. Which copywriter is going to make more money? And how much more is that copywriter worth?

You can see the point. And that's why successful copywriters often demand between $10,000 and $25,000 plus royalties for every campaign that they write. And that's for projects that can take as little as a single week to complete.

You can see the potential. And it's not just for copywriters. Graphic artists, list consultants, and marketers who understand direct marketing can earn very substantial part-time incomes.

You can learn about direct marketing by taking courses at your local college, by reading books on the subject, or by enrolling in home-study programs. As I've said earlier in this book, it will take you about a thousand hours to become a competent copywriter, marketing manager, graphic artist, or something comparable. You can reduce that time requirement by learning under the guidance of a pro.

Once you have the skills, set aside four or five hours a week to promote yourself to local, regional, or even national direct-marketing businesses.

You can—and probably should—specialize in a particular medium: mail, print (newspaper or magazine ads), Internet marketing, or television. You can—and probably should—focus on a subject area, too (health, financial, business, self-help, nonprofit, etc.). Specialists always make higher incomes because they have more rarefied skills. It may seem at first as if you are limiting yourself, but you'll soon experience the benefits of narrowing your focus once you start feeling like a true expert.

Your Best Bet: Selling Your Own Products or Services through Direct Mail (or E-Mail)

Agora Learning Institute (www.agoralearninginstitute.com) publishes an excellent resource for the would-be direct-response entrepreneur. The book, *Made to Order: The Top E-Mail & Mail-Order Businesses* (available from Agora), highlights 50 major categories perfect for direct response, each with its own niche market. It also identifies various sources to obtain your products, specific marketing strategies in each area, the major players to learn from, pricing, and how to get started.

If you have an interest in direct marketing, here are some samples of profitable mail-order businesses (taken from *Made to Order*) to consider:

1. *Artist supplies.* The market for art supplies is a \$30 million–plus industry, and it's growing at more than 10 percent a year, according to the Hobby Industry Association. Direct-response art supply companies sell professional-quality painting, sculpture, and woodworking materials, as well as beads and jewelry stock. Working artists like high-quality equipment. If you can give them something that lasts, they'll remember the brand and reward you with repeat purchases. Be aware of pricing, since this is a price-sensitive market, and offer a strong guarantee.

2. *Audiocassettes and CDs.* There are all sorts of subjects that lend themselves to audiocassette, CD, and DVD sales. In the business-to-business arena, there are training programs, and in the consumer arena, you have books on tape, language programs, and music, just to name a few. The trend toward electronic forms of information, advice, and entertainment is unstoppable. One example is the Audio Book Club, which sells more than 65,000 audiobooks a year via mail order and the Internet. Online sales are growing, and there is a strong demand for companies that can sell audio products by allowing consumers to download the information online after paying by credit card. Buyers are interested in availability (the sooner, the better), the quality of the audio, the quality of the content, and value.

3. *Diet and weight-loss products.* The direct-response market for diet and weight-loss products is enormous, encompassing everything from videos and books to exercise equipment, pills to curb the appetite and burn fat, support groups, weight-management programs, and simple products like bathroom scales and fat monitors. Body-conscious Americans spend \$40 billion each year to lose weight, and the industry is growing at 5.6 percent annually. The National Center for Health Statistics tells us that an estimated 64 percent of Americans are considered overweight or obese and more than 50 million will go on diets this year. It's best to feature only one product in each mailing. Build a solid customer base, and then sell additional products on the back end. To charge the premium prices necessary for profitable mail-order marketing in this category, you must give your prospect hope that your product can provide a

solution to his or her weight problem. And, of course, you must offer a strong money-back guarantee.

4. *E-mail publishing.* There are e-mail publications for virtually every area of interest. Especially profitable market segments include financial investors, sports enthusiasts, hobbyists, business opportunity seekers, and people interested in personal growth. Sources of income for e-mail publishers include subscription fees, advertising revenues, and back-end sales. E-publishers earn money on the back end by offering products and services related to the topics covered in the publication. An extraordinary benefit of e-publishing is that there is very little cost associated with distribution (via the Internet as compared with U.S. mail). The key to success is to maintain a large subscriber base. To do this, you must offer valuable information, adhere to a delivery schedule, provide an easy-to-read and consistent format, and not badger your readers with too much advertising. Once you have built a subscriber base, there are companies that will market your space to potential advertisers.

5. *Fitness and exercise videos.* Mail-order fitness companies specialize in exercise videos featuring aerobics, boxing workouts, yoga, Pilates, and dozens of other systems. Buyers in this segment are men and women of all ages who are interested in self-improvement. They are generally middle to upper income, and respond well to targeted direct-response advertising. It's best to feature only a single product in each mailing. To justify charging a premium price, you must offer a unique routine or regimen, expert instruction, simple and quick workouts, or a unique venue or location. Sources for all of these products can be readily found on the Internet.

6. *Gardening seeds and tools.* Some 85 million households participated in one or more types of do-it-yourself lawn and garden activities in 2002, according to the National Gardening Association. The indoor and outdoor gardening industry achieves revenues totaling $40 billion per year, and this number is growing by 4 percent annually. Mail-order gardening companies specialize in sales of tools, outdoor power equipment, magazines, books, seeds, bulbs, and plants. To set yourself apart

in this industry, provide high-quality products, ease of ordering, and free educational information via editorial content in your catalog or on your website. It's also a good idea to consider producing a newsletter.

7. *Hobby and craft products.* Mail-order companies in this category specialize in kits and supplies for projects such as stained-glass decorations, decorative painting, woodworking, jewelry, and scrapbooking. The industry is very lucrative and growing rapidly, as it is being fueled by several consumer trends. Many consumers are concerned about the shaky economy and are choosing to save money by making their own gifts, decorations, and clothing. Others are making these items to create a second income. The majority of successful mail-order craft companies not only specialize in a particular category, but also offer their products online. This is a seasonal business. During spring and summer (the slow seasons), the focus is on wedding- and anniversary-themed crafts. In the early fall, it's Halloween and Thanksgiving. The Christmas season, as you might expect, is when you'll make your biggest money.

8. *Natural health products.* Mail-order health and nutrition companies specialize in organic foods, vitamins and supplements, and other minimally processed natural products. There is enormous opportunity in this industry, because sales continue to grow. In 2002, they topped $36.4 billion. Sales of health foods alone exceeded $10 billion in 2002. Sales of natural personal care products were more than $1.7 billion, almost half of which occurred outside of traditional retail channels, according to *Nutrition Business Journal.* Buyers in this category are affluent, well-educated men and women of all ages. These buyers respond well to direct-response advertising, and good mailing lists are plentiful. In addition to natural health products, it may be possible to market other related goods to these customers, including information publications and exercise equipment.

9. *Newsletters.* According to the Custom Publishing Council, more than 50,000 unique newsletters are produced annually, resulting in revenues of $20 billion each year. Most of them

provide financial, health, business, and travel information— subjects that all have one thing in common: They provide information that would be difficult for customers to find in mainstream media publications. The more highly specialized the information, the higher the subscription rate that can be charged. Because they are an information product, you can make a substantial profit with newsletters. The physical product you send customers will be very inexpensive to produce. In addition to subscription revenues, you can also offer your subscribers related products and services that will appeal to them. For example, if you're targeting salespeople, you can offer seminars, books, and CDs with special strategies to help them improve their sales skills.

10. *Pet supplies.* The pet industry is a major segment of the U.S. economy. Last year, American pet owners spent $26 billion on their pets. Sales of pet supplies alone are expected to exceed $8 billion by the year 2007. Demographic trends are at work here. More baby boomers are purchasing pet supplies because they increasingly view their pets as family members. And as empty nests become refilled with dog beds and litter boxes, older adults have new ways to spend their money. The direct-marketing strategies in this area are similar to those in other markets. Online marketing is especially effective, as is producing a catalog featuring a series of front-end products that the customer can order directly. To distinguish your business, offer quality products at competitive prices, expertise in all areas of pet care, excellent customer service, and free information about the latest trends in pet care.

ONE MORE GOOD IDEA FOR YOU: BUYING AND FLIPPING REAL ESTATE

Investing in real estate has historically been one of the most consistent ways to build wealth. In Chapter 5, we'll talk about how you can accelerate your wealth-building goals by investing in rental properties. Since this chapter focuses on income, let's take a look at how you can create a second stream of income with real estate.

Normally, when you think "income," you think rental units. But rental real estate provides income only after rents go up and expenses go down. During the early years of an investment in rental property you will usually be lucky to break even in terms of income. Yes, your net wealth will be increasing every year (because the equity you have in the property will become more valuable), but your cash flow will be break-even or even slightly negative.

This is especially true today, when real estate is so highly valued. In most parts of the United States, prices are at historical highs. As a real estate investor myself, I find it nearly impossible to buy rental properties that give me positive cash flow right away. It can be done, but I wouldn't create a wealth-building plan that depended on it.

I love rental real estate, but I think of it as an equity play—at least for the first 5 or 10 years. That said, where do you get income?

That's what I want to talk about here: creating a substantial second (or third) income by buying and selling properties.

How to Flip Your Way from a $10,000 Purchase
to a $28.5 Million Sale

One of the most successful real estate investors I know is Frank McKinney, who lives in my local area. By his own admission, Frank was the black sheep of his family. He had been in trouble as a teenager and barely graduated from high school. At the age of 20, he left Indiana and arrived in South Florida with just $50 in his pocket.

He went to work digging golf-course sand traps for $2 an hour at a resort. When he learned that a friend was making $40 an hour giving tennis lessons, Frank convinced the resort manager to pay for him to take a course that would get him certified as an instructor.

Soon, Frank had built a successful tennis-pro business, targeting affluent residents of new oceanfront condominium developments. He was making $100,000 a year. Life was good. But Frank wanted to do more—he just wasn't sure what that might be. So he decided to learn from his wealthy students.

He ran them ragged for 45 minutes of their scheduled one-hour lessons. The last 15 minutes, they were happy to just sit, sip water, and recuperate. During that time, Frank would pepper them with questions. What he learned was that they all had one thing in common. In some way, they had all invested in real estate.

That inspired Frank to buy his first foreclosure.

He started by learning as much as he could about real estate. Not only from his students but also by reading everything on the subject that he could get his hands on. He researched the local market and attended foreclosure auctions for 10 months. Then he scraped some money together and bought his first property. It was a roach-infested former crack house in a rundown part of town. He picked it up for $30,000, fixed it up, and sold it just a few months after buying it—for a profit of nearly $20,000.

Frank went on to do hundreds of these types of deals, eventually flipping dozens of properties in a single year. Still shy of his 30th birthday, he invested in his first oceanfront property. When it was renovated and sold, he pocketed nearly $1 million on this single deal—about what he would have made on 30 of his smaller deals.

Then he invested in another oceanfront property . . . and another and another. Since 1998—when Oprah Winfrey interviewed him as one of the country's most innovative young entrepreneurs—he has become the leading developer of ultra-high-end oceanfront homes in South Florida.

Today Frank enjoys the lifestyle of the rich and famous. He's written a book about his success called *Make It Big! 49 Secrets for Building a Life of Extreme Success* (Wiley, 2002). Recently, he attended a wealth-building conference sponsored by *Early to Rise* in Delray Beach, Florida. Attendees were struck by his enthusiasm for real estate. "Why shouldn't I like it?" he said. "It's given me so much— a great career, the chance to meet all sorts of interesting people, a way to get involved with charitable activities, and a very substantial income."

So let's talk about income—how to make $25,000 to $125,000 a year, part-time, buying and selling real estate.

You Make Your Money by Buying Right

According to Frank McKinney, Donald Trump, and countless other real estate experts, you can make good money buying and selling real estate so long as you stick to a few basic rules.

First, make sure you buy at a good price. If you can snatch up a property significantly below its current market value, chances are you'll be able to easily turn it around and sell it for a nice profit.

It's difficult to become an expert on the value of real estate all over town, so focus on one or two neighborhoods that you are familiar with. Properties that are selling at a discount to market value won't last long, so you'll have to do some legwork to uncover deals and be ready to jump on bargains the moment they appear.

Start by figuring out the average cost per square foot of properties in your target area. To do this, you'll need to research a representative sample of homes that sold in the recent past. The best time frame is within 12 months, and the larger the sample, the better.

Use a spreadsheet to map out the details of each property, including the sale price and square footage. By dividing the sale price by the square footage, you get the cost per square foot. By averaging all of your results, you will get the average cost per square foot for homes that have recently sold in your area.

Next, put together a list of the homes that are for sale right now. Do the same sort of calculation (using asking price instead of sale price) to come up with the average current asking price per square foot of property in your area.

Armed with these numbers, you now have a reliable benchmark to help you quickly determine whether a property represents a good value and a potentially profitable investment.

Finding the Best Deals on the Market

Once you know the property values in your target area stone cold, you are ready to recognize true bargains the moment they appear.

Scour the paper every day or two and call about every property for sale. You can also do some valuable research on www.realtor.com. When you have the address, square footage, and asking price, compare it with the comparable values you've already established for the area.

You'll soon get to a point where you'll be familiar with all the properties being offered in your target area, and you'll be looking only for new listings. At most, that will take 15 minutes a day—15 minutes that could pay off big with just one or two hits a year.

Regularly scouring the paper and the Internet for new deals as soon as they appear should become a regular part of your routine. But that's not the only way to find undervalued properties. Look for tell-tale signs that an owner may be thinking of selling, even before he or she advertises it.

Buying and Flipping Preconstruction Properties

Flipping real estate means there's a new development in town. You know it's going to be hot, and you can buy a preconstruction unit for $125,000. You are relatively positive you'll be able to flip it (sell it quickly) when construction is finished for $160,000.

This is a very nice business. No mess, no hassle. And you can make a lot of money. The trick here is to make sure you have the legal right to sell the property when you want and for the price you want. Beware: These deals often come with contracts that need to be amended.

Flipping is a very nice and rosy way to make good money in real estate. It's something you can't do all the time, but when you can, it's golden. The idea is to buy preconstruction homes or condos in very promising local developments.

Here's an example:

DL bought two condominium apartments in a Miami Beach high-rise three years ago, just at the beginning of construction. He bought one for himself at $375,000 and a smaller one for investment purposes at $205,000.

The building was completed in about 14 months. At that time, the larger apartment had appreciated by more than 20 percent—similar units were selling for $450,000. And the smaller unit did even better than that. A year later, prices had moved up again. He sold his investment property for $375,000.

Another example:

BM (a guy who has mastered buying and selling expensive cars, watches, etc.) bought two preconstruction condominium units in our town for $265,000 each. The property is not yet finished, but all the units have already been sold. The last six were sold for more than $300,000 each. BM has made almost $100,000 in less than 18 months.

It Can Be a Very Nice Business

This gives you an idea about what can be done by buying and flipping preconstruction properties.

It won't work if property values are falling. And it won't work if the particular development you choose turns out to be a clunker. That's why it's so important to *stick to your local market*—so you can truly know it.

HERE'S HOW I APPROACHED THIS BUSINESS

I made a deal with AK. She is basically doing all the day-to-day work: the forms, the filing, the footwork, and so on. I'm putting up the money, using my contacts to make good decisions, and taking financial responsibility. We are going to buy several properties every year—but only if we can get good deals—totaling a particular figure.

For the purposes of illustration, let's say that figure is $800,000. This will require an initial investment on my part of between $100,000 and $200,000. We are going to try to sell that $800,000 worth of property—when it is ready to be sold in about a year—for as close to $1 million as we can. In addition to the initial down payment, we have to consider closing costs, mortgage costs, and marketing costs (including commissions if we use a broker) when it comes time to sell. Our goal is to net, after expenses, $100,000. If we can do it once, we will reinvest the profits to do it again the next year. By the third year, if we are successful, I'll have taken out all of my at-risk capital and will be playing with the house's money—that is, money that is pure profit from the previous sales.

For this to happen, two things need to take place:

1. The local market needs to stay strong.
2. Good new properties need to be developed.

By sticking with developments in my hometown—an area I know and whose real estate investment climate I understand—I will have a pretty good idea about which direction prices are going in general. I don't yet know how to determine beforehand whether individual developments are good, but several criteria are obvious:

- The developer has to have an established track record and good references.
- The location has to be one that is very good or moving up.
- There shouldn't be anything seriously wrong with the development (such as lack of adequate parking or proximity to railroad tracks).
- The size of the development should be appropriate for the local market (neither too many units nor too few).

I met this year's commitment by picking up two units. One is (and again I'm using figures to illustrate) a $205,000 town house in a very good part of town. I bought it when the development was already half-sold and therefore already appreciated, but I thought the unit could go up another $30,000 or $40,000 in the future.

The second is a home in a development of eight units, six of which sold at $1 million and two of which (smaller and not facing the water) are priced at $500,000. My thinking is that I'm buying a cheap house in a nice neighborhood. The value of the more expensive homes will pull this up regardless of the market.

So far, the cheaper unit has gone up $10,000. I've just turned down $550,000 from the developer for the other one. So, on paper at least, it looks as if I should be able to meet my target of making a hundred grand this year from this particular part-time business. If I do half that well, I'll be happy.

You'll need to decide for yourself whether properties are appreciating in your area. If so, look around and see whether there are units you can buy that meet your own financial requirements.

If you're a novice at this, you ought to severely limit your investment. That said, wouldn't it be nice to have a little part-time, buy-and-flip business that could give you $20,000, $50,000—even $100,000—a year in extra cash flow?

One great thing about real estate: It goes up much more often than it goes down. And the good properties in the good areas go up much stronger and longer than the rest.

Once Again, the Most Important Rule: Invest in What You Know

I've talked about profits in the simplest terms. If you want to maximize your returns and minimize your cash outlay, you'll be borrowing money—up to 90 percent of a property's sale price. Thus, you could, for example, control $100,000 worth of real estate with a down payment (and transaction costs) of as little as $15,000. Some people put down even less. The better you can judge the market, the less risk you take and the better advantage you can take of the power of leverage: *borrowing most of the money you need.*

Perhaps the best thing about this particular form of real estate investing is that it requires the least amount of day-to-day work. Once you've selected the property, the hard work is done. After that, all you do is check on the development's progress from time to time to make sure it's on schedule. If your hunch about the market is right, you'll soon be selling your property for a very nice profit—because the development itself will be doing the selling for you.

Anatomy of a Great Real Estate Deal

RJ just sold a town house condominium for $341,000. He bought it, with a 5 percent down payment, eight months ago. He paid, after all expenses and upgrades, $291,000. After sales commission (he negotiated 3 percent with the lady he bought the unit from) and closing costs, he'll net about $226,000. After paying off the mortgage, he'll make about $35,000 on an investment of $15,000 eight months ago. Annualized, that comes out to more than 300 percent.

What's going on here?

This is an example of what happens when you buy a preconstruction home or town house and flip it on the day of closing. That way, you can market a new property—always more in demand—and never have to worry about maintenance, condo fees, or the like.

To make this work, you need to find good developments (by good builders and promoters) in hot areas. If the market is hot, that helps, too. You also need to buy the property right (which usually means early in the construction process so you get the lowest price) and sell it aggressively by every means possible.

In RJ's case, he went to the best source—the company that sold him the unit—the moment he heard that it had sold out its units. He figured they'd get people coming in looking to buy and would be happy to sell his unit at a 3 percent commission rather than get nothing. It worked!

To Make Money in Real Estate, You've Got to Buy Right

To buy right . . . be prepared to drive around and do some work. The big secret about real estate (at least for making money in the short term) is to buy good property at or below market value. Buy low and sell higher. And no matter what the popular books tell you, you won't be able to do that on a regular basis unless you take the time to get out there and find the best deals yourself.

Seven Rules for Buying Investment Properties

When you buy property as an investment for quick resale, you should adhere to the following seven basic rules. Most of these apply to rentals as well. However, if you're buying rentals for long-term ownership and profit, you will have to revise Rule 6 so you are actually improving the quality of the rentals.

1. Don't own real estate from afar.
2. Buy only in proven, up-and-coming neighborhoods or those that border on the same.
3. When buying a single-family home, make sure the gross rental income is at least one-tenth of your purchase price including improvements. In most areas this should limit the purchase price of the home to the $150,000 range and below. When you buy single-family homes above that range, you'll usually find that the rental value as a percentage of the purchase price will fall. If you're purchasing homes in the $150,000-plus range, your strategy will often be to fix and flip.
4. Figure out how much you're paying on a square-foot basis, trying to keep it as close to $100 per square foot as possible. That number is relative to the particular market, of course. In most nice neighborhoods, for example, some homes sell for $200 per square foot. But it's better to be down around $100 to leave room for improvements and margins for commissions.
5. Buy only homes where you can get a $2 to $4 return on every $1 you spend fixing them up. This is actually easier to determine than you might think. The trick is to buy a house priced considerably under the market and then redo it as cheaply as possible.
6. Spend money improving the house, but only where it matters. Paint. Put up inexpensive shutters and awnings. Replace cabinet doors and carpeting. Put ceramic tile on countertops. And landscape the entryway. Those are the main upgrade opportunities. Everything else you might do—including plumbing and electrical work—will probably not be good investments.
7. If possible, have a renter for your house before you buy it. If you get the word out sufficiently often, your friends and colleagues will think of you when they meet someone who is looking for a place to live.

That said, there is still much that is nebulous about determining value.

For example, is that two-bedroom ranch house that you saw on 13th Street and Olive Avenue worth the $150,000 being asked for it? What about that three-bedroom colonial a few blocks away? Is it over-priced at $120,000?

You can't answer those kinds of questions unless you have a very good feel for the neighborhood. And as I said, you can't have a very good feel for a neighborhood unless you limit your investing to a particular area, preferably in your own hometown—and unless you are willing to drive around that neighborhood and ask questions.

If you can do those two things, real estate can work for you. Think about it. And start looking.

When Buying Real Estate, Always Insist on an Inspection

Never buy a house or commercial property without an inspection—a good inspection from someone with a long-term reputation for fairness and honesty. If you don't know a good inspector, get referrals from other real estate investors you might know and from reputable contractors. Do not seek recommendations for inspectors from the realtors.

Never go to contract without inserting a clause that gives you back your deposit if the inspection identifies something unanticipated and unwanted.

A case in point: JJ signed a deal on a four-bedroom, two-bath $100,000 house in a marginal neighborhood. According to the seller, the monthly rental income was $1,200. That would make the deal look fantastic. But when he had it inspected (by someone he has used in the past and trusts), he found out that it was a double-wide trailer. It had been put up on a permanent foundation and covered in clapboard, so it was not apparent. But to the professional who inspected it, and to the bank that told JJ it didn't finance such structures, there was a world of difference.

1. *The home-alone technique.* Whenever you see a vacant home in your target area, stop and jot down the address. Look up the owners in the county property records and call or write to ask if they'd be interested in selling the property. If the house is in desperate need of a paint job or has a severely overgrown lawn,

you may have found motivated sellers before they've actually put the property on the market. If they want to sell, you may have found a property at a very good price.

2. *The garage sale.* Sometimes, before owners put their property up for sale, they'll hold a garage sale to clear the house of all clutter and get it into showing shape. So keep an eye on your local paper for garage sales and moving sales in your target areas. Don't waste time attending the sales. Just call to find out what they're selling. During the conversation, explain that you're looking for a home in the area—and ask if they know of any that are coming up for sale. Occasionally, you may find that you can buy not only what's in the garage, but the house itself.

3. *Out-of-state owners.* Whenever you're researching local property values, be sure to make note of all out-of-state property owners. The property rolls should list the mailing address of the owners—in addition to the details of the property itself. When the owners' address is out of state, send them a letter or look them up in the phone directory and call to find out whether they might be interested in selling.

4. *Code violations.* A property with a number of code violations can be a signal that the owners cannot afford to keep the property up or may no longer be interested in taking care of it. Some towns will physically tag a property that has code violations. Learn to recognize that tag and keep an eye out for it as you drive through your target areas.

Buying and Selling Fixer-Uppers

The skill needed here is an eye for what could be—the ability to see a house in shambles and imagine how much better it would look with some paint, a little gardening, and new carpet.

The secret to making fixer-uppers work is to keep your improvement expenses in line with your budget. If, for example, the two-bedroom mess you are looking at is $40,000 under the market, your fix-up budget should be significantly less than that—$10,000 to $15,000 would be a good bet. Creating a realistic budget and then sticking to it are the two essential skills needed to make this sort of income-producing venture work for you. There are three rules to buying and selling fixer-uppers:

1. Buy undervalued property. You can't make a fully valued property become more valuable by fixing it up. The idea is to find a property whose value is less than what it should be (compared to similarly sized and configured properties in the area) and then bring it up to its full value by spending a little money on it.

2. Create a fix-up budget that leaves you with enough profit to meet your overall financial goals. Buying and selling fixer-uppers is fun work. But it's work. So you want to be sure you make good money for it. You can do that by deciding beforehand how much income you want this business to provide and then dividing that by the number of transactions you can reasonably expect to achieve on a part-time basis. For example, if your goal was to make an extra $60,000 the first year, you might decide that you need to net $20,000 on three transactions. If you want to net $20,000 on an individual transaction, make sure that your budget shows you making that much or more. (I like to cheat in my favor by budgeting a profit of $25,000 if I want to make $20,000 because I've learned that there are always some unanticipated expenses.)

3. Just as expenses usually exceed your expectations, prices sometimes disappoint you. To deal with that reality, you must be disciplined about selling. You can't make money in a buy-and-sell business if you never sell. You must be prepared to drop your asking price to move the property if local selling conditions dictate. A good rule of thumb: Never hold onto a property for longer than one season (or one year). In the long run, you'll make more money taking smaller profits on each transaction but making more transactions.

Always Have a Plan B

The single most important principle in reducing risk and increasing your profit potential on every property flip is to have a solid backup plan in place. Even though you may have no plans to rent out a property you intend to flip, it's best to make sure you *could* rent it out at a profit (or at least break even) if you had to.

We've all heard stories about the investor who buys a house, hangs a new front door, touches up the paint, plants a few flowers, and sells it a month later for a $50,000 profit. While this kind of success is not uncommon in a fast-moving market when the property is purchased below market value, it is certainly not the rule.

Go into every real estate deal—whether you're planning on flipping or investing long term—with a good defense. And your best defense is to make sure the rental income the property would produce will cover your carrying costs plus at least 10 percent—just in case. Your carrying costs on a property are the sum of your monthly principal, interest, taxes, and insurance (PITI).

Find out what the rental values are in your area by calling about rental properties listed in the newspaper and calling agencies that specialize in rentals. The Department of Housing and Urban Development (HUD) also publishes fair market rent (FMR) guidelines for certain areas—and although this is not always an accurate reflection of reality, it can serve as a good base number.

To determine your margin of safety on a particular property, calculate the *gross rental yield*. To do that, divide the rental income it would bring in each year by the asking price.

So if the asking price for a home is $100,000 and the rental income is $750 per month, the gross rental yield would be 9 percent ($750 × 12 = $9,000; $9,000 ÷ $100,000 = .09).

In most markets, a 10 percent rental yield provides a comfortable margin of safety. In other words—worst-case scenario—if the property does not sell, you could rent it out and more than cover your costs.

The rental yield also gives you a quick way to determine the maximum amount you should pay for a property. In our example, let's say your target is a minimum 10 percent rental yield. At $100,000, the house does not meet your criteria. So reverse the math a little bit. Take the annual rental value of the property and divide it by the yield you need to get.

In this case, $750 times 12 gives you $9,000 in annual rental income. Divide $9,000 by 10 percent (.10) and you get $90,000. This is the maximum amount you can pay for the property and still earn the 10 percent rental yield that you want.

The rental value will always serve as your anchor, preventing you from offering a ridiculously high price in a fast-rising market.

Make Any Deal a Potential Quick Flip with an Assignment Clause

Even if you're looking to buy for the long term, you should give yourself the legal option to flip the property. You do this through an assignment clause. If your only goal is to flip the property, an assignment clause is mandatory.

It simply means that on every contract you sign, make sure you have the right to assign the contract to another buyer. In principle, it's similar to the idea of endorsing to someone else a check that's made out to you. The assignee would then close on the contract with the seller—under the time and terms stipulated in the contract.

The primary benefits for you are that you make a very quick profit and you can avoid all closing costs. In many standard contracts, the language will refer to "the 'Buyer' (and/or assigns and nominees)." This automatically grants you assignment rights. If it's not in the contract, you can add it by putting "and/or assigns" where you fill in your name on the contract.

If the contract comes from the seller, read it carefully to make sure it doesn't have a clause forbidding assignment of the contract without the seller's written permission.

Besides the ability to assign the contract to another buyer if the opportunity arises, the assignment clause will also enable you to take on a partner for the property after you get it under contract—if you should decide to do so.

For example, let's say you find an absolutely screaming deal. You can buy it for $250,000 and you know it's easily worth $325,000. And it's got great rental value in relationship to the price so that—even financing 90 percent of the purchase—it will kick off cash flow at $250,000 like a slot machine.

Only problem is . . . it's a bit out of your reach. You've got the financing contacts and qualifications to qualify for a $150,000 property only. So what do you do?

Go ahead and make the offer to get the property under contract. Just make sure the contract has a standard clause making it contingent on your obtaining financing within a certain period of time. Even though you probably can't get the financing on your own, because of the assignment clause you can get the next best thing: an equity investor.

How Not to Flip a Property

Flipping real estate can lead to quick and sizable profits when you find the right property. But these deals are not always a sure thing, and inexperienced investors often lose money. Remember the lessons you just learned in this chapter—and keep the following three points in mind.

1. If you have to rehab the property, remember that this is not the time to create your dream house. Focus only on the areas that would bring up a red flag at closing and the relatively inexpensive things that will help the house show better—such as fresh paint, new windows, landscaping, and a thorough cleaning.
2. Don't get emotionally caught up in a fast-rising market. The most common mistake people make when they lose money flipping a property is that they pay too much for it, expecting that the price will skyrocket. If prices stall and you don't have a rental yield to cover your costs, you could be looking at a loss.
3. Don't be looking to flip properties if you are always in a crunch for money. You could become a desperate investor— and you never want to buy or sell in desperation.

If you follow the rules I laid out regarding buying the property at a discount to its true market value, and if you are certain that in a worst-case scenario the rental yield would still create a positive cash flow, you have a comfortable margin of safety. And flipping real estate might just be your key to *automatic wealth*.

PLAN YOUR SUCCESS

Set specific objectives in terms of both learning about real estate and then investing in it. Make these specific (e.g., "become the marketing manager for my company's hair products by the end of the next fiscal year"; "start one side business within six months"; "invest in one potential flip within three months"). Then incorporate these objectives into the yearly, monthly, weekly, and daily task lists that I showed you how to do in Chapter 2.

At first, your plan will be somewhat general. But as you spend time thinking about it and working on it, you will come up with countless ideas that will help sharpen your vision and spur your personal progress.

Some of these ideas will be large, some small. Some will be solo efforts. Others will require the help of colleagues. Some will meet with success and some will meet with failure. Most—in the early stages of your learning—will fall somewhere in between.

But the more you work at your plan, the easier it will get.

If you want to become wealthy in a short to moderate amount of time, you will need a six-figure income. The higher you get your income, the faster you can achieve wealth. This chapter has discussed several ways to boost your income:

- Make a higher (possibly radically higher) salary.
- Become a freelance consultant.
- Start your own income-generating side business.
- Invest in income-producing real estate.

Think of each of these four methods as separate streams of income. You can start each stream flowing simultaneously. By this time next year perhaps you can be depositing four separate paychecks into your personal account each month—each making you wealthier and better able to accelerate your wealth in the future.

All these income streams stem from the same wellspring: knowledge. And the knowledge that they require is fundamentally the same: how to create, develop, and sell products and services.

To accelerate your income goals, begin to learn as much as you can about sales and marketing today. Focus on how customers are acquired and then resold, and concentrate first on an industry or business that you already know. Master direct marketing and understand how it can be applied to every business you get involved in. Apply the concepts you learn to everything you do: your main job, your freelance work, a side business, and real estate.

It's not necessary that all four of these income streams produce for you. Any one of them can make you rich. But since they all require the same fundamental knowledge, you can edge yourself into all of them—or at least several—simultaneously. And that means a much bigger and better chance of earning a radically higher income.

STEP 5

GET RICHER WHILE YOU SLEEP

There's no way around it—radically increasing your personal income will take some work. Maybe even a lot of work. However you boost it—by getting more from your employer, by buying and flipping properties, or by creating a second income—it will require focused, energized, self-initiated work.

But creating wealth through *equity* can be different. It doesn't usually require ongoing, stress-producing work. It does demand making a financial investment. And that implies risk. But if your investment is a good one (i.e., if the investment structure is fair and the business grows and profits), the equity owner can get rich without working. He or she can get richer continuously, 24/7—even while sleeping.

If you invest in a good business at a fair price, you can expect that the share you have of that business will become more valuable. Just how valuable it becomes will depend on a number of things—the industry, management, capitalization, marketing, and so on—but it doesn't have to depend on you.

That's what's good—and what's bad—about equity investing.

Random House gives us three financial definitions of equity:

1. "The interest in the ownership of common stock in a corporation."
2. "The monetary value of a property or business beyond any amounts owed on it in mortgages, claims, liens, etc."
3. "Ownership, especially when considered as the right to share in future profits or appreciation in value."

And that's how we'll address this important part of your wealth-building future, in terms of stock, real estate, and direct investments.

INVESTING IN STOCK FOR EQUITY APPRECIATION

During the Internet-company-fueled stock market bubble, just about everybody I know was investing in stocks. Not just colleagues in the financial-information industry, but my friends, my family members, my jiujitsu teachers, my tailor, the people in the doctor's waiting room, and, yes, the guy in the airport who shined my shoes. Many of these people were new to the stock market and looking for a quick buck. But many, too, were long-time, self-described "conservative" investors who were trying to enjoy the 25-percent-plus yearly returns that just about everyone seemed to think would go on forever.

There were a few exceptions: a handful of investment writers who had been predicting a stock market collapse for as long as I've known them (and who therefore missed out on the enormous market appreciation that occurred in the last 30 years of the twentieth century) and two or three experts who had been in the market and profiting from it, but pulled out when their indicators flashed "sell."

One, Steve Sjuggerud, had been bullish on the market since the October 1987 correction. He had made himself and his readers a lot of money for many years. About six or eight months before the top of the market, he began to reduce his stock investments drastically. By the time the correction (crash?) occurred, he was 90 percent out.

Steve has had a very impressive record of timing the market, but what I like most about him is how humble he is. When it comes to investing in stocks, he is the first to acknowledge that however much he knows about the industry sector and however much he discovers about the stock he likes, he can never know enough to confidently predict the future value of its shares.

The Stock Market Is a Very Complicated Animal

There are so many factors involved in determining the price movements of individual stocks. (I shouldn't even use the word *determining* in such a statement.) For example, there are fundamental factors such as price-earnings (P/E) ratios, revenue growth, and earnings history. There are basic business considerations such as leadership, market share, and debt. And there are technical considerations—tools and indicators that attempt to track and predict price movements. Finally, there is the overarching and overwhelming influence of market psychology at work—the fear and greed of ordinary and institutional investors. Add up all these elements and you have a living organism whose growth, habits, and movements are the equivalent of free will.

So when investing in stocks, Steve follows a stock selection protocol that respects that organic, impulsive, sometimes erratic nature of the market:

- *Invest in what you know.* Your chances of being right about a particular stock's price future improve as your knowledge of its business, its industry, and its management increases. Since you can't know enough about everything, develop expertise by narrowing your scope. Identify several industries that interest you and learn as much as you can about them: how they create customers, how they develop products, how they maximize profits.
- *Be suspicious of stock stories.* The stock brokerage and information businesses work on the basis of drama. Create a great story about a start-up company with a revolutionary technology headed by a genius billionaire, and you've got a proven formula for sales. Brokers, stock analysts, and investment gurus all make their livings by discovering, packaging, and presenting such stories. A good story works by evoking emotion. Emotion overrules logic. With your logic put aside, you allow yourself to make investments you will probably regret later.
- *Be conservative with each investment.* However well you know the business, never invest more than you can afford to lose. My personal limit is 1 percent of my investable wealth. That means that

if you have an investment portfolio of a million dollars, you should never put more than $10,000 in any single investment.

- *Have a Plan B.* When I invest in small businesses, I always have a Plan B. A Plan B is what I do if the business doesn't work out like I think it will. A good Plan B should limit your losses. When it comes to stocks, Steve does the same thing with *stop-loss orders.* "When a stock hits an established stop-loss," he told me, "it's a signal to me that the market knows something about it that I don't. I'm not smarter than the market. So when I get a chance to get out with most of my investment intact, I am happy to get out."

How I Look at Stock Selection Strategies

Steve's approach to investing reflects his conservative nature and the recognition that the market is too big, complex, and alive to treat it like some finite, comprehensible, mechanical contraption.

That's the way I feel about the world of business generally. Although I have developed some expertise in certain specific sectors (information publishing, consumer health products, etc.) and certain business skills (direct marketing, back-end sales, etc.), I recognize that if I stray even a little bit from these areas of expertise and invest in something somewhat new and different, the chances of being successful are very small.

I didn't always feel that way. When I began my career in the information publishing industry, I had enormous enthusiasm for every new idea I ran into. Whenever someone would suggest a new book, audio-cassette series, or periodical, I was all ears. If it had—or seemed to have—a big potential and a great story (see my previous comments on stories), I'd usually fall in love with it. Over the course of the next few days, weeks, or months, I'd do everything I could to give birth to this next great brainchild.

I was fortunate to have at that time the counsel of a partner/boss who understood reality a bit better than I did. He was able to douse many of my hottest ideas by asking me simply, "Do you believe in it enough to put in half of the capital?"

"Well," I thought, "*you* own the business. That should be your job." But I was wrong. And I learned the hard way how wrong I was. Because every three or four times I was crazed on some great new idea, he let me test it in the marketplace. And three out of four times (my track record might have been even worse . . . it's too painful to remember), the idea bombed and our business—the business he owned and was funding—lost money because of me.

I am prone to guilt, so this laissez-faire approach to teaching me about start-ups had a much greater effect on me than his challenges or his counseling. ("Michael," I remember him saying a hundred times, "you have to decide if you are fish or fowl. You can't be in every business that looks interesting. Choose one area and focus on it.")

To make a long, embarrassing personal history short, in the period of time that I worked under his mentorship, I changed from being a very quick and enthusiastic backer of new moneymaking ideas to a very skeptical and conservative investor.

The fact is, most new business ideas fail, and many, if not most, old businesses slow down and eventually die. If this is true in the world of the businesses I know, shouldn't it be true of the stock market that represents them?

When Investing in Business, Take the Short Odds

And that's an important point.

As I explained, my early experience as a promoter of hot new ideas has taught me the danger in good stories. The better they sound, the more skeptical I've learned to become. As an investor in small businesses, I'd much rather put my money into something with *reasonable but probable* prospects, as opposed to something that has *fantastic but only possible* prospects. Twenty-five years of investing experience has taught me that I'm not that good at spotting winners.

And I'm talking about businesses I can examine, CEOs I can interview, industries I know, and investments that give me an actual say in what's happening. If I can't make a killing with all those advantages working for me, how can I expect to be successful investing in little companies about which the only thing I know is that they have a good story?

So, as I said, I make it a habit to invest only in what I know, to limit my investment, and to have a Plan B already in place so I can get out if my great idea turns out to be a bummer.

There is one exception to the "invest in what you know" rule: the "invest in who you know and trust" exemption. I have sometimes invested in businesses I knew very little about because they were headed up by people I knew to be bona fide moneymakers and they gave me their personal assurance that the deals were good ones.

This is a tricky exception to the rule, so I wouldn't actually recommend it to most investors. To make it work, you have to be right about the person's genius and correct, too, about the value of his or her personal assurances. For most people, this kind of opportunity comes around rarely, if ever.

Larger versus Smaller Stocks

There is some debate in the investment world about which kind of stocks will provide the best equity appreciation. Large-cap stocks (Fortune 1000 type of companies) give you more stability but less performance. Small-cap stocks are riskier, but they can provide a very substantial ROI.

I like a mixture of both. When I invest in larger, more established companies, I take a very conventional, old-fashioned, fundamentalist approach. I like to see a solid balance sheet, a history of earnings growth, and a P/E ratio that's good by contemporary market standards. That's the foundation, but I need more. I need to believe that the company is an active player in a trend that is hot within an industry that is growing. Since I recognize that good fundamentals are only part of the game (market psychology is a major part, too), I want to see something that tells me all stocks of this sort will be heading up, even if I'm wrong about the particular company I've invested in.

THREE CHARACTERISTICS OF GREAT START-UP VENTURES

When I invest in smaller companies, I look at all those things I look at with larger companies—but I also focus on three factors that are, in my experience, the best predictors of a new business's future growth:

1. *Efficiency of customer acquisition.* The first and most important job of a businessperson is to make a sale. Without that first sale, nothing else can happen. Natural entrepreneurs understand this. In starting a new business, they devote 80 percent or more of their time and money to that objective: selling the product.

HOW INVESTING IS LIKE DIETING

Have you ever been on a diet? Can you remember being tempted to eat something, resisting the impulse, and then allowing yourself to take just one bite?

What happened? If you're like me (and most people), that one bite simply stimulated your appetite and led to other bites, which led to a virtual food fest. You begin with discipline, make one compromise, and before you know it you are stuffing your face while telling yourself that tomorrow you'll start your diet anew.

The same pattern holds true with investors. In a rational moment, they commit to a sensible strategy for buying and selling stocks. It works well so long as the stocks are working well. But the moment something negative happens, they abandon their selling protocol and do whatever everyone else is doing.

This is why most individual stock investors lose money. It's not about luck or intelligence. It's about fear and greed.

Fear and greed are the investor's worst enemies. Fear will prevent you from buying good companies, simply because they are cheap. Greed will make you buy bad companies, simply because you are convinced their share prices will go up, even though they are already too high.

Fear and greed. Cardinal sins. But there are other moral failings a stock investor must watch out for.

Insecurity is one. Insecurity—a sin of the ego—makes it difficult for investors to admit that they were wrong about one of the stocks they put their money into. Not admitting you were wrong means not selling a bad stock when it's going down. Many stock investors never sell their stocks, even when they are left with pennies on the dollar. A healthy attitude about investing is one that says, "Although I invested in this stock in good faith, I'll never know enough about the stock or the market generally to be 100 percent right all of the time. When the market causes a particular stock price to come down, that is just its way of telling me that I didn't have all the facts."

Besides greed and insecurity, laziness prevents people from doing the right thing—or *anything* at all. Much easier to sit back and let your stocks play out. Stock prices moving up is not exactly a clarion call to action.

(continues)

Moving down? Also not a time to panic. The worm will turn. Some people think they are being patient. Patience *is* a virtue in investing in stocks, especially when applied to big, established companies whose stock you want to hold onto for 5 to 10 years. But patience should not be confused with running on empty out of sheer laziness.

If you want to be successful as a stock investor, you must be virtuous:

- *Modesty.* You don't need to be the best and most successful investor in the world. Set modest objectives—10 percent to 15 percent—and you will have a good chance of hitting them.
- *Humility.* You don't know enough to predict the future. Admit it by setting stop-losses and sticking to them.
- *Consistency.* Umpteen studies have shown that the single most important factor in stock market success is the consistent application of a rational system. Which system you follow (whether it is the one described here or some other one) is not as important as your consistency in adhering to it.

When investing in start-up businesses or evaluating someone's idea for a new business, my first two questions are: How are you going to acquire new customers? and How much is that new customer going to cost you? Unless I get good answers to those two questions, I take no further interest in the project, because I know that its chances of success are very slim.

Compared to making the first sale, every other aspect of the business—from creating a good product to providing good customer service to taking a share of the industry—is insignificant. Prove to me that (a) you know how to bring in new customers and (b) you can bring them in without going broke, and I'll be interested in your business.

2. *Gross profit margin.* I prefer businesses that have substantial markups. Being in the information publishing business, I've been spoiled in this regard. Since we sell analysis, interpretation, and advice (as opposed to raw information, which is like a commodity), we can charge significant markups—sometimes

500 percent to 1,000 percent—depending on how valuable we believe that advice is.

Higher margins give beginning business builders more money to spend on marketing. Having more money to spend on marketing gives them a better chance of finding an efficient way to acquire new customers. Although I acknowledge that there are plenty of interesting and profitable businesses in the world that operate on small margins, I prefer not to invest in them—especially as start-ups.

Success in business is all about learning from mistakes. Growing a successful business is about making all the mistakes you need to without going broke in the process. Companies that operate on big margins allow for a lot of mistakes. I like that kind of allowance.

3. *Back-end potential.* A large margin allows a new business to discover a formula for acquiring new customers, but unless the business can find a way to convert those initial transactions into substantial, longer-term business relationships, the business model is faulty. A business that depends entirely on new sales for growth and profit is like a vehicle driving uphill on a road coated with oil. It may have enough traction to travel for a while, but eventually the work involved in moving exhausts the engine and wrecks the car.

I like businesses that can expand geometrically—businesses that can acquire an increasing number of customers from an expanding market and then improve the value of those customer relationships by selling them more, better, and more-expensive products. If acquiring new customers is the front end of the business, making those customers more valuable (by selling them more, better, and more-expensive products) is the back end.

So when I look to invest in a new business, I want to see all three components in place: an efficient customer acquisition protocol, a high profit margin, and the potential for big, back-end profits.

Expectations of an Equity Position in Stocks

It's reasonable to assume that, over the long haul, the stock market will give you a return of about 10 percent on your money. (I don't think it will do that well in the near future, because it's overvalued today. But if you have 10 or 15 years to wait for the right time, you will probably do all right.)

You could do better than 10 percent—12 percent to 15 percent is my current target—by following the rules I laid out:

- Invest in what you know.
- Limit the size of any individual investment.
- Have a Plan B ready in case you are wrong.
- Invest in both large- and small-cap stocks.
- With growth stocks, favor companies that have (1) an efficient customer acquisition protocol, (2) a large profit margin, and (3) the potential of a big back end.

A 12 percent to 15 percent ROI may not make you wealthy in 7 to 15 years, but if you stick to this formula and don't abandon it when you hear an irresistible story, chances are you will do much better than your friends and colleagues.

As I said at the beginning of this chapter, the best thing about equity investing—and this is most true of stock investing—is that, after the work you do investigating a particular investment, you don't have to do anything else to get richer. You just lock in a stop-loss in case the price moves against you, and watch your wealth build.

Building a Stock Portfolio

My portfolio reflects my belief that no one can ever confidently predict the behavior of any individual stock or any sector or the stock market as a whole.

Currently, I have less than 2 percent of my net worth invested in stocks. In the past, it has been higher, but I don't think I've ever had more than 10 percent of my money tied up in stocks. To most financial planners, that would seem like an ultraconservative position—especially for someone who recently turned 50. But for me, it feels smart. Not just because I'm skeptical about stocks, but also because I invest heavily in real estate and small businesses.

I prefer to have most of my money in investments that are more interactive than stocks. By "interactive" I mean investments about which I can have more intimate knowledge and over which I can have more control. Take real estate, for example. It doesn't take a genius to know when the residential housing market in the neighborhood is over-valued. All you have to do is keep an eye on prices and buyers and make some commonsense decisions about whether this trend can continue.

When I invest in start-up enterprises, I always restrict myself to businesses I know. And when I take a position, I make sure it comes with some influence so that, if things should start heading south, I can step in and effect some changes. This combination of inside knowl-edge and active control makes me feel much more confident about investing my money. And that's why I have about 50 percent of my investable wealth tied up in real estate and new businesses.

What Others Say

My portfolio may be too conservative for you. If so, consider follow-ing a more traditional approach:

- *Safe portfolio—20 percent stocks, 80 percent bonds.* For more than 70 years, this portfolio has averaged 7.0 percent a year. Its worst year was a loss of 10.1 percent. It lost money 17 percent of the years.
- *Balanced portfolio—50 percent stocks, 50 percent bonds.* During the same time period, this portfolio has averaged 8.7 percent a year. Its worst year was a loss of 22.5 percent. It lost money 22 percent of the years.
- *Risky portfolio—80 percent stocks, 20 percent bonds.* This portfolio has averaged 10.0 percent a year. Its worst year was a loss of 34.9 percent. It lost money 28 percent of the years.

You see the pattern, don't you? The riskier the portfolio, the more robust the growth was in the good years. But losses were greater dur-ing the bad years and there were more bad years.

In choosing which portfolio suits you best, take your age into con-sideration. The older you are, the less risk you should want to bear. Why? If you're retired, the practical consequences of your losses can-not be assuaged by your current job income. Even if you're not retired, you simply lack the luxury of having several decades to make up for moderate-to-heavy losses.

Another consideration is the current direction of the stock market. Is it going up or down? It's not always easy to tell. Just because it's down today doesn't mean that tomorrow it will begin to rebound. Or if it's up today, it may begin a long decline tomorrow. I'll let you in on a couple of secrets in just a few pages that will help you decipher the direction and trend of the market. Bear in mind that in a down market, you should lower your stock holdings even more than suggested in the preceding three recommendations. If the market is making hay, increase your stock holdings accordingly, let's say by 20 percent. So, if you're holding 50 percent in stocks, you would increase it to 60 percent.

One way to divvy up your portfolio is this: 30 percent U.S. stocks, 30 percent foreign stocks, 10 percent high-quality corporate bonds, 10 percent high-yield bonds, 10 percent U.S. Treasury bonds (TIPS), 5 percent real estate stocks, and 5 percent gold and precious metals.

A Closer Look at Stop-Losses:
The Exit Strategy That Professionals Use

One thing that both Alex and Steve agree on is this: Whatever your approach, you're bound to make some bad stock selections. In fact, there's no guarantee that your good decisions will outnumber the bad ones. Here's the good news: *It doesn't matter.*

If you make twice as many bad stock purchase decisions as good ones, shouldn't you lose twice as much as you've earned? No. Because stock investing is not just about buying. It's also about selling. As important as buying the right stocks at the right time is, it is equally important to sell the right stocks at the right time. And you're not going to make the same selling decisions for depreciating stocks as you would for appreciating stocks.

Cut your losses. Ride your winners. Professionals know when to sell a stock and when to hold it by using a *trailing stop-loss.*

The trailing stop requires you to track the price of your stock and sell it as soon as it drops to a certain level. The sell point can be triggered at 10 percent, 20 percent, 30 percent, or whatever, below the stock's highest selling price. I recommend 25 percent.

There's nothing magic about this number. It just seems to suit most stock exit situations. But it does carry one strong implication as to what your risk tolerance should be. A good ratio is one to three. That is, if you are willing to risk a 25 percent loss, you should reasonably expect at least a 75 percent return on your investment. If you are told, for example, that a 30 percent return but no higher is expected from a particular investment, your stop-loss point should be triggered at 10 percent, not 25 percent.

Let's use as an example a stock you bought for $100. For the sake of convenience, you're using my recommended 25 percent rule. The stock climbs to $110. If it drops 25 percent from that price, to $82.50 or below, the stock is sold. You've lost 17.5 percent of your investment. In another scenario, let's say the stock climbs to $150 before losing altitude. Under the 25 percent rule, the instruction to sell would be triggered if the stock falls to $112.50 or below at the end of the trading day. You've made $12.50 on the stock, or 12.5 percent. In this case, you are using the trailing stop technique not to cut your losses, but to ride your winners. You have allowed your stock to reach its highest price. Once it starts to drop off, you sell. By not keeping the stock excessively long, you cut your losses. By not selling it prematurely, you've let your winner ride.

Placing the Stop-Loss Order

This technique is so important for you to use each and every time you buy stock, I am going to tell you exactly how to set it up. You place a stop-loss order with your broker, instructing him or her to sell a stock that you own at a certain price. Using the 25 percent rule, that price would be 25 percent below the market price. As the current market price moves higher, your stop-loss price moves higher in lockstep.

If you deal with a full-service broker, you simply need to tell your broker to put the 25 percent trailing stop-loss order into play. There's no charge for doing so until or unless it's activated. At that time, you would have to pay the regular broker's commission fees.

If you trade online, it's up to you to regularly track your stocks and move your trailing stop-loss orders as needed. Use only end-of-day prices. It gets too complicated otherwise.

If you are dealing with a low-priced stock, it wouldn't take much price movement to trigger a stop-loss order at 25 percent. In such cases, increase the 25 percent so that the downward price movement would have to be more than just a few dollars to trigger the stop-loss order.

Let's say you bought $10,000 worth of two stocks. After a month, the first stock's worth climbs to $12,000. The second stock drops to $8,000. After two months, the first stock reaches $15,000 and the second one drops further, to $5,000.

Here's what you may be tempted to do . . .

You've made $5,000 on the first stock. You're pleased. That's a 50 percent profit. You're going to get out while the going is good and keep your $5,000 profit. Unfortunately, the second stock has lost 50 percent of its value. You're $5,000 in the hole. You could call it quits, take the loss, and figure that between the $5,000 gained and $5,000 lost, you're even. But you're convinced that the stock has dropped so low that it's bound to pick up again. So you decide to hold onto it. Not only that, but at half of its former price, it's a good buy. So in order to really benefit from the bounce you're sure the second stock will take, you use the $5,000 earned from your first stock to buy more of it.

Is there anything wrong with this picture? There sure is.

You've made two bad decisions. You gave up on a still-rising stock, anxious to lock in the profit you made. How much more could its price have increased? "It already grew 50 percent," you thought, "so why push my luck?" The fact is, you don't know how much further it could have risen. It's not unheard of for a stock to go up 100 percent, 200 percent, or more. You just don't know. Still, you took it upon yourself to put a ceiling on what you earned. The stock didn't necessarily stop growing. But by your action, it did stop growing *for you*. Bad move. It makes much more sense to ride your winning stocks as long as possible. I'll show you how in a few minutes.

The other unwise decision? You stuck with your losing stock. To make matters worse, not only did you stick with it, you invested more of your precious money in it. The stock *might* have hit bottom by the time you reinvested in it. It *might* then rebound and soar to new heights. But let's face it, you really don't know. The only fact you do know is that the stock's price fell 50 percent. You think that's a lot—and it is. But you know what? It could fall much further . . . all the way down to zero.

Maximizing Profits and Minimizing Risk

Not all your stock purchases will make out well. Perhaps not even a majority of them will make you money. But if you stick with stocks and sectors you know, you'll maximize your profits and minimize your risk. A good way to start is to focus on stocks that are closely related to your profession, expertise, and/or interests. Add to your knowledge by learning. Read. Take courses. Talk to experts. Try to develop an inside feel for the market.

And even when the market seems to be going against you, stick with your game plan. Warren Buffett, the most successful investor of all time, never strayed from the companies and industries he knows best and believes in (such as razors and soda—Gillette and Coke), even when the market fell in love with high-tech companies. When the high-tech bubble burst, Buffett's investments stayed strong and his commitment to what he believed was vindicated.

Sticking to a good system is a lot harder than it sounds. You will be tempted to invest outside your area of knowledge frequently. Sometimes the stories will seem almost irresistible. Remind yourself: The better they sound, the worse they probably are.

And do the other conservative things that great investors like Warren Buffett do: Pay attention to the fundamentals, limit your ownership of individual investments, and be conscious of your goal in terms of time.

In analyzing every stock investment, ask yourself, "What will this be worth in X years?" Remember, the reason you are investing in stocks is for medium-term (7- to 15-year) appreciation. If the stock isn't likely to give you a good return in that time frame, skip it.

I Don't Think You Can Predict the Stock Market,
but If I Did . . .

The advice I've given you in this chapter will give you a solid foundation to invest in stocks safely and steadily. You don't need to read a half dozen magazines, subscribe to newsletters, and go to seminars. Just stick to one or two specific areas and be faithful to your system.

And forget about trends. Or try to.

If you simply can't resist trying to figure out the market, indulge yourself. But realize that what you are doing is nearly impossible. And keep the money and time you spend doing it to a minimum. Consider it a bad habit, like playing video games or smoking cigars. A little bit once in a while can be entertaining, but too much too often can be dangerous to your financial health.

That said, I have a two thoughts on predicting trends.

1. *More often than not, it pays to follow the trend.* Most of the big money I've made in business has come from enterprises that were riding the crest of a market trend. Although I am con-

trarian by nature and enjoy reading contrarian speculations, I've never made any money by investing against the grain. I read somewhere that, at any given point in time, there is a 70 percent likelihood that an existing trend will continue for the short term. That is, what's happening today will happen tomorrow. Although I can't cite the source, this is a statistic that feels correct. When you are investing in real estate or in a private business in an industry you know, it's not too difficult to get a feel for where in the trend you find yourself. It's more difficult to make this judgment with stocks.

2. *Your chances of figuring out your place in a stock trend depends on your knowledge.* The better you know the industry, the better your chances. But with the stock market, you are dealing not just with business trends but with market psychology, too. Consider that bear markets always begin in good times and bull markets always in bad times.

SIX SENSIBLE STOCK INVESTING RULES TO LIVE BY

Here are a few rules of smart investing that you can bank on:

1. Most quick-buck deals turn out to be losers. If it seems too good to be true, it probably is.
2. Let your winners run . . . and cut your losses short.
3. A rising tide lifts all ships. Whenever possible, invest in a sector that is appreciating.
4. A buy-and-hold strategy works only if you are investing in a solid company and can wait out a bad market almost indefinitely.
5. If you don't understand an investment, don't buy it. You will be at the mercy of your stockbroker and adviser. And they're never wrong, right?
6. There's no such thing as a hot tip. Getting inside information may seem like the next best thing to winning the lottery. But you could go to jail if you act on it. And if it's not the real inside dope, you could lose all your money.

If You Were on a Desert Island and Had Only
One Trend to Follow

The most time-tested market indicator comes from Charles Dow, who developed his Dow Theory in the late 1800s. He developed two market indexes, the Dow Industrials and the Dow Rails (now called the Dow Transports). Dow theorized that these two indexes represent production and distribution, respectively—and that when they are in agreement, the trend in the market is confirmed.

The theory has proved to be remarkably accurate. When Dow Theory says we're in a bull market, stocks rise by an average of 35 percent. Dow Theory has made only seven incorrect bull-market calls over the entire 100-plus years of the Dow Industrials. And most of those wrong calls were not wrong by much. When Dow Theory indicates a bear market, stocks lose an average of 6 percent.

At the beginning of this chapter, I said that what I liked most about equity investing in stocks is that you could do it without a lot of active work.

You can't say that about investing in small private businesses and real estate. Most of the time, you have to monitor, analyze, and often direct the operations and activities of the business. That extra work, though, can bring you significantly greater returns. Whereas 12 percent to 15 percent is the target I set for my stock investments, 25 percent to 100 percent is what I look for in real estate and small businesses.

Let's talk about real estate.

THE POTENTIAL OF REAL ESTATE

There is sometimes an argument among real estate investors about what's better: buying and holding properties or buying and flipping them. There are pluses and minuses to each. But there's no point in arguing. If you want to acquire wealth quickly, you need to do both.

You need to buy rental properties for equity appreciation and buy-and-flip properties for income. This statement may sound confusing to the inexperienced. Aren't rental properties for income? And isn't the idea of buying and flipping to take advantage of the increased equity you create?

SIX STATEMENTS YOU MUST PROMISE YOURSELF YOU'LL NEVER SAY—ESPECIALLY TO YOURSELF

If you hear these words coming out of your mouth, brace yourself for a loss:

1. *"It's only $3 a share. What can I lose?"* You can lose your entire investment in this stock, same as if you were investing in a more expensive stock.
2. *"Eventually, they always come back."* As if all companies emerge from bankruptcy filings intact and healthy. Do you remember WorldCom, Enron, Global Crossing, and all the dot-coms?
3. *"When it rebounds, I'll sell."* When your patience is finally being rewarded and your stock is worth more with each passing day, who's kidding whom? You're more likely to keep it than sell.
4. *"What, me worry? Conservative stocks don't fluctuate much."* Even blue chips can get hammered. They're worth at least a little attention.
5. *"It's taking too long for anything to ever happen."* Stocks that inch their way to higher value can be fine medium-to-long-term investments. A stock that grows 1 percent a month won't dazzle you, but it will make you good money on an annual basis.
6. *"Look at all the money I lost because I didn't buy it!"* Peter Lynch, who managed the ultrasuccessful Fidelity Magellan Fund and wrote a book about it, titled *One Up on Wall Street: How to Use What You Already Know to Make Money in the Market,* says this thinking "leads people to try to play catch-up by buying stocks they shouldn't buy, if only to protect themselves from 'losing' more than they've already 'lost.' This usually results in real losses."

Yes and no. Yes, rental properties will eventually give you equity. But this won't happen—or shouldn't happen—until you have become financially independent and are ready to shift your lifestyle and investment profile into a retired or semiretired orientation.

While you are building wealth (for the next 7 to 15 years), you should treat your rental real estate portfolio as an equity play. You will want to use leverage (by taking mortgages) to get the maximum appreciation on your cash. Remember, if a property appreciates 6 percent a year and it is mortgaged at 20 percent, you are getting, in effect, a 30 percent appreciation (6 percent × 5).

To take advantage of this enormously beneficial, wealth-producing effect, you need to use debt to your advantage—by having each property mortgaged. As your equity increases in each property, you should consider taking some of that money out of it and reinvesting it in other properties.

If you follow this program, you won't be making any income from your rental properties. And that's why I am categorizing rental real estate as an equity play.

When your wealth increases and you reduce your debt, income will start coming in. Eventually—and certainly when you've reached retirement age—you will want to reduce your leverage by paying down your mortgages. As you do that, your income will increase. Eventually, you may have a very nice income stream from your rental properties.

Buying and flipping real estate—however much it relies on equity appreciation—is an income play. Or at least you can approach it as such during your wealth-building career. You should think about this activity as a sort of business unto itself. You capitalize the business with an initial down payment, and every profit you make from a sale can be plowed back again into the business.

This, again, should be thought of as an income play. And that's how I've arranged it in this book.

The wonderful thing about real estate is how quickly your equity in it seems to expand. You buy a condo this year with the cash you got back from last year's taxes. It's barely enough to get you to closing, but you throw some extra dollars at it and fix the property up.

Eventually, as your rent increases to match the property's appreciated value, what was a net cash expense becomes a net cash positive.

Year after year, you purchase more and better properties. Some you keep for the long haul. Others you sell for a profit and then invest that money in two (or more) up-and-comers. You develop an intimate knowledge of the market. You can see the specs for a property in a given neighborhood and, sight unseen, know just how much you should pay for it. You learn to separate your feelings from your actions. You buy value and you sell into a rising demand.

Before you know it, 5 years have passed. Then 10. And then 15. One day, you add it all up and realize you have accumulated more than $10 million worth of real estate. What seemed like a part-time hobby has become, in retrospect, a retirement windfall.

In Chapter 4, I described how to create a second income by buying and flipping local properties—both fixer-uppers and higher-end properties. This chapter is about buying and holding onto rental real estate.

Buying and Managing Local Rental Properties: An Overview

There are two big secrets in making rental real estate work for you. One has to do with the old "location . . . location . . . location" axiom. The other is about the condition of the property you buy.

Let's start with these four rules, keeping in mind that rules are made to be followed until you understand the principles behind them.

1. *Buy properties in your local area.* To be a successful investor, you have to know what you are doing. And if you've been living where you are currently living for any number of years, you already have more knowledge about local real estate than you think. You have a clear idea of the good neighborhoods, the not-so-good ones, and the ones you need to stay out of. And you may have developed a feeling for the up-and-comers. By staying in your local area, you give yourself the chance to really know the market. And this is the most important factor in limiting your risk and increasing your chances for profits.

2. *Invest in good or up-and-coming properties.* The old saying about the three rules of real estate being "location . . . location . . . location" is true. But there are *two kinds of good locations:* those that are already established as good and those that are on their way to becoming good. You can make good money with both. Here's how:
   - In good neighborhoods, buy the least-expensive property you can find. That way, any money you spend fixing it up (if you fix it up wisely) will bring you double or triple your invested dollars. When you buy a poor piece of property in a good neighborhood, you get the benefit of the neighborhood to lift your selling price once the property looks acceptable. Of course, it's not easy to get the least-expensive

piece of property in such a good neighborhood cheaply. Most of the time, the property owner realizes what's going on. But with really dilapidated homes, and sometimes with owner-sold properties, you can get a real bargain.

- In up-and-coming neighborhoods, buy properties in clusters—either by yourself or with a consortium of buyers. You will upgrade the look of the area, and this will bring up prices—sometimes even more than you'd guess.

3. *Whenever possible, buy newer, solid structures.* There's nothing worse than managing a rundown building. The tenants complain. They are reluctant to pay the rent. They treat you like a crook. It's bad. Be extra careful about the critical and costly things. Don't buy any property that has major problems—a bad roof, rotten plumbing, or burned-out electrical. The cost will eat up any profit you can make.

4. *Develop a network of reliable contractors.* You'll need a plumber, an electrician, a heating/ventilation service, a painter, a landscaper, and, most important, an inexpensive handyman. Choose wisely. Hire reliable workers who will give you eight hours of *competent* work for eight hours of pay. If you find contractors who are giving you substandard work or charging too much, let them go.

There is a natural tendency in this business for things to go from bad to worse. Don't lull yourself into passivity by hoping for the best. Be tough. Be fair. And act decisively.

As in So Many Businesses, Real Estate Is
All about Buying Right

If you get a property for a good price and don't overinvest in fixing it up, you'll be 95 percent certain to do well in the long run.

What do I mean by a "good price"? A price that allows you to make a sizable (say, 25 percent or more) medium-term profit. And how can you figure that? There are several ways.

One way is to make sure that the net rental income you'd get would be at least 11 times the gross investment. Say, for example, that you found a $90,000 triplex that needed about $10,000 worth of work to make it attractive. Your total investment in such a building would be

$100,000, and so you'd want to be able to get about $11,000 a year in rental income.

An $11,000 net return would be the equivalent of about 9 percent, cash on cash. But that's not counting the appreciation on the property—how much more it will be worth over time. If the triplex in question appreciated at the historic average of 6 percent, you'd have an ROI of 15 percent—again, cash on cash.

But if you leveraged this investment by mortgaging the property, you'd do a lot better. In this case, for example, your cash outlay might be a $20,000 down payment plus the $10,000 in fix-up costs, for a total investment of $30,000.

Having a mortgage would increase your costs—roughly by the amount of the interest you would pay (the cost of the money you are financing)—and so you might end up paying an additional $7,000 a year in financing costs. Subtract the $7,000 from the $11,000 net rental income and you get $4,000, which is a 12.5 percent return on the $30,000 you put down.

This, again, is without considering appreciation. Add the $6,000 a year appreciation to the $6,000 and you have a return of $10,000 on $30,000, for a 33 percent ROI.

That's an amazing number compared to, say, stocks, but it's not unrealistic if you are investing in solid, well-priced rental properties in up-and-coming neighborhoods.

Here's the point.

Owning rental properties—if you own good ones (which means better tenants and fewer complaints)—can be a very manageable way to make a lot of extra money on the side, while you are working for someone else or running your own business.

In fact, of all the on-the-side things I've done to increase my wealth, rental real estate has definitely been among the very best.

My Disastrous Beginning as a Real Estate Investor

I bought my first rental property in 1980 in Washington, D.C. This was probably the worst investment I ever made. It was a condominium on Massachusetts Avenue, a remodeled building just down the block from the projects.

I didn't know it at the time—because I understood nothing about what I was doing—but I overpaid for the apartment by about 25 percent. I also took out a negative-amortization mortgage (that I wasn't qualified to have) that ballooned every three years and couldn't be refinanced except by the bank that issued it (because it wasn't Freddie Mac/Fannie Mae approved). And so I ended up losing money every month—not just on the net rental income but on the appreciation . . . which was going down!

To top it off, I had to scrape together three or four thousand extra dollars every time the balloon matured. And if that wasn't enough, the attractive young lady to whom I rented the apartment turned out to be a deadbeat hooker. That meant threatening letters from the homeowner's association, bounced rental checks, and two years of fighting with the D.C. government to try to get her out of there. (I was told that if I changed the locks—even though she hadn't paid me rent at the time and was plying her illegal trade to the detriment of her neighbors—I'd be arrested and put immediately in jail. So much for sensible legislation and police work in the inner city.)

But the Story Gets Better . . .

That first experience cooled my jets for a while. But then, about 15 years ago, a business associate and I began investing in nineteenth-century mansions in Baltimore. These were beautiful but neglected town houses in the historic section of town, which was, at that time, overrun by drug dealers and hookers (maybe my old tenant was there—who knows?) because the local government had, in its infinite wisdom, decided to put Section 8 housing smack-dab in the middle of the city's best neighborhood.

The good news is that we were buying majestic ruins . . . with potential . . . for $30 a square foot. By the time we had them completely restored, our cost was $50 a square foot—about what you'd pay to have a cinder-block warehouse built today in the Midwest.

At this sort of entry price, we figured we couldn't lose. And we ensured against losing by putting some of our little businesses into these buildings and charging them reasonable (but sufficient) rents. This worked out in the short run. We were break-even for the first two or three years while paying off reconstruction and mortgage costs, but were able to accelerate the rental payments as the businesses grew. By year four or five, we were cash positive.

Today, these buildings produce a high cash flow and, thanks to a new mayor who moved the Section 8 housing and replaced it with student dorms, the neighborhood has become safe and property values have soared.

If you have a business and lease your space, start shopping for a property now. Renting your business to yourself is the single best, most cash-flow-productive, and most tax-wise real estate investment you can make.

My Small Investments Started to Add Up

A few years after we began buying the Baltimore properties, I moved to Delray Beach, Florida, and started buying property there. My first purchase was a very small house on a large lot, which I rented to my brother. The next was a small condominium in an up-and-coming neighborhood a few blocks away.

I never had to come up with a lot of money at any one time— never more than 25 percent of what I had saved that year, even when I was saving less than $10,000. But the small investments added up. Frequently, I was able to swap a piece of property that had appreciated (in some cases, doubled in value) for another one that I thought had greater potential. Sometimes, I traded one unit for two.

Most important, I bought a lot of properties in partnership with friends and colleagues. Having had the very good experience of owning the Baltimore property with partners, I reasoned that it was better to own 50 percent of two buildings rather than 100 percent of one. I wanted to put as much diversification as possible into my local rental real estate portfolio.

And it worked. In less than eight years, I accumulated more than 20 properties—the smallest being a condominium apartment I bought for $65,000 (that is now worth $160,000 and producing $12,000 a year in cash) and the largest one being a 21-unit apartment complex. All totaled, these properties are worth millions of dollars. Yet, except for the big one that came later, I never laid out more than $20,000 at any one time.

The appreciation I've enjoyed has been tremendous—more than a million dollars in eight years. And best of all, it happened with so little work on my part. My partners found the properties. They, or someone we hired, did the renovations. A management company I hired does most of the rentals. What it doesn't do, my partners take care of for some modest fees. The equity I have in these buildings is probably going up at least $250,000 a year right now. And what am I doing? Nothing!

And this is just my residential rentals in South Florida. I've also enjoyed some equally wonderful deals in the commercial arena. The building I'm writing from at this moment was an 11,000-square-foot warehouse that my friend and I bought for $400,000 about seven years ago. We fixed it up and bought an adjacent parking lot (another $200,000). Today, it is generating about $70,000 in net cash income—plus, the value has increased by considerably more than a million dollars.

With this kind of experience under my belt, how could I not be enthusiastic about real estate?

A Few Cautionary Words . . .

But I must issue the required cautionary warnings. Real estate does not always appreciate. The national historical average might be 5 percent or 6 percent, but there are plenty of regions where land has not appreciated a nickel in a hundred years.

When investing in real estate, you have to think about trends. When it comes to real estate trends, I like growth areas and especially waterfront growth areas.

Another caution: As I write this, I believe real estate is at the peak of a very significant bubble. I expect to see single-family home prices in most of the country's major growth areas decline by 15 percent. Commercial real estate could drop 20 percent or more, and condominiums—always the riskiest part of the residential real estate market—might drop by as much as 40 percent.

That said, I'm still shopping. If you can find properties, as I'll explain later, that can sustain themselves through such downturns, you will eventually come out richer for it. (A good example: that Washington, D.C., disaster I told you about. I eventually got out of it after losing $35,000 on my $65,000 investment because I couldn't afford to put more cash in it. Yet if I had held onto it, I'd be smiling. Because today, that unit is worth at least $650,000.)

I was able to get into real estate in a small way, learn from my mistakes, leverage every investment with mortgages, and use the cash returns to buy other properties, which compounded the equity I was earning in leaps and bounds.

And as I said earlier, I did this without ever coming out of pocket more than $20,000 and without ever spending more than four or five hours on a single deal. The entire time I devote to managing my real estate portfolio today is less than four hours a month.

If you are an investor in local real estate rentals, you probably have good stories of your own to tell. If you are new to the game, we're going to go through a few basic things you need to know right here.

Don't forget the most important secret in building your fortune in real estate: *Knowledge is everything.*

Net Rents Are Your Safety Net

There are four ways wealth builds in a real estate investment: compounded appreciation, leverage, net rents, and amortization. In Chapter 4, we looked at an example of buying a property for $100,000 that appreciated at an annual rate of 6.5 percent. In the first year, it went up $6,500. But in year 11, your *annual* 6.5 percent appreciation worked out to $12,200 because the value of the property had compounded to about $187,700.

You leveraged your investment by financing 90 percent of the purchase price. That means you put down $10,000. When we factored in closing costs ($2,000), the appreciation in year 11 alone worked out to be more than 100 percent of your original investment (since $12,200 is more than 100 percent of your original $12,000 total initial investment).

But the deal is even sweeter. Because, in the meantime, you've also been getting net rents. That's the money you put in your pocket every month after paying all the carrying costs of the property. And those net rents should steadily rise every year, since you can fix the majority of your carrying costs (principal and interest).

The best part is that your mortgage payments are being paid out of the rents you receive on the property. And the rents pay for all other expenses, too—from insurance to taxes to maintenance and management (if you're not managing it yourself). That's what I mean by the property "paying for itself."

But beware. If you pay too much for a property—way too much—and get bad financing, you could end up on the flip side of each one of these forces (as I was with my Washington, D.C., apartment). Instead of appreciating, the property may depreciate. In that case, your leverage could actually compound the problem. If you get the wrong type of financing, you could even end up with *negative amortization* (meaning your loan balance goes up, even though you're making your regular monthly payments). And net rents could turn into negative net rents if you don't know your rental market.

To see what I mean, let's lay out some numbers. We'll examine three scenarios.

- *First,* we'll see the kind of wealth you can build up as a very occasional real estate investor, buying just one property a year.
- *Next,* we'll suppose you've gotten some experience under your belt and are now buying two properties a year.
- *Finally,* we'll see the kind of wealth you may achieve as a very active investor—perhaps with the intention of eventually doing it full-time.

The Lazy Real Estate Investor's Route
to a Comfortable Retirement

Let's suppose you're going to buy just one property a year. And let's suppose you'll average a down payment of 10 percent of the purchase price on each property. Some will be less, some will be more. But overall, you'll average 10 percent down.

Let's keep it in line with historical numbers and assume your property will appreciate, on the average, 6.5 percent a year. To keep the math simple, we'll also say that every property you buy costs $100,000.

We'll also suppose that after paying all costs (principal, interest, taxes, and insurance—PITI for short—and maintenance) and making an allowance for some rental vacancies, you initially net $100 a month on each property. Finally, we'll assume that your net rents increase by 5 percent a year.

Let's see what can happen with one property over the course of 15 years.

EVEN A SINGLE INVESTMENT PROPERTY CAN MAKE
A BIG DIFFERENCE IN YOUR RETIREMENT

YEAR	EQUITY AFTER EACH YEAR AT 6.5% APPRECIATION*	NET RENTS INCREASING AT 5% A YEAR	TOTAL NET RENTS RECEIVED TO DATE
1	$17,542	$1,200	$1,200
2	$25,574	$1,260	$2,460
3	$34,128	$1,323	$3,783
4	$43,239	$1,389	$5,172
5	$52,941	$1,459	$6,631
6	$63,274	$1,532	$8,162
7	$74,279	$1,608	$9,770
8	$85,999	$1,689	$11,459
9	$98,481	$1,773	$13,232
10	$111,775	$1,862	$15,093
11	$125,932	$1,955	$17,048
12	$141,009	$2,052	$19,101
13	$157,067	$2,155	$21,256
14	$174,168	$2,263	$23,518
15	$192,381	$2,376	$25,894

*Equity is built up in two ways: from appreciation and from paying down the loan balance (amortization). For amortization purposes, this table assumes a 30-year fixed-rate mortgage at 6.5 percent.

Just by purchasing one investment property, you'll end up with an extra $192,000 in equity 15 years down the road. And that's on top of nearly $26,000 in net rents you've collected over the years.

That's not bad. But what if after doing this for one or two years, you understand the concepts and enjoy the process, so you decide to be just a little more active? Instead of buying just one property, you buy one property every year. How would that affect your retirement?

By picking up just one property a year, you have amassed almost $1.4 million in equity in just 15 years. During that time, you've also collected more than $180,000 in net rents. And you get a rent check every month of nearly $2,200.

And that's just buying one property a year.

If you expect to be more active than this, multiply these numbers by two or three or more to get an idea of what you can achieve.

BUILDING WEALTH WITH JUST ONE PROPERTY A YEAR

YEAR	NEW PROPERTIES BOUGHT	TOTAL PROPERTIES OWNED	TOTAL NET EQUITY TO DATE	TOTAL RENTS TO DATE	TOTAL EQUITY + NET RENTS TO DATE	NET RENTS	MONTHLY RENTAL INCOME
1	1	1	$17,542	$1,200	$18,742	$1,200	$100
2	1	2	$43,116	$3,660	$46,776	$2,460	$205
3	1	3	$77,245	$7,443	$84,688	$3,783	$315
4	1	4	$120,483	$12,615	$133,099	$5,172	$431
5	1	5	$173,425	$19,246	$192,671	$6,631	$553
6	1	6	$236,699	$27,408	$264,107	$8,162	$680
7	1	7	$310,978	$37,179	$348,157	$9,770	$814
8	1	8	$396,978	$48,638	$445,615	$11,459	$955
9	1	9	$495,459	$61,869	$557,328	$13,232	$1,103
10	1	10	$607,233	$76,963	$684,196	$15,093	$1,258
11	1	11	$733,165	$94,011	$827,176	$17,048	$1,421
12	1	12	$874,175	$113,112	$987,286	$19,101	$1,592
13	1	13	$1,031,242	$134,367	$1,165,609	$21,256	$1,771
14	1	14	$1,205,410	$157,886	$1,363,295	$23,518	$1,960
15	1	15	$1,397,791	$183,780	$1,581,571	$25,894	$2,158

Accelerating Your Success

As a final supposition, let's say you want to move at a very brisk pace. We'll suppose you start with three properties in your first year. Then, every year after that, your goal will be to buy one more than you bought in the previous year. So you'd buy three in year one, four in year two, five in year three, and so on.

This method can work very well for those who are willing to put a good deal of time into their property investments. (If you rely only on friends and colleagues to spot good properties for you, you may not have as much opportunity as you need.)

You increase your buying activity only as you increase your experience. And with each new successful property, your equity grows. As your track record develops, you also get more opportunities with lenders and potential investment partners. So let's see what this might look like.

ACCELERATED PROGRESS

YEAR	NEW PROPERTIES BOUGHT	TOTAL PROPERTIES OWNED	TOTAL NET EQUITY TO DATE	TOTAL RENTS TO DATE	TOTAL EQUITY + NET RENTS TO DATE	NET RENTS	MONTHLY RENTAL INCOME
1	3	3	$52,626	$3,600	$56,226	$3,600	$300
2	4	7	$146,890	$12,420	$159,310	$8,820	$735
3	5	12	$292,392	$28,296	$320,688	$15,876	$1,323
4	6	18	$499,353	$53,301	$552,654	$25,005	$2,084
5	7	25	$778,660	$89,766	$868,426	$36,465	$3,039
6	8	33	$1,141,908	$140,307	$1,282,215	$50,541	$4,212
7	9	42	$1,601,445	$207,847	$1,809,292	$67,541	$5,628
8	10	52	$2,170,421	$295,651	$2,466,072	$87,803	$7,317
9	11	63	$2,862,842	$407,346	$3,270,189	$111,696	$9,308
10	12	75	$3,693,625	$546,966	$4,240,591	$139,620	$11,635
11	13	88	$4,678,654	$718,977	$5,397,631	$172,011	$14,334
12	14	102	$5,834,847	$928,323	$6,763,170	$209,346	$17,445
13	15	117	$7,180,223	$1,180,461	$8,360,684	$252,138	$21,012
14	16	133	$8,733,969	$1,481,410	$10,215,380	$300,950	$25,079
15	17	150	$10,516,523	$1,837,798	$12,354,321	$356,388	$29,699

Under this accelerated scenario, you build over $1.6 million in equity and receive more than $65,000 a year in net rents (after all expenses) by year seven!

As you're about to discover, each property you buy should provide you with a good rental return plus sizable capital appreciation potential. Do this consistently, and you can build hundreds of thousands of dollars in equity, cash, or both in a few short years.

So what's the first step?

The First Commandment of Successful Property Investing:
Cover Your Downside

The best way to limit your risk and maximize your profit potential is to make sure you're buying every property at a good value. What's a good value? Well, to answer that question, let me make the analogy to stocks.

First, companies that regularly pay dividends regularly make money. And psychologically, when the price of a company's stock is falling, it's easier to hold onto it if the company is profitable than it is if the company is losing money.

Second, investors are at least receiving some dividend payments from the company while waiting for its stock to come back. So they don't feel much pressure to sell.

So how does this apply to real estate?

Well, dividends are like net rents in real estate—the money you put in your pocket every month or year after paying all the carrying costs of a property. But instead of the current, miserable 2 percent yields offered by today's blue-chip stocks, you can find net rents in the range of 8 percent, 10 percent, 12 percent, or more.

Not only is this a very respectable return in itself, it gives you a very important margin of safety in case market values drop. Even if you have to lower your rent 8 percent to 10 percent in a down market, you can cover your mortgage and expenses while waiting for a recovery or planning an exit strategy.

If you invest carefully in a growing market, you may never experience the downside of real estate investing. But smart investors cover their downsides—by having an exit strategy (or Plan B) before they make the investment.

You can do that with real estate by making sure that, if rents go down 10 percent or 15 percent, you can still make all your payments and hold onto the property. If you can survive when things get bad, when things go well, they'll go *very* well. And when they don't go well, they won't be a disaster. You'll be ready to fight another day and take advantage of the next opportunity when it comes along.

Let's take a look at why it is so important to take care of the downside. Consider the following $265,000 swing on a single property.

Why One Investor Made $164,000 and Another Lost
$101,000 on the Same House in a Few Short Years

Several years ago, I bought a beautiful home in a quiet neighborhood a block from the Intracoastal Waterway. I paid $182,000 for the property and sold it about four years later for $390,000.

With an initial 20 percent down ($36,400) and counting all costs and upgrades, I'd put about $65,000 into the property. After paying real estate commissions on the sale and picking up roughly $6,000 in amortization, I walked away with about $225,000 in net equity when

I sold. (My original $65,000 plus about $159,000 in profits from appreciation and amortization.)

In addition to that, I also picked up nearly $5,000 in net rents over the four years, pushing my total profits to about $164,000. About a 250 percent gain on the deal in four years—a very nice return!

Here's how the deal looked for me:

Sale price of	$390,000
Less purchase price of	$182,000
Equals appreciation of	$198,000

But not all that appreciation was profit. To see what my actual profit was, let's look at my gross equity and net equity when I sold the house.

The gross equity is the money I had on hand before paying the real estate agent's sales commission and before my part of the closing costs on the sale. To figure my gross equity, simply subtract the loan balance due from the sales price:

Sales price of	$390,000
Less loan balance due at sale of	$139,630★
Equals gross equity of	$250,370

Now, we take the gross equity and subtract the real estate agent's commission of 6 percent and the seller's (my) closing costs on the sale. The result is my net equity:

Gross equity of	$250,370
Less sales commission of	$23,400
Less seller's closing costs of	$2,000
Equals net equity of	$224,600

Net equity is the amount you receive from a sale that you get to put in your pocket, before taxes. (And there are ways to postpone the capital gains taxes on property indefinitely.) But net equity is not your

---

*The original loan on this property was 80 percent of $182,000, which works out to $145,600. For a 30-year loan fixed at 7.5 percent, about 4.1 percent of the loan is paid off during the first four years. That's why the loan balance due at this point is $139,630.

profit. To calculate that, you have to subtract your initial costs and any net carrying costs from your net equity.

In this case, the house originally cost $182,000—but I didn't pay that out of pocket. I used leverage in the form of a standard property loan equal to 80 percent of the purchase price. So my down payment was $36,400.

As the buyer, my closing costs were $4,000. I also put $25,000 worth of renovations into the house. So, my initial costs were:

Down payment of	$36,400
Plus closing costs of	$4,000
Plus renovations of	$25,000
Equals total initial costs (or investment) of	$65,400

I had no net carrying costs because the property had a positive cash flow. That is, it paid for itself . . . and then some. So now we subtract my total initial costs from the net equity I received at the sale and we get my profit:

Net equity of	$224,600
Less total initial costs of	$65,400
Equals profits from appreciation and amortization of	$159,200

But those aren't my total profits. I actually made more because I collected net rents every month. To get an idea of what I netted monthly, let's calculate my monthly costs.

The monthly principal and interest payment on a $145,600 loan at 7.5 percent for 30 years works out to about $1,020. My taxes were $250 a month, insurance was $75 a month, and I averaged about $75 a month in maintenance. So my total monthly carrying costs were $1,420:

Principal and interest of	$1,020
Plus taxes of	$250
Plus insurance of	$75
Plus average monthly maintenance of	$75
Equals total monthly carrying costs of	$1,420

Now we subtract those monthly carrying costs from my monthly rental income and we get my monthly net rent:

Rental income of	$1,500
Less monthly carrying costs of	$1,420
Equals net rent of	$80

Rents increased at about 5 percent a year during the four years I owned the house, so my net rents increased, too. Yes, insurances, taxes, and maintenance expenses went up as well—also by about 5 percent a year. But the bulk of my costs—principal and interest—were fixed. So my monthly net rents increased by $55 to $60 each year. The following table shows why:

RENTS RISE 5 PERCENT A YEAR AND NET RENTS RISE $55–$60 A YEAR

	YEAR 1	YEAR 2	YEAR 3	YEAR 4
Monthly Rent	$1,500	$1,575	$1,654	$1,736
Monthly Costs				
Principal and interest	$1,020	$1,020	$1,020	$1,020
Taxes	$50	$263	$276	$289
Insurance	$75	$79	$83	$87
Maintenance	$75	$79	$83	$87
Total Monthly Costs	$1,420	$1,440	$1,461	$1,483
Monthly Net Rent	$80	$135	$193	$253
Yearly Net Rent	$960	$1,620	$2,313	$3,041

As you can see, even though rental values rose just 5 percent a year, my net rents *more than tripled* by year four! That's because the bulk of the carrying costs are fixed.

If we add the yearly net rents together, you can see that during the four years, the property brought in net rents of $7,934. However, it was vacant for two months—one in year one during renovations and the other in year three during a tenant transition.

My actual net rents over the four years were $7,934 minus $1,500 (one month of rent in year one) minus $1,654 (one month of rent in year three). So my net rents for the four years were $4,780 (an average of about $100 a month).

If we add this to my profits from appreciation and amortization, we get my total profits:

Total net rents of	$4,780
Plus profits from appreciation and amortization of	$159,200
Equals total profits of	$163,980

So in four years' time, I made about $164,000 on a property I bought for $182,000. But that doesn't mean I almost doubled my money. I made much more than that because of leverage.

I didn't pull $182,000 out of my pocket to buy the house. My initial investment was the down payment, renovation costs, and closing costs on the purchase. Those, as we've seen, totaled $65,400. So my profit, as a percentage of my original investment, was actually 251 percent.

Total profits of	$163,980
Divided by total initial investment of	$65,400
Equals leveraged profits of	251%

Same House, Very Different Results

I made a significant profit on this house. Yet the woman who bought it from me wasn't nearly as fortunate. She is also an investor. And she had made great money on various properties here in town as the market rocketed up 15 percent to 20 percent in recent years. She bought my house at $390,000, moved in, put $20,000 into it, and then put it on the market for $475,000.

But there were no buyers at that price. Or at $450,000, or $425,000, or $400,000. After a year on the market, she unloaded it for $350,000—representing roughly a $101,000 loss.

Here's how her deal looked. First, we calculate the appreciation (or, in this case, the *depreciation*):

Sale price of	$390,000
Less purchase price of	$350,000
Equals depreciation of	$40,000

Next, we look at her gross equity when she finally sold the house:

Sales price of	$350,000
Less loan balance due at sale of	$308,600★
Equals gross equity of	$41,400

Then, we take out sales commission and closing costs to get her net equity:

Gross equity of	$41,400
Less 6% sales commission of	$23,400
Less seller's closing costs of	$2,000
Equals net equity	$16,000

Now, let's figure her total, out-of-pocket expenses:

Down payment of	$78,000
Plus closing costs on purchase of	$6,000
Plus renovations of	$20,000
Equals total initial investment of	$104,000

Add to that what she lost from the depreciation:

Net equity of	$16,000
Less total initial investment of	$104,000
Loss after depreciation and amortization of	−$88,000

And now her carrying costs, which were more than mine since she paid more than twice what I did for the house and because taxes and insurance go up with higher sales prices:

Principal and interest of	$1,875
Plus taxes of	$500
Plus insurance of	$150
Plus average monthly maintenance of	$150
Equals total monthly carrying costs of	$2,675

★Buyer borrowed 80 percent of $390,000, or $312,000. Interest rates had fallen to 6.5 percent by this time. After one year at 6.5 percent, her balance due on the loan, or *payoff amount,* was $308,600.

Since we now know what she has to spend to keep the property and since we know what she receives in rent, we can figure her net rents. In this case, the net rents are negative:

Rental income of	$1,825
Less monthly carrying costs of	$2,675
Equals negative net rent of	$850
Yearly negative net rent	−$10,200

In addition to this, she had one month of vacancy in the year she owned the property. So her net rents for the year were −$12,025 ($10,200 − $1,825).

Total negative net rents of	−$12,025
Plus loss after depreciation and amortization of	−$88,000
Equals total loss of	−$100,025

So why did this woman lose so much money when I made so much on the same house?

Autopsy of a Bad Deal

The number one mistake this buyer made was that she didn't have a margin of safety going into the deal. Her purchase price wasn't anchored to reality by rental values. By contrast, when I first bought the house, at $182,000, it had a $1,500 monthly rental value. Since interest rates were 7.5 percent at the time, my rental income covered my loan payments, taxes, insurance, and maintenance and still gave me a 5 percent margin of safety.

That's not a huge margin of safety but a fair one, given the strong appreciation potential of the neighborhood. What's more, as rents rose, my margin of safety increased every year. By year four, I was receiving rent of around $1,736 a month and netting $253 after all expenses.

That meant rents could fall as much as 15 percent at that point without my experiencing negative cash flow. And if the rise in housing prices suddenly dipped, or even stopped, I could afford to bide my time.

By contrast, by the time this woman bought the house from me, the rental value had risen to only about $1,825. Even though interest rates had come down to 6.5 percent at that point, the rent still wasn't nearly enough to cover her loan payments—let alone her other costs.

She had let the fast profits in the market of the previous few years go to her head. She speculated in the worst sort of way.

She was betting on a quick flip and had no backup plan. For her to make the kind of money she was hoping to make, everything had to go perfectly. If anything went wrong, she had set herself up to fail big. And that's just what she did . . . to the tune of $100,000.

The Same Principles Apply If You're Buying
with Little or No Money Down

As it happened, in the preceding example, both buyers (I and the woman who bought the property from me) put 20 percent down. Yet the same principles apply even if you're buying a property with 10 percent down, 3 percent down, or no money down.

If you are able to pull off one of these low/no-down-payment deals, just realize that the less you put down, the higher your interest payments will be, for two reasons:

1. You're borrowing more money, so you're paying principal and interest on more money.
2. Usually the more money you borrow (as a percentage of the purchase price), the higher your interest rate. This means the more you borrow as a percentage of the purchase price, the higher your gross rental yield should be.

Gross rental yield is simply the monthly rental value of the property multiplied by 12 and divided by the purchase price. It doesn't take into account carrying costs or vacancies.

When I bought the property in this example, the gross rental yield was 9.9 percent.

How did I get that number?

The rental value when I bought the house was $1,500. Multiplied by 12, that works out to $18,000 a year. Divide $18,000 by the $182,000 purchase price, and you get a gross rental yield of 9.9 percent.

After all expenses, I had a net rental yield of just 1.5 percent my first year. By year four, it had risen to 4.6 percent.

Now, how did I get *that* number?

I netted $80 a month, or $960 a year, in year one. So $960 divided by my total initial investment of $65,400 works out to 1.5 percent.

By year four, I netted $253 a month, or $3,041 for the year. Thus, $3,041 divided by the original investment of $65,400 works out to 4.6 percent. If you buy distressed or significantly undermarket properties, it's possible to get even better yields than these. For instance, an associate recently bought two multiunit properties with an average gross yield between them of just over 11 percent. By locking in an interest rate of about 6 percent, he was able to buy both with 100 percent financing and still have positive net rents on the properties.

Those net rents are his margin of safety. And the fact that the rents are 5 percent below market is an additional margin of safety, because he can raise them when current leases come due—if he so chooses.

The moral, then, is to always take a hard look at what your carrying costs for a property are going to be. Then make sure your rental income will more than cover those costs.

And the bigger the margin, the better.

How to Use Rental Values to Know When the Price Is Right

Asking prices and actual sales prices can't tell you whether the property you're investing in has a built-in margin of safety. For that, you need rental values.

For any neighborhood that you're thinking of buying into, you should thoroughly research the rental values as well as the sales prices. You can easily do this in a number of ways.

First, make it a habit to call on every property you see for rent and find out what they're asking. Browse through your local newspaper. You can also call real estate agencies that specialize in rentals and ask what they have available.

Any time you get a rental quote—whether it's on a house or an apartment—file that information. Investing just a few minutes a day in this kind of research can make you very knowledgeable about your local rental values in a matter of a week.

If there are not many rentals currently available in the neighborhood and you're having a hard time gathering information, call your local office of HUD and ask to speak to the person in charge of the Section 8 program.

Section 8 is the rent-subsidy program I was complaining about at the beginning of this chapter. It's usually bad for the neighborhood because it brings in junkies, prostitutes, and drug users (as well as some very nice single mothers with numerous children from deadbeat lovers), but it's great for the landlords who get subsidized rent for their overpriced buildings. That's because HUD pays for all or some of the rent of low-income people. The pay scale is based on the income the person makes and the size, type, and location of the property.

HUD has FMR guidelines for different areas. For instance, the HUD FMR for a 2/1 apartment in Smithtown might be $700. I haven't invested in HUD programs myself, but my colleague Justin Ford, with whom I collaborated in producing a home-study course on real estate (Main Street Millionaire—www.earlytorise.com/mainstreet.cfm) has. He says that HUD's guidelines are often close to the market price for non–Section 8 renters as well. Sometimes, however, you may come to the conclusion that the market will bear more than the FMR number. However, the FMR can serve as a good base number.

Making Sense of the Rents

Once you've collected at least a dozen rental quotes, create a table similar to this one:

AVERAGE RENTAL VALUES

ADDRESS	TYPE	SQUARE FEET	MONTHLY RENT	NO. OF BED/BATH	PRICE PER SQUARE FOOT	AVERAGES
755 Lee Ave., Unit 3	Apt.	875	$750	2/1	$10.29	—
10 Atlantic Ave., Apt 1A	Apt.	750	$700	2/1	$11.20	Avg. $725, 2 BR Apt.
120 Enfield Rd., #6B	Apt.	1,025	$925	3/1	$10.38	—
5 Glenwood Ct., 3D	Apt.	925	$875	3/1	$11.35	Avg. $900, 3 BR Apt.
1201 5th St.	House	1,100	$950	2/2	$10.36	—
1450 5th St.	House	1,500	$1,200	2/2	$9.60	Avg. $1,075, 2 BR House
22 4th Ave.	House	1,850	$1,350	3/3	$8.76	—

Residential rental values depend on a lot of factors that aren't shown in the preceding table. But mostly they're about location, number of bedrooms, and square footage. And since all of the properties you're looking at are in the same general area, getting an average rental value for a dozen properties should give you a good yardstick that you can use to quickly estimate the rent you might receive on any property you buy.

Even though I listed only 7 properties in this table (and you really should have 12), it's apparent that the average annual rental value per square foot for an apartment in this neighborhood is $10.25. A 2/1 is likely to rent for somewhere around $725. And if it has a third bedroom, you might expect $900.

RENTAL RESOURCES ON THE WEB

The best way to get a handle on your local rental market is to check out "for rent" signs in the area and scour the newspapers. However, there are also a few websites that can help you gauge local rental values or help you find resources for rental values in your market:

- www.affordablehousingonline.com
- www.hud.gov/offices/pih/programs/hcv/index.cfm

For a complete set of fair market rents directly from HUD, go to:

- www.huduser.org/intercept.asp?loc=DatasetsFMR/FMR2004f/ ScheduleB_FY2004F_FMR5.pdf

A somewhat more user-friendly version of the same information can be found at:

- www.affordablehousingonline.com/affordit.asp

You'll enter your state and county to get HUD's FMRs in your area.

I got the annual price per square foot for each of these properties by dividing its monthly rent by its square footage and multiplying that number by 12.

For example, the last property on the list—22 4th Ave.—is an 1,850-square-foot home that rents for $1,350 a month. So . . .

Divide $1,350 by 1,850 square feet and you get $0.73 per square foot monthly. Multiply $0.76 by 12 months and you get $8.76 per square foot annually.

The location is usually the residential renter's first consideration—in tandem with the number of bedrooms he or she needs.

All other factors being equal, a 1,250-square-foot, two-bedroom house will get a higher rent than a 1,000-square-foot, two-bedroom house. But it's not likely to be 25 percent higher rent just because the square footage is 25 percent higher; it might only be 5 percent or 10 percent more.

By listing a dozen properties for rent in a table like the preceding one, you'll quickly develop a sense for what any given property could rent for.

Sometimes, There's the "Rental Value" . . .
and Then There's the Real Rental Value

If the property you're looking to buy currently has tenants, your task is easier. It has an established rental value—the amount the tenants are currently paying.

If the tenants are on a lease, better still. Chances are, you won't immediately have to seek a tenant. Plus, leases tend to make banks happy and improve your chances of getting a loan to purchase the property.

But beware: Not all rental values are what they seem.

I recently saw a listing for a 15-unit motel. It was listed at $1.1 million and claimed to have yearly rents of $159,000. This looked like it could be an excellent deal with plenty of positive cash flow. But on a closer examination, it turned out to be a dog at that price.

The $159,000 was based on weekly rentals at 100 percent occupancy. But the weekly rental rates seemed high by 10 percent at least. The building was also a bit run down. And it was in a location in South Florida where weekly occupancy rates would fall off sharply during the summer. None of that was reflected in the gross rental number of $159,000.

I asked for the owner's actual income statement on the property, which he didn't produce. (If we had gone to contract, I would have also requested his tax returns.)

I ultimately figured that the property probably pulled in about $90,000 a year in actual income, not $159,000. The asking price was too expensive by at least $200,000. Because the property wasn't in very good condition to boot—and because I had higher-yielding opportunities elsewhere—I didn't even bother making an offer.

WHAT ABOUT UTILITIES AND OTHER COSTS?

To keep things as simple as possible, I've assumed, for all the examples in this chapter, that the tenants pay the utilities. That's the case with most of my properties. Even on most of my multiunit properties, each unit has individual water and electric meters.

On one of my multiunit properties, however, there are no separate water meters. So I pay the water bill. In addition, there is a common-area electric bill (i.e., lighting in the hallway). And I pay a monthly landscaping fee. As a result, I estimated and added these costs to my total monthly costs when I was figuring the minimum monthly rents I would need to cover my expenses on the building.

Work with Legitimate Rental Values

Here's another example of an inflated rental value on a property from Justin Ford:

Recently, I bought a three-bedroom house in an improving neighborhood. The seller was originally asking $105,000. And to justify the price, the real estate agent told me he could rent it out "all day long" for $1,200 a month.

What he meant by that was that he could get that much by stuffing the house with transient tenants, perhaps three to a room.

A house two doors down was rented in just that way. That landlord got the maximum cash she could—all off the books, since local codes don't permit that density. And because she had so many transient renters, she figured there was no reason to do anything but the bare minimum of upkeep on the property. The house was an eyesore.

But I had no intention of being a slum landlord. I get great satisfaction from renting out properties in good condition at fair prices—prices that also give me my rental margin of safety.

After doing research on normal rental values on a month-to-month basis (including checking with Section 8), I figured I could get $850 a month for that house. So I made my offer in line with what I considered to be the realistic rental value of the property. And I ended up buying it for $90,000. At that price, the rents would be enough to cover the hard carrying costs on the property, even though I bought it with no money down (that is, with 100 percent financing).

After cleaning it up, painting it inside and out, and doing some landscaping and minor rehab work, I ended up renting the property for $900 a month. I wound up with one of the nicest homes in the neighborhood—and with good tenants who pay on time and take good care of it.

I also now have another property that I can happily show to the bank when I purchase my next property. In the eyes of the bank, this property won't be a liability with visible carrying costs but invisible income. It will be an asset that pays for itself as it increases in value.

Along with my other properties, this will be further proof to lenders that I am a borrower they should compete for and offer their best terms and rates.

How Much Should You Be Willing to Pay?

As far as hard numbers go, there are two major criteria you want to use in determining how much you're willing to pay for a property. The first is the comparable sales values of similar properties in the neighborhood. The second is your rent versus your carrying costs.

Your first step is to calculate the gross rental yield that a property offers at different prices. To do that, you simply take the price of the property and divide it by the annual rental value. So, if the asking price is $100,000 and the monthly rent is $800, you'd have a gross rental yield of 9.6 percent—if you paid the full $100,000 asking price.

Why?

The $800 monthly rent multiplied by 12 equals an annual rental value of $9,600. Divide that by the asking price of $100,000 and you get a yield of 9.6 percent. But, again, that's the yield you would get if you paid the $100,000 purchase price.

What if you negotiated the price down to $90,000?

At that price, your yield would be 10.7 percent. Why? Because the $9,600 annual rental value divided by the $90,000 purchase price is 10.7 percent.

Here's another example:

The owner is asking $100,000 for a two-bedroom house. Based on your research, you estimate the rental value to be $700 a month. So now you . . .

- Multiply $700 by 12 to get a gross annual rental value of $8,400
- Then take that $8,400 and divide it by the asking price of $100,000 to get a yield of 8.4 percent

Again, that would be your yield if you paid the $100,000 asking price. If the owner accepted an offer of $90,000, your yield would be greater. How much greater? Well, the rental value stays the same. It's $8,400 a year. So you divide $90,000 by $8,400 and you get 9.3 percent. That would be your gross rental yield if the owner accepted your $90,000 offer.

Start with Your Carrying Costs . . . Then You Can Figure Out the Minimum Yield You Need

We'll suppose you're putting 10 percent down on this $100,000 property. So you're borrowing $90,000. And you're taking a fixed loan at 6.5 percent for 30 years. That means your principal and interest will be about $570 a month.

At a sales price of $100,000, you learn property taxes will be $1,500 a year, or $125 a month. You also get an insurance quote and find out that it will cost you $420 a year to insure the property, or $35 a month.

So your hard costs of principal, interest, taxes, and insurance are $730 a month.

Principal and interest	$570
Property taxes	$120
Insurance	$35
Total hard costs	$725

Obviously, to cover your PITI costs, you'll need to be able to rent the property for at least $725 a month. But the fact is, PITI won't be your only costs.

Make an Allowance for Maintenance and Vacancy

PITI are your hard costs. You know you'll have to pay them every month, quarter, or year. Other costs are not so hard, meaning you don't know exactly what they'll be. But you should make allowances for them. You'll also have maintenance expenses, for example.

YOUR MAINTENANCE ALLOWANCE HAS NOTHING TO DO WITH MAJOR REPAIRS

Monthly maintenance figures will vary, depending on the condition of the property. The maintenance allowance I'm using here is *not* for renovation, rehab, or major repairs. It is an allowance for maintaining a property that is already in good shape to begin with.

If the property you're considering buying needs major repairs, you should account for that as part of your initial investment. So if you're buying a property for $50,000 and it needs $5,000 in repairs, consider the total price to you to be $55,000.

If you're paying for those repairs with cash, it increases your initial investment, but not your carrying costs. If you're financing the repairs, your initial investment doesn't increase, but your carrying costs do.

For example, let's say you take out a $5,000 loan to pay for those repairs. Terms are 30 years at 6 percent—so your monthly payments on it are $30. In this case, you would add that $30 to your monthly carrying costs. And that means the minimum monthly rents you'd need to cover all your carrying costs would increase by $30.

Once you've made those repairs and brought the property up to a condition that is safe, functional, and presentable, however, you should still expect ongoing minor repairs and maintenance. That is what your maintenance allowance is for. By putting it into your expected costs and using those costs to help determine your maximum offer, you're creating a cash-flow cushion for those contingencies.

According to the Census Bureau's American Housing Survey, maintenance averages about 1 percent of the property value per year. So let's say you expect to have $1,020 a year in maintenance expenses (a little more than 1 percent of the property value). That works out to $85 a month.

You should also make an allowance for some vacancies. National statistics put this at around 10 percent a year. That means, whatever the rental value of the property, you can expect to receive, on the average, about 90 percent of that value.

To make an allowance for vacancies, take 10 percent off the monthly rental value. So if the monthly rental value is $900, expect to receive about $810 a month, on the average, over the course of the year (because $810 is 90 percent of $900).

Then, you'll want to make sure that the $810 covers at least your PITI and maintenance. In this case, it does that, exactly. So you have, at the very least, a potential deal.

Even When You Initially Break Even on Cash Flow,
You Can Still Make Sizable Profits

In our example, you've put just $10,000 down on this $100,000 property. And let's say you pay $2,000 in closing costs. If you've chosen a good neighborhood with strong appreciation potential, you have a property that should pay for itself—and *you* get all the appreciation and amortization.

With average appreciation, the house would go up by about 13 percent—or $13,000—in two years, more than doubling your investment in that time *while the property pays for itself.*

Plus, you'd pick up about $2,000 in amortization (reducing the loan balance), for a gross profit of about $15,000 on $12,000 invested for two years.

And that's in a market rising by historically average rates of appreciation. In a fast-rising market, you might make three or even four times your money in two or three years.

On top of all this, as rents rise, you should eventually collect positive net rents, too. Even though you originally bought at a price that was just enough to cover your carrying costs, over time that property could produce hundreds in net rents every month.

Your rents are paying all your carrying costs. And if your rental value covers your PITI plus allowances for maintenance and vacancy and then some, all the better. You'll have a positive cash flow from the get-go, one that should grow steadily in coming years with the rise in net rents.

Coming Up with a Handy Guideline Number

Wouldn't it be nice to have a guideline number you can use with any property in your target investment area?

For instance, let's say you see a property for $100,000 and you immediately know that if it has annual rental income of $10,000, it's a possible deal. Or you see a property that has a rental value of $6,000 a year and you immediately know that it's a potential deal if you can get it for $60,000 or less.

In this case, your magic number would be 10 percent. (I was alluding to a guideline like this at the beginning of the chapter.) You're potentially interested in properties with a gross rental yield of 10 percent or more of the purchase price. I say "or more," because any property you'd be interested in has to have that yield as a *minimum*. That's your minimum gross rental yield.

Why is this important?

Because if you can get a property at a price that gives you that rental yield, you know your rental income will likely cover your PITI and maintenance costs, and provide an allowance for vacancy. The property should pay for itself. So you can probably use this 10 percent magic number with virtually any property in your target area.

At least, you can use this number right now.

As I write this (in 2004), a 10 percent gross rental yield is a pretty good number. As I said in the beginning, I shoot for 11 percent, because I live in a high-growth area, by the beach, with plenty of reasons to believe growth will continue despite some dips here and there (especially in the condo market).

If I can get 10 percent or 11 percent, I know I have a potentially very good deal. I still have to check out other things, of course, such as comp values, condition of the building, and how this opportunity stacks up against others that are available. But I know that as far as the rental anchor goes, we're close.

Whether I'll accept less than 11 percent will depend on a number of things—first and foremost, how much I'm putting down on the property. Why? Because the more I borrow, the higher my carrying costs are and the bigger the yield I'll need if I'm going to have the property pay for itself.

What does this mean in a nutshell?

Well, 10 percent or 11 percent might be a good number for you, too, at the present time. But it will change if interest rates change.

Also, even if interest rates stay the same as they are today, 10 percent might be a little low or a little high for you. That's because your carrying costs on a $100,000 property may differ radically from mine.

To buy that $100,000 property, you may intend to borrow more or less than I do. You may get better or worse interest rates from your lender. Your property insurance and taxes may be much higher or lower in your region than in mine.

So let's get to work to help you figure out *your* guideline number for your area.

Finding Your Gross Minimum Rental Yield

This number is *gross,* because it's before expenses and before making an allowance for maintenance and vacancy.

It's the *minimum,* because if your yield is less than this, chances are you won't consider the deal.

It's a *yield,* because we're talking about the annual rental value of the property as a percentage of the sales price.

Calculating your gross minimum rental yield begins with figuring your carrying costs and making an allowance for maintenance and vacancy.

Let's go back to the $100,000 property example we've been using. And let's assume these numbers apply to you and your situation.

We know you intend to borrow 90 percent of the purchase price, or $90,000. You've talked to lenders, and you know you qualify for a fixed-rate, 30-year loan at 6.5 percent. So we know your monthly principal and interest payments will be $570.

We also know that at a $100,000 sales price, your property taxes will be about $120 a month and your insurance will cost about $35 a month. So your PITI will be $725 ($570 + $120 + $35 = $725).

We're making an allowance for maintenance equal to 1 percent of the purchase price. That's $1,000 a year, or $85 a month (rounded up). Now, we know that your PITI plus maintenance are $810 a month ($725 + $810).

All we need to do now is to make an allowance for rental vacancy. If you know the rental value, that's easy.

For instance, if you've found out that the property's rental value is $900 a month, you take 10 percent of that as your monthly vacancy allowance. That's $90. Add that $90 to the $810, and you've got $900. That's exactly equal to the rental value you need to cover your PITI and allowances for maintenance and vacancy. If this property has a $900 monthly rental value, you have a potential deal.

But what does this mean in terms of the magic number? It means you need at least $900 in monthly rental value to be potentially interested in paying $100,000 for a property. And that means you need at least $10,800 in annual rental value ($900 × 12) to justify a $100,000 purchase price.

In other words, you need a gross minimum rental yield of at least 10.8 percent.

Why 10.8 percent? Because . . .

The annual rental value of	$10,800
Divided by the purchase price of	$100,000
Equals a gross rental yield of	10.8%

And that's the *minimum* rental yield you need to cover your carrying costs. This is your magic number. And now you can use it for other properties as well!

To keep things simple, let's take that 10.8 percent and round it to 11 percent. And let's say you see a property for sale at $60,000. You can now immediately determine that to justify that price, it would have to have an annual rental value of at least $6,600.

Why $6,600? Because 11 percent of $60,000 is $6,600 (0.11 × 60,000 = 6,600).

That annual rental value of $6,600 translates into a monthly rental value of $550 ($6,600 ÷ 12 = $550). That $550-a-month rental value is really what you'd be looking for, since rents are usually quoted on a monthly basis.

What If the Asking Price Is Too High?

Bad luck. The property doesn't rent for $550 a month. It rents for only $500 a month. So what's the maximum offer you'd be willing to make? Well, reverse the math a little bit and you'll get your answer.

Multiply the monthly rental value of $500 by 12 ($500 × 12 = $6,000). Then divide that number by your gross minimum rental yield of 11 percent ($6,000 ÷ 0.11 = $54,545). So $54,545 is the most you would be willing to pay.

Of course, if you can get the property for $50,000 or $45,000 or less, all the better. But now you have a ballpark number for the maximum price you should pay if *at the very least* the property is going to cover your PITI and allowances for maintenance and vacancy.

The More You Put Down, the Less Rent
You'll Need to Cover Your Carrying Costs

The magic number we just came up with assumes a down payment of 10 percent. Change that, and you change the gross minimum rental yield you'll need to cover your carrying costs.

If you put down more—say, 20 percent—the amount of interest you'll pay on a monthly basis will come down, reducing your overall carrying costs. And your interest bill will come down for two reasons: First, you're paying interest on a smaller loan. Second, as a rule of thumb, the more you put down, the lower the interest rate the lender will require.

All other costs stay the same, except for the amount of the loan and the interest rate. And if, for example, your effective interest rate comes down by half a percent to 6 percent, you're now paying a lower interest *rate* on a smaller loan *amount*—$80,000 instead of $90,000. As a result, your principal and interest payments will now be $480 a month instead of $570 a month. Taxes and insurance stay the same. So your PITI are now $635 instead of $725.

Your maintenance allowance still works out to $85 a month. So your PITI plus maintenance are now $720 ($635 + $85).

Now, you don't need a $900 monthly rental value to cover your PITI plus allowances for maintenance and vacancy. You need a monthly rental value of only $800. Here's why:

Monthly rental value of	$800
Less 10% vacancy allowance of	$80
Equals expected average monthly rent of	$720

That $720 is exactly equal to your PITI plus maintenance costs of $720.

In other words, putting 20 percent down, you'd cover your carrying costs on this $100,000 property with an $800 monthly rental value, instead of $900. This means you need an annual rental value of only $9,600 ($800 × 12). Divide that annual rental value of $9,600 by the $100,000 price, and you get a minimum gross rental yield of 9.6 percent.

Your yield has gone down from 10.8 percent to 9.6 percent because you're putting more money down and so you have lower carrying costs.

Now you can use this as your new magic number for any property in your area that you might buy with 20 percent down.

If you see a property for $50,000, for instance, you'll know it's a potential deal if it has an annual rental value of at least $4,800 (which works out to $400 a month).

Why $4,800? Because $50,000 × 0.096 = $4,800.

The Problem with No-Money-Down Deals

We've just seen how putting more money down reduces your carrying costs—and so it reduces the minimum rent you need to get in order to cover those carrying costs. Consequently, it reduces your gross minimum rental yield.

By the same token, if you were going to buy this property with no money down, you'd be increasing your loan amount to $100,000. The higher loan amount, in itself, makes your carrying costs go up. It's also likely that you'd pay a higher interest rate by putting zero down than if you were putting 10 percent or 20 percent down. And that means your total carrying costs are going to go up even more.

Now, instead of $800 or $900, you may need $1,000 or more a month to cover your PITI and allowances for maintenance and vacancy. So your minimum gross rental yield might go up to 12 percent or more. It depends on what your ultimate interest rate is.

When I invest with a 20 percent down payment, I like to get 11 percent. But when I invest with Justin Ford, we are happy with a minimum gross rental yield of 10 percent for 20 percent down . . . and 10.5 percent for 10 percent down . . . and about 11.5 percent if we can do a zero-down deal.

These benchmark numbers help us quickly determine the viability of a property. They don't tell the whole story. We still have to do the comps. Justin does the homework, figuring out the appreciation potential of the overall neighborhood. He has to thoroughly check out the condition of the building. And he has to be reasonably sure there's not a much better deal for our money right down the block.

But our benchmark rental numbers are a very important part of the equation. If we've got good cash flow, we'll have a property that gives us a margin of safety and that has the potential to make us money on its own after we buy it.

Exactly what your minimum gross rental yield will be likewise depends on your down payment and interest rate and on your local costs for property insurance and taxes.

Local property taxes and insurance can vary significantly. So, depending on where you live and your financial situation, your required minimum gross rental yield may be a few points lower or higher than mine.

But once you determine that number, it becomes very helpful. When you go looking for properties, you can immediately gauge the maximum price you'd be willing to pay on any property . . . then go about trying to get it *for less.*

After all, it is a *minimum* gross rental yield we're talking about. If yours is 10 percent and you pick up a property with a yield of 15 percent, all the better. You'll start out with healthy positive cash flow from the get-go.

Begin Slowly . . . but as You Become Familiar with the
Numbers and See Some Good Returns, Crank It Up!

If you haven't already begun investing in real estate, start doing so today. If you are a budding real estate tycoon, resolve to add to your empire this year.

You'll find that actively investing in real estate can give you much-better-than-the-stock-market returns, the comfort of knowing your investments can't disappear, and a lot of fun fixing up old buildings.

Here's a promise: If you haven't ever invested in rental real estate but start this year, you'll be glad you did. If you keep investing—buying at least one new property a year (which will be easy once you get going)—you will be a real estate multimillionaire when you retire.

Real estate has been very good to me. Although it would be difficult to say with precision, I'm very sure that my real estate investments have provided me with an average return of well above 25 percent over the years, including the money I lost on the worst investment I ever made (my first investment in real estate) and the two or three real estate limited partnership deals that provided relatively meager (5 percent to 15 percent) returns.

Simply put, my real estate investments alone have made me wealthy. But I never would have had the money to invest in real estate had I not (1) dramatically increased my income by becoming an extremely effective marketer and (2) used that extra income and skill to start a bunch of side businesses.

That's what I'd like to talk to you about now: how to create wealth by investing in small and start-up businesses.

When you look back on all the wealth you acquired, you'll see that real estate was not only the easiest but also perhaps the most lucrative.

Spend some time today thinking about your financial picture this year and set goals for yourself in terms of real estate investing. Give yourself some time to find a good piece of property or a good deal.

MAKING YOUR FORTUNE IN YOUR SPARE TIME BY GETTING EQUITY IN A BUSINESS

In thinking about this part of the program, I realized something curious about my own career that illustrates an important truth about building wealth.

When I first decided to become wealthy, I was making about $50,000 a year. During the next 12 to 18 months, I boosted it to about $100,000. Since then—and it's been more than 20 years now—my salary has never gotten much larger than that. Except for a single year with a single company, I have never been guaranteed more than $120,000 a year (or $10,000 a month) by any client or any business that I owned or had a stake in. My income has always been very high—but it was profit shares and dividends that brought it into the seven-figure category. In other words, the high income I've enjoyed for so many years has been directly dependent on the wealth I've been able to generate through small businesses I've been part of.

I think this observation is interesting, because it suggests both the limitations of salary-based income goals and the vast potential of equity-generating income. I say "equity-generating" income because profit sharing and/or dividends, over any length of time, are possible only when you have a stake in the business. You don't need to hold stock. But you do need to be in a position to get a piece of the action.

In other words, to make a lot more than $100,000 a year consistently, you will have to do something more than simply be an excellent employee. Getting equity in a business—whether by getting stock or having a long-term profit-share arrangement—should be a very important part of your wealth-building strategy.

Getting Equity from Your Employer

In Chapter 4, I talked about ways to get your current employer to pay you a radically higher income. I said that if you develop a financially valued skill and put your mind and heart squarely in the center of your company's profit-making game plan, your chances for making $100,000 to $150,000 a year are good.

But it is also sometimes possible to persuade your business to give you a stake in its equity. If you can do that, the rewards can be much greater than the $100,000 to $150,000 you can get from your salary.

This is not going to be possible if you work for a Fortune 1000 company. It's highly unlikely to happen if you work for a public company. But if you are employed by a small to medium-sized business in a thriving industry, there are ways to induce the boss to give you a piece of the pie.

What I did was straightforward. After developing strong marketing skills and coming to figure out how the industry really worked, I conceptualized, developed, and created the marketing plan and materials for a brand-new, very exciting product. The product was different enough from the company's existing products to call it new and different but close enough to take advantage of some of the resources the company had.

I created the product in my spare time. And when it was done and ready to be marketed, I handed it to my employer with no strings attached (or so I thought). I didn't ask for a piece of the business that my boss already had—that was his. However good I was in working for him, I realized I had no right to the business he had created before I came or to anything I created during company time and using company resources. I asked for—and asked only for—a small piece of the product I created. And I told him that I'd be more than happy to fund its launch by risking my own money in proportion to my equity.

He was smart enough to recognize in me someone who was going to be successful. He must have figured that he could deny me and risk losing me (and my future wealth-producing potential) or agree to my terms and see what I could do for him.

He gave me 25 percent of my product, made me pay good money for it, and told me he hoped that one day it would make us both lots of money.

I don't have to tell you how motivated that made me. With his help and guidance, I went back and took another look at that product and refined it and then refined it again and then again and again . . . till it was twice as strong as it had been originally. And once we got the product right, we went to work on the promotion. It took about three months of working nights and weekends to take this new venture from very good to very likely. And all that extra work I was happy to do because I had a 25 percent share in its future.

The result was about as good as you could imagine. Within days of the launch, we'd recovered our initial investment. A week later, I had an extra $7,000 in my bank account. And before 12 months had passed, I had made my first million.

And that was all besides the money I was earning—and the profits my boss was making—on the first business.

As time passed, I came up with many other new and original product ideas. Most of the time we put them into the core business. But every once in a while, my boss/partner felt that an idea was sufficiently unique and/or risky to merit being launched independently. When that happened, we negotiated my equity. In some cases, I got less than the 25 percent he gave me in that first deal. But in most cases, I got more. At the end of an 11-year stint together, our combined businesses had sales of more than $135 million, and I had a significant stake in many of them.

Now the Shoe Is on the Other Foot

Since then I've used this model backward with superstar employees who have worked for me. Although I don't believe that giving employees equity increases the quality of their ideas or the value of their work, I do recognize that every once in a while you hire someone who is an unstoppable wealth builder and you realize that unless you make it worth that person's while to stay with you, you'll lose him or her to a competitor or to the person's own ambitions.

In such cases, I try to work out some sort of flexible, long-term financial arrangement that either includes equity in a new start-up or provides substantial bonuses and payouts that resemble equity in some portion of the business that this person will create and grow.

Again, the vast majority of employees—and I include even the best employees here—do not qualify for this type of treatment. I'm talking only about that very rare individual who understands how your business works, knows how to create sales, and can and will produce new products and a never-ending stream of profits. That's the kind of person with whom you want a longstanding, mutually rewarding business relationship.

So this game works both ways: If you are employed, you should turn yourself into a superstar, create a new line of products, and then try to get equity in their future. If you have employees and are lucky enough to have a superstar among them, make a lifelong deal with that person now so you won't have to compete with him or her later.

No matter which side of the field you are playing from, this game has the same basic rules:

- You can't expect equity in a business that was there before you.
- You can't begin a new business that is the old one in different makeup.
- You can't work on the new business during company time.
- You can't use company resources.
- You can't demand equity. You can only ask for it.
- Your boss/company deserves the lion's share of the equity, even though you did all the work.
- You have to pay a fair price for the equity—even if it's only in the risk you take.

- You must maintain the primary relationship, even if it means making some sacrifices. Keep in mind that the opportunity came from your company/boss. No matter how good you are or how hard you have worked on your project, without your boss's consent and approval you'd have nothing.

One Million-Dollar Company Leads to Another

I have made at least a dozen deals like this in the past 15 years. The vast majority of them were very successful. Here's a recent example:

Jeremy quit his accounting job to work for me. He had no marketing or sales skills at the time, so I mentored him. He was a quick and enthusiastic learner and worked productively for a business I ran for two years.

Then an opportunity came up—a joint-venture proposal from a colleague—that I had neither the time nor the inclination to pursue. I knew it was going to be a moneymaker, but I had other irons in the fire.

Instead of simply saying no, I offered the opportunity to Jeremy. He discussed it with his wife and accepted the job the next morning. The new position demanded not only solid marketing skills, which he had, but also the ability to attract clients with one-on-one salesmanship. This was something he had no experience with and it was something I wasn't good at, either. I told him that if he wanted to develop this skill on his own, I'd give him a 25 percent stake in the company.

He did just that and—to make a seven-year story very short—developed it into a business that today is making almost a million dollars a year.

The story doesn't end there.

About two years ago, while vacationing at a house I have in Nicaragua, he got together with his cousin and plotted out a new, unrelated business venture. Taking a note from my book, he told his cousin that he would fund the business if his cousin would run it. They agreed on a split on equity, and the cousin quit his job and went to work full-time to make their dream a reality.

Today, in less than three years, the business is growing and producing profits. Recently, the two cousins got back together again at my home to talk about the nice, new toys they would buy themselves (big toys, with motors and fenders) and how they would grow the business in the future. This second business, as successful as it is, requires only an hour or two per week of Jeremy's time. It doesn't interfere with his main business—the business I had an interest in—and yet it brings him a substantial additional income.

There are other wonderful stories I could tell you. But you get the point: In considering second incomes, think first about the business/person you are working for. Is there a way to leverage the relationship you have already established? Is there a chance that you can springboard your wealth-building plans by bouncing off the resources that are already at your fingertips?

Rule No. 1 for Starting a Home-Based Business

If your boss is not a likely partner, don't despair. For every person who has made a fortune going into business with the company he or she worked for, there are tens or hundreds who have started profitable businesses on their own.

The classic business start-up occurs at the kitchen table. The first real business I began—the pool-installation business I talked about earlier—happened just that way. The great thing about starting a business from your home is that you don't have to spend extra money on rent, furniture, and utilities. You use what you have at home and devote all of your time and money to other, more important matters.

Having recently entered my sixth decade, I have had the opportunity to have many, many conversations with friends and family about starting new, second-half-of-life careers. By and large, the people I speak to want to be in businesses they know nothing about.

- An engineer wants to start a commercial airline.
- A corporate lawyer wants to sell exotic travel vacations.
- A high school teacher wants to open a health spa.

Most of these fantasies are held by 40- and 50-year-olds who have been working in one area for many years and can't stomach the idea of starting a business doing what they've been doing. "I'm through with that," they tell me.

The old work bores them. They would much rather start something new and different, something that inspires them with romantic thoughts of fun, tranquility, excitement.

This sort of escapist approach to business is understandable but inadvisable. Your chances of being successful are much, much better if you start with what you know.

Successful start-up businesses depend primarily on knowledge—specifically knowledge of the customers and the products.

Knowledge of the customer includes knowing:

- Who are my buyers?
- Where are they located?
- How can I reach them?
- What do I need to say or do to sell them?
- How do I get them to buy more?

Knowledge of the product includes knowing:

- What kind of product does the customer want today?
- What are its necessary features?
- What are its possible benefits?
- How much should I charge for it?
- How can I replicate it?
- How can I increase its value?

The answers to some of these questions are obvious, even to an outsider. But the most important knowledge about customer acquisition, retention, and product development in every business I've ever been involved in has been difficult to decipher.

Much of this critical industry knowledge is counterintuitive. As a once-outsider in the health-information industry, for example, I thought that top-notch analysis and advice about disease prevention could fetch a reasonably high price in the marketplace. My thought process was this: If my customers are willing to pay hundreds and thousands of dollars for advice about how to pick good stocks, surely they'll be happy to pay that much and more to find out how to fight cancer and defeat pain.

Well, I was wrong for a number of reasons that I discovered later—after having lost a good deal of money following my logic.

Logic might dictate, for example, that you should open your shoe store in a town that doesn't have a shoe store. But anyone who has been in retail knows that such a conclusion is the basis for disaster. Much better to put your store in a town that already has 50 shoe stores, even if the rent is considerably higher.

When you start a home-based business in a field in which you have no experience, the chances are very high that you'll make many such logical mistakes. And unless you have a lot of money set aside to cover your failures (and if you have enough, you probably have enough to retire!), you'll go broke learning what you already know about the business you are already in.

So that's the first rule: Begin with what you know. Start a business that sells to essentially the same market, using essentially the same marketing techniques as the business you are in right now.

And don't worry too much about being bored. Consider this: Every business is different. Your new venture will look, sound, and feel different from the business you are in. It will deal with a different, better product. And it will be sold to a different, perhaps more interesting part of the market. Most important, everything you do in your new company will have your imprint on it. It will reflect your idea of ingenuity, practicality, quality, and customer service. This factor alone should revive your spirits.

ANOTHER WAY TO START WITH WHAT YOU KNOW

If you are lucky enough to have a lifelong hobby, it's quite possible that you can create a successful business by leveraging your knowledge and contacts there. I've mentored several people who have made this transition—from marketing executive of a publishing business to CEO of a business that teaches children about financial responsibility, to give just one example.

The trick to turning a hobby into a business is to use the experience you currently have in marketing and sales and couple it with the knowledge you have about your hobby. If, for example, you make a living selling vacuum cleaners door-to-door and you want to turn your passion for cooking into a business, consider creating your own cookbook (or better yet, home-study cooking program) and selling it door-to-door.

This sort of marriage—linking what you know about selling with what you know about your hobby—isn't always possible. For example, I can't think how you could sell vintage cigar lighters door-to-door.

But if you think you can do it, you probably can.

Rule No. 2: Choose a Business That Has
These Three Qualities

I don't invest in businesses unless they have three qualities:

1. An efficient marketing model
2. A substantial profit margin
3. A considerable back-end potential

AN EFFICIENT MARKETING MODEL

By "efficient marketing model," I mean a proven way to acquire customers without going broke. This may seem ridiculously obvious, but the truth is that many start-up businesses do not have this.

Most of the business plans I look at have unrealistic expectations about marketing. Two key issues, in particular, are usually off the mark:

1. How much it will cost to acquire a new customer
2. How many new customers can be acquired in a given time

If you get the wrong answer to either of these questions, you will usually go broke because you'll be spending money on other aspects of your business—product fulfillment and administration, among others. That will deplete the funds you need to reach the point at which repeat and back-end sales begin to cover expenses.

The primary benefit of Rule No. 1—starting with a business you know—is the knowledge you have of this one aspect of business: how to acquire new customers efficiently.

Every sector of every industry has its own model. And many individual businesses within a particular sector have their own peculiar formula for bringing on new customers. You can't possibly expect your home-based business to succeed unless you have a very good idea how you are going to attract new customers efficiently. And you can't do that unless you have working knowledge of how other, similar businesses have done so in the past.

When people I know insist on starting businesses outside of their knowledge base, I usually encourage them to get a job in the marketing department of a business like the one they want to enter. I would recommend this even if you have to volunteer your services. The knowledge you'll gain—and particularly the knowledge you'll gain about the three essential qualities of the business—will be worth much more than any financial compensation you could get.

It's a long shot, but it is possible to decipher an acquisition model by reading books and interviewing people. If you insist on going that way, read only books written by people who have achieved their success by doing, not talking about it—and secure personal interviews with the same sort of experienced individuals. (You may be surprised at how much successful people are willing to tell you about how they became successful.)

A SUBSTANTIAL PROFIT MARGIN

Knowledge of how to acquire new customers efficiently is, as I said, the first and most important thing I look for when investing in a new business. But it's not the only thing. I like to see a large gross profit, too.

By "gross profit," I mean price minus cost of goods and refunds. A paperback book on building wealth, for example, that sells for $7.95 might have a $3.95 production cost. That's a gross profit of $4.00 on $7.95—the cost of product (including refunds) being about 50 percent of sales. That's a gross profit margin many businesses find acceptable, but it's the kind of number that makes me nervous.

I like big profit margins—the bigger the better. That's why I like information products. The paper and ink are cheap. And the initial cost—that pays for the intellectual product—can be amortized over the life of the product.

Take the aforementioned example of the wealth-building book. A 100 percent markup (from about $4 to about $8) doesn't leave me a lot of room for marketing costs. But if I could put that same information into a different format and sell it as a home-study course, I might be able to charge $99, $199, or even $399 for it. My product and fulfillment costs would increase, but only marginally. Yet my gross profit margin would soar.

In the twenty-first century, there are many businesses that offer large margins. The obvious ones are information based, but entertainment and prestige products offer large margins, too.

The best thing about big margins from a start-up perspective is that they allow you plenty of room for error. As a general rule, the larger the gross margin, the more cash you can generate with each sale. And the more cash flow your business has when it begins, the better able you'll be to keep the business going while you figure out the perfect customer acquisition model—the one that will allow your company to keep on growing.

A CONSIDERABLE BACK-END POTENTIAL

The third and final quality I look for in start-up businesses is the potential for back-end sales. By "back-end" sales, I mean more, better, and higher-priced products and services sold to the existing customer base.

I like businesses that have customers who keep on buying. I like the feeling that the work that is done to acquire a new customer will be the hardest work done. I like the thought that for every dollar I get bringing a new customer into my business, there will be 3 or 4 or even 10 more dollars down the road.

It's much, much easier to make a second sale to an existing customer than it is to get that customer in the first place. Businesses that have this potential are natural moneymakers, because they allow the business to reinvest 100 percent or more of its front-end sales into acquiring more customers.

When you have an efficient marketing model, a good profit margin, and a substantial back end, you have everything you need to make your business grow exponentially. Your margin allows you to continuously build your active customer base, even accounting for those customers who expire or drift away.

As your customer base grows, your back end explodes—because a good back end stimulates itself. The more back-end products you have, the higher the response rate (and income yield) you'll get from each existing customer. When you are dealing with small business development in industries with back-end characteristics, supply-side economics is a wonderful fact of life.

Rule No. 3: Make Sure There Is an Active Market

The most common fatal mistake would-be entrepreneurs make is the failure to find out whether there is an active market for their intended product.

The mistake occurs most commonly when people violate Rule No. 1 by starting a business that they know little or nothing about.

It's an understandable mistake. You have a special interest or a pet peeve and you think of how to turn it into a great business. You assume there are plenty of people in the world who share your feelings and imagine it would be very easy to sell your new product or service to them.

You talk to a few friends about your idea and they bolster your courage (though they don't know anything about it, either). And before you know it, you've spent a year and most of your life savings getting a business going that falls flat on its face with the first promotion.

"What went wrong?" you wonder.

Answer: You forgot to see whether there was an active market for your bright idea.

We would all like to think that we could create the next Wite-Out or Post-it pad or AOL. In fact, 99.9 percent of such brand-new ideas result in dismal, disappointing failures. The reason is simple: There is practically nothing new under the sun. Although you may feel sure that your brainchild is unique to you, chances are that it, or something very similar to it, has been thought of by countless other people—and months, or years, ago!

This is true in every aspect of business, but it's especially true when your great idea is outside of your experience. That's because most "good ideas" don't work for reasons that are invisible to outsiders (including new employees) but are obvious to anyone who's had the benefit of seeing such ideas fail in the past.

The solution is to follow Rule No. 1. If you do, you'll probably avoid most of the mistakes you're likely to make. But if you must (or simply really want to) get into a business you know nothing about, don't invest a nickel in it until you've determined that there is an active market for your product.

What do I mean by that? I'm talking about lots and lots of buyers already out there purchasing similar, if not identical, products.

When it comes to investing your time and money in a side business, you want to be very careful not to blow everything on your first effort. A good way to increase your odds is to make sure that there is already a ready market for your business.

I'm not recommending getting into a crowded market with a weak, copycat product. But your chances of success doing that would be much greater than trying to create a new market with an untested product.

When it comes to launching a new product, a very good position to take is second or third place. The marketability is proven with the first success. By coming in second or third, you reduce your risk while still enjoying the momentum that the first product may have created in the marketplace.

But even if you are fourth, fifth, or tenth into the market, you can still be successful so long as you price your product competitively, sell it forcefully, and develop its own peculiar benefits to distinguish it from the competition.

Rule No. 4: Develop a Unique Selling Proposition

As you learn more about your customers, continually redesign and improve your product so that it better fits their needs.

There is a theory in business management courses called *incremental degradation*. The idea is that you can ruin a product gradually by reducing the cost of manufacturing it by slight amounts over time. The example I heard had to do with a soda that originally had, say, 32 flavorings that were part of its formula. A taste study by an enterprising, cost-conscious executive revealed that the company could remove one of the 32 ingredients without any of the customers noticing it. The savings in production costs were substantial, so the ingredient was eliminated. Several months later, the same executive did a second test and found also that another ingredient could be removed without anyone noticing. The idea was repeated a dozen times over a two-year period, with each successive degradation going unnoticed. Then, all at once, the market crashed. Sales dropped in half and nobody could explain why.

The explanation, the theory goes, is that although you can't distinguish incremental degradations from one another, the cumulative effect is noticed by consumers. Thus, the decision not to degrade a product is one that can't be subject to short-term, narrow-basis testing.

If a product can crash because of incremental degradation, why can't it also soar because of incremental augmentation?

Why can't a good product get better, in terms of both its intrinsic qualities and its success in the marketplace?

I think it can. And I am a strong advocate of incremental augmentation with clients. In recommending improvements, however, I'm not so foolish as to fix what's not broken. Every change must be tested in two ways: first subjectively by insiders—who must feel that the improvements are, in fact, improvements—and then objectively by measuring the reaction of the buying public.

In improving products, think always in terms of benefit: How does this change improve the experience of the buyer? Think also in terms of a unique selling proposition: Is this change something I can talk about in my advertising? Does it convey a benefit that the competition does not have?

If you improve your product carefully and continually, you'll keep it alive much longer . . . and that will make your business thrive.

Rule No. 5: Forget Retail and Glamour Businesses

We can make this section very short. If your idea for a side business involves a retail store or just about any business you think is glamorous (travel and entertainment are the two biggest culprits), save your money.

Retail businesses can succeed, but they are very difficult and very time-consuming, and they almost never provide the ROI you want from them. Travel and entertainment businesses are even worse.

If you are already in one of these businesses, you know what I'm talking about. If you aren't, take my word for it. You'll be glad you did.

Rule No. 6: Sell First, Tweak Your Product Later

Another very common cause of failed start-up businesses is forgetting that making the first sale is the first job.

Many people go into business with the idea that they should get all the details worked out before they open shop. They get all their plans done (sometimes to the nth degree), rent and equip an office, print business cards and brochures, and then get busy with operational and fulfillment issues before finding out whether they can sell the product.

Good start-up businesses have efficient marketing models (see Rule No. 2), and the only way to find out whether your marketing plans will work is to test them. Testing them doesn't mean marketing studies, prospect surveys, or even simulated sales situations. Most of that stuff is a waste of time.

To give your little business its best chance of succeeding, you have to find a way to bring in customers profitably before going out of business. There is only one way to do that properly, and that's to create a great advertising campaign and expose it to your prime audience.

If you employ a direct-marketing-driven marketing program, you won't have to spend a fortune testing your advertising. You need only target a handful of very strong, very vertical lists (i.e., addresses of buyers who bought products very similar to yours) and a very strong promotion. (Don't be penny-wise with copy. Pay for the best copywriter you can afford.)

By focusing the lion's share of your time, money, and talent on advertising, you can very quickly find out the most important thing you need to know about your new business: how to effectively acquire new customers.

Nothing else you can do in the beginning is as important. And everything else you may feel like doing—with the exception of creating the product, of course—can probably be done later.

Rule No. 7: Don't Throw Good Money after Bad

If you create a great advertising campaign and it fails, stop everything immediately and regroup.

You may be tempted to throw good money after bad by testing other marketing ideas. You may decide that if you reinvented the product, the next promotion would succeed. Any or all of your post-failure ideas may be valid, but you'll waste a lot of money and undermine your chances of succeeding by keeping the business open while you get set up for a second chance.

When I think back on all the products I've launched in my career (and there have been several hundred, at least), I can think of only a handful that started out weak and then gained strength afterward. Most new product launches that begin with a whimper eventually fade and die. Those that begin poorly do even worse.

It is usually only ego that compels you to go forward with a business idea that the market has told you it doesn't like. This mistake, this business hubris, is common not only among new entrepreneurs but also among mature and successful people.

To make your cut-and-run decision easier, set a stop-loss before the first test. Figure out what kind of return you expect from the advertising campaign and stick to it, even if the results are close.

If you don't expend all your money, time, and patience by pursuing a not-so-good or bad idea, you'll have enough of each to come back with a winning promotion the second time around.

STEP 6

RETIRE EARLY

If you follow the program I laid out for you so far, you will be able to retire in 7 to 15 years—maybe sooner.

And if your personal wealth-building program includes at least one side business, chances are you'll end up with more money than you really need.

The purpose of this book is to help you develop one or several wealth-building skills and specific financial *behaviors,* so that getting wealthier becomes almost automatic. Once these skills are mastered and the new habits are acquired, you will get richer with every passing day, even after you have abandoned wealth building as a primary goal. In fact, as an automatic wealth builder, your net worth will continue to increase even if you never spend another moment thinking about money.

That's a good thing—being free to think about other things, not just money-related issues. But you'll decide for yourself once you become wealthy.

In this last chapter of the book, I'm going to do three things:

1. I'm going to explain the logic behind my investment philosophy.
2. I'm going to give you four model investment portfolios—to give you an idea of how your investment mix should change as

you progress toward and ultimately achieve financial independence.

3. I'm going to explain why, after you achieve financial independence, you shouldn't entirely retire. I'll tell you why retirement doesn't work for most people—but how to make it work for you.

STOCKS AND BONDS VERSUS REAL ESTATE AND ENTREPRENEURSHIP

Since a big part of my e-zine *Early to Rise* (earlytorise.com) is devoted to entrepreneurship, many first-time readers mistakenly believe that I favor taking risks. Long-time readers know better than that.

I am and always have been a very conservative investor. As someone who started out with nothing and earned my money by working hard for it, I'm very uncomfortable seeing it disappear.

In one of Donald Trump's books—I think it was *Think Like a Billionaire*—he recommended a somewhat commonplace rule about investing. To determine what percentage of your investment portfolio should be in stocks, he said, subtract your age from 100. If you are, for example, 30 years old, you should have 70 percent of your invested assets in equities (stocks) and 30 percent in debt instruments (bonds). If you are 60 years old, you should have 40 percent in stocks and 60 percent in bonds.

This is not bad advice—if you believe, as most financial advisers do, that there are only two ways to invest: in stocks and in bonds.

The reasoning behind this rule is simple: The younger you are, the more risk you should be willing to take (stocks being more risky than bonds). I can understand the sense in that stance—especially for people who have a single income and whose only hope of financial independence is investing their savings for 40 or 50 years. But as I said at the beginning of this book, I don't have anything to say to people who have that much time to get rich—first, because they are so few and far between, and second, because they don't need my advice.

Early to Rise and *Automatic Wealth* are for people who want to get wealthy in 7 to 15 years. And the only way to do that—as I've attempted to prove in the preceding pages—is to (1) achieve a radically higher income than you have right now and (2) invest a sizable portion of that extra income into at least one side business and/or local real estate.

A side business, if it is successful, can give you returns of 20 percent to 100 percent per year. Real estate, prudently purchased, can give you 15 percent to 25 percent, or more. If you invest in both a side business and local real estate, you'll quickly lose your appetite for gambling on stocks.

The reason is simple: Successful stock investing is very, very difficult. First, you have to have an intricate, insider's understanding of the business you are buying. Next, you have to be able to know its market well enough to project future earnings. Third, you have to be able to correctly guess Wall Street's future thoughts and feelings about that company. And finally, you have to be able to divine investor confidence.

That's not to say that stock investing can't be made to work. In any 10-year period, there are at least several investment advisers whose track records exceed, by far, the market average. Still, those advisers are the exceptions. If you have normal or bad luck (as I have), you'll end up on the losing side of the equation.

That's why I've always been very reluctant to commit a large portion of my wealth to stocks. Since the bulk of my money is tied up in small businesses and real estate, I don't feel inclined to. I'd rather put most of my nonactive money into risk-free and relatively risk-free investments.

To put it another way, I look at investing more broadly than most financial advisers do. I like stocks and bonds, but I like real estate and entrepreneurship even better. If I had to rate each on a risk/reward basis, this is how it would look:

Reasonable Profit Potential per Year in a 7- to 10-Year Period

Stocks:	Range: 4% to 15%	Target: 12%
Bonds:	Range: 2.5% to 6%	Target: 5% (nontaxable)
Side Business:	Range: 25% to 100%	Target: 30%
Rental real estate (mortgaged):	Range: 15% to 50%	Target: 25%

What about risk? On a scale of 1 to 10, with 1 being the least risky and 10 being the most, here's how I'd rate these four investment alternatives:

Stocks: 8
Bonds: 2
Side business: 6
Real estate: 3

These are not scientifically determined assessments. They are better than that. They are the numeric equivalents of what my gut tells me. After 30 years of investing (and being in the investment publishing industry), I believe I've done and seen enough to know.

My Confidence in Small Businesses Is Rooted in Personal Experience

Small businesses contribute much more to the overall economy than they are given credit for. Most new jobs are created by small businesses. And most breakthrough ideas, too. Small business operators work harder than their larger competitors because they have to. And in working harder, they create innovations that improve the world.

I've had the good fortune of having started dozens of successful small businesses over the years. Most of them became multi-million-dollar enterprises. A few got much, much larger. This sort of track record is likely to give you a positive attitude. But I believe my optimism is valid. My evidence is the tens of thousands of other entrepreneurs who successfully launch businesses every year. Many people fail in business, but many more succeed. If you subtract the foolish failures—restaurants being the most foolish, followed by any sort of glamour business (think travel, bed-and-breakfast, sports, celebrity) or retail business—the successes far outnumber the failures.

When I think about my own experience and the experience of people I've coached, and I reflect on the larger numbers, it doesn't feel like starting a small business is all that risky.

You can reduce the risk in starting your own small business by sticking closely to what you already know. By "what you know," I mean (1) the product or service you are selling and (2) the primary method by which you are going to sell it.

Serially successful entrepreneurs follow this formula. They spend thousands of hours figuring out how a particular business works—and once they understand it, they seldom jump into something entirely different.

My own rule for starting a new business is this: One baby step at a time. By that, I mean that I'm willing to try something new—but just a little new. If, for example, I've learned how to sell cat food with banner ads on the Internet, I might consider setting up a business that sells cat food with small ads in magazines. (That's one baby step. If I can't figure out magazine advertising, I can get out quickly and safely.) But I wouldn't let myself get into a business that sold cat health-care products through direct mail—even if I could convince myself that I'm an expert in selling cat products. Selling cat health-care products through direct mail is simply too many steps away from my core competence.

If you develop expertise in a particular business and don't stray too far from it, you'll always feel confident that you can create a new business without taking a lot of risk.

Real Estate Has Always Been Good to Me

I'm bullish on entrepreneurship. And I'm at least as bullish on real estate.

Stocks are much riskier than real estate—to me—because (1) I've lost money investing in stocks and/or stock funds time and again and (2) I've seen so many others lose money. Again, I do believe that the stock market has been and will continue to be a pretty good long-term investment. But long term as far as the market goes is a 10- to 20-year time frame. Since we are concerned with getting wealthy in 7 to 15 years (and since the market is currently overvalued, from a fundamentalist's point of view), I don't feel confident in stocks.

Nevertheless, since I began actively investing in real estate—about 11 years ago—I have never lost money on a single transaction. The worst two deals I've been in since my first big lesson (i.e., disaster) produced yields of 7 percent and 12 percent annually. And that's not including tax benefits—which were significant. Most of the real estate investments I've made have been good to great.

Three recent examples:

1. A house I bought about eight years ago for $175,000 and on which I put in $25,000 in upgrades was sold four years later for $395,000.
2. A triplex my friend JP and I bought four years ago for $250,000 is producing cash-positive rent every month and is worth at least $400,000 today.

3. A 19-unit apartment complex I bought with another friend last year for a down payment of $400,000 has already appreciated at least $500,000—giving us a very substantial one-year return on our money.

I'm no Donald Trump. I don't even consider myself a professional real estate investor. I'm a professional marketer who has made real estate investing a nice sideline business. But in the 11 years that I've been doing it, my real estate portfolio has grown and grown. As an income producer, real estate has never failed to provide me with less than a very substantial income. As an asset builder, my rental real estate properties have all paid for themselves and provided me with a rate of return that is at least 10 times what I've been able to get from stocks and bonds.

I believe we are at the tail end of a nationwide real estate bubble. By any fundamental perspective, property prices have gotten out of hand. In some locations, this may mean a significant depreciation. In other, better locations (the Sun Belt, certain cities), it may mean a two- to four-year deflation of 10 percent or 15 percent. The worst depreciation will probably occur with condominiums, which are traditionally overpriced, overfinanced, and too heavily owned by speculators during bubble periods. That said, I'm confident that you will be able to find good real estate deals this year, next year, and each year thereafter during the downturn.

FOUR MODEL INVESTMENT PORTFOLIOS—ONE FOR EVERY STAGE OF YOUR WEALTH-BUILDING CAREER

So now you know how I feel about stocks, small business, and real estate. Bonds? I love bonds. Especially if you invest in them the way I do: Buy them. Be happy with the guaranteed return. And forget about them.

With this perspective made clear, you will see some sense in the following four model portfolios, each based on a stage of wealth building.

- Stage One: Your investable net worth is less than $25,000.
- Stage Two: Your investable net worth is between $25,000 and $100,000.

- Stage Three: Your investable net worth is more than $100,000 but less than you need to be financially independent.
- Stage Four: You are financially independent.

Stage One: What Your Portfolio Should Look Like When Your
Investable Net Worth Is Less Than $25,000

At a cocktail reception at a recent *Early to Rise* wealth-building conference, a gentleman approached me with a complaint. I suggested we take a seat together so I could give him the personal attention he seemed to want.

"What is it that disappointed you?" I asked.

"You spend too much time talking about working hard, starting a second income, and investing in real estate. That's too much trouble for most people," he contended.

"But it works," I replied.

"Maybe it does. And maybe it doesn't," he said. "But what I'm interested in is stocks and stock options. You should give more information on that."

I explained that while most "investment" conferences focus exclusively on stocks and options, we wanted to talk about safer and more lucrative ways to build wealth.

He didn't seem to hear me. "Also, I wanted to hear about how I can get into futures and make some money by leveraging gold or natural resources," he told me.

"I'm not going to give you individual advice about your passive investing," I said—although I couldn't help but wonder how many millions or billions of dollars this guy had. So I asked him. And this is what he told me: *His entire net worth consisted of about $250,000 worth of equity in a home he loved and about $18,000 in the bank that he was actively investing in stocks.*

This wasn't the only conversation I had of this nature. Of the 80 wealth builders who attended the conference, at least a third of them were small-fry investors. Interestingly enough, when asked on the registration survey to rate their interest in various types of investments, there seemed to be an inverse relationship between net worth and the stock market. The wealthier attendees were very interested in real estate, side businesses, and alternative forms of investing, while the beginners wanted to make their fortunes by buying and selling stocks.

The next day, speaking to the attendees as a group, I made a point of explaining what a beginning wealth builder shouldn't do.

1. First, when figuring your *investable* net worth, you really shouldn't count the equity in your present home unless you plan to sell it and buy a less expensive home during retirement. And even if you do that, you can count only the difference between what your house is currently worth, the mortgage, and what it will cost you to buy another house that you'll be happy with. Using the example of our dissatisfied conference attendee, he admitted that there was little or no hope of finding a nice retirement home in a community he liked for less than the equity he had in his present house.

2. Next, you shouldn't be investing in stocks and options if your investable net worth is less than $25,000. In our example, the gentleman was playing the stock market with his entire savings: $18,000. Think about the risk this guy was taking!

It's true. And you will probably never hear this from any other wealth-building "expert." Unless you have more than $25,000 to invest, you probably shouldn't be investing in individual stocks—and you definitely shouldn't be trading options and futures.

The reason is simple: You want to get wealthy in 7 to 15 years—preferably in less than 7. There is no way that $25,000 can turn into something that even sounds like wealth in that amount of time—though there are a lot of professional investment gurus who will tell you otherwise. In fact, there is a huge, multi-billion-dollar business that is determined to snow you on this issue.

So what can you do with $25,000? Or $18,000, for that matter?

If your scope is seven years or less, there is only one answer: Start a business. You can't start a capital-intensive business with $18,000. You can't, for example, open a restaurant or create a new line of pharmaceuticals. But you don't want to be in those businesses anyway. (The risk/reward ratio isn't working for you.)

Much better to start a business selling something you know about—such as gardening or collecting beer steins or taking care of pets. You can start a little business like this for a few thousand dollars if you start small and go slowly—at first.

I've mentored several friends and relatives in starting up small businesses. The first years were always a struggle, because they were trying to find ways to efficiently bring in new customers. Once a way was found, things got much easier. Developing a back end (i.e., selling other, usually more-expensive products to existing customers) is relatively easy, as is refining operations.

A typical business start-up of this kind will break even or lose a little money in year one, make a decent salary for the owner in year two, and provide a substantial bonus—in addition to a good, arm's-length management salary—in year three. After that, it's usually straight uphill.

You can invest a small amount of money (and a lot of hard work and well-spent time) in a small business and see it grow into a business that is worth a million in seven years. I've done it many times. I've coached people who have done it. Stories are published in magazines every month about people who have done it.

But let's be frank. With only $18,000 to $25,000 to invest, it won't be easy. That's why I like to encourage *Early to Rise* readers who are at this first wealth-building stage to focus most of their time and efforts on building their income. Doubling your income in a year or two is entirely possible if you follow the advice I gave you in Chapter 4. And if you double your income and don't double your lifestyle, you'll have a lot more money left over to ensure the success of your small side business.

Here are five things I recommend if you are in this situation:

1. Find a way to radically increase your salary by making yourself radically more valuable at work.
2. Resist the temptation to spend more money as your income rises.
3. Put some of your savings down on an undervalued, small, single-family house, fix it up fast, and sell it for a profit.
4. Reinvest that original capital plus the profit in another buy-and-flip deal. Keep doing this until it becomes a very pleasant habit.
5. Invest another portion of your savings in a part-time, weekend business. Sell a product or service you know and understand. Make sure you are not a pioneer. Unless there are others actively selling the same thing, you don't want to be in the

market. The idea is to enter an active market with a better/ cleverer/cheaper version of what others are selling. Sell only by direct response—print, mail, and Internet. Go carefully and learn from your mistakes.

Stage Two: What to Invest in When You Have between $25,000 and $100,000

When you get to the next stage—that is, when you have between $25,000 and $100,000 to invest—you can take a multilayered approach to your investing. I like the following simple five-part formula.

1. *Cash.* The first money you save should be marked for emergencies. This needs to be put someplace that is secure but easy to access, such as a home safe or a safe-deposit box. The amount you should keep for emergencies depends on your personal situation: how much you typically spend, how reliable your income is, and so on. As a rule of thumb, though, I'd recommend about 10 percent of your investable net worth. If you have $100,000, that would be $10,000.

2. *Income-generating real estate.* I recommend buying and flipping real estate for everyone, even beginners. If you start when you have less than $25,000 to invest and make a few deals, by the time your investable net worth hits $100,000, you should have a pretty active, nicely profitable second stream of income.

3. *Side business(es).* If you didn't want to get involved in a side business when you had less than $25,000 to invest, you should consider it at this stage. You don't have to risk a ton of money. Invest $10,000 conservatively in a business you understand and see where that takes you.

    You could, for example, create a side business selling a skill you currently have (accounting, legal, writing, editing, purchasing, etc.) or could develop (graphic design, copywriting, resume writing, etc.). Or you could turn a hobby or passion (stamp collecting, gardening, pets) into a profitable, Internet-based direct-marketing business.

    As your side business grows, it will require that you reinvest some of the profits into creating new products, hiring employees, and developing new advertising campaigns. You should allow for growth, but limit it to avoid growing so fast that you end up losing control and getting into trouble.

4. *Equity-building real estate.* Buying equity-building real estate means buying rental properties. The trick to making this work for you at this second stage of wealth is to buy conservatively—that is, to make sure that the rent you'll get will at least meet (but should really exceed) your cost of maintaining the property. I recommend duplexes, triplexes, and quadruplexes to start. They'll give you the best chance to achieve zero or positive monthly cash flow. How much equity-building real estate should you develop? If you have a net worth of $100,000, I'd recommend a little more than half. Let's say $60,000.

5. *Fixed-income instruments.* The rest of your money should be in Treasuries, municipal bonds, or quality corporate paper. Fixed-income instruments like these don't provide a high return, but they are safe.

In Stage Two, safety should be your main concern.

You will notice that in this second stage there are no stocks, options, futures, metals, rare coins, or derivatives in the portfolio. And there is a good reason for that. When you have less than $100,000 to invest and less than a long time to get rich, you should focus on only two things:

1. Continuing to increase your income by continuing to perfect a financially valued skill such as selling, marketing, product development, or profit management
2. Investing the surplus in high-return equity ventures

If you focus on this for a few years, chances are that you'll end up with a surfeit of cash—that is, more cash than you need for your side business and real estate ventures. This extra cash should be kept safe. *Extra safe.* Remember, this is the beginning of your retirement nest egg.

So place this surplus cash in bonds, and reinvest the interest in bonds, too. Make it a primary objective to have this safety reserve grow substantially every year. Once your bond savings become significant, you'll start to appreciate what a valuable, comforting investment bonds can be.

As Will Rogers is reported to have said, "It is not the return on my investment that I am concerned about; it is the return of my investment."

Building the critical skills that will make you wealthy—and that includes learning as much as you can about your local real estate market—is plenty to keep a novice investor busy. Trying to simultaneously develop expertise in stocks or futures or options is foolhardy—foolhardy and unnecessary. By buying up-and-coming properties in your local market and having the bank finance 80 percent of them, you can easily make 20 percent to 25 percent on your money every year. With this being 60 percent of your investment portfolio, who cares if the other 40 percent earns less than 5 percent?

You will make practically nothing on your cash and only about 4 percent on your tax-free bonds (which will probably be worth about 6 percent on a taxable basis). Admittedly, that's not much. But if you invest reasonably in real estate, financing 80 percent of your investments with bank loans, that larger (60 percent) part of your portfolio should appreciate at 15 percent to 25 percent. That will give you an overall return of between 12 percent and 15 percent.

While you are going through this first, pre-$100,000-net-worth stage of wealth building, a return of 12 percent to 15 percent of your hard-core retirement savings is plenty.

So here's my basic advice to you if you are in Stage Two:

1. Continue to buy and flip local real estate. Use bank financing to increase your ROI.
2. If you didn't do it in Stage One, invest some time and money in a side business that you understand.
3. Invest the rest of your savings ultraconservatively—in cash and bonds.

Stage Three: What to Invest in When You Have More Than $100,000 but Less Than You Need to Retire

In the first stage of wealth building—when you have less than $25,000 to invest—the only investment to consider is to start a side business. In Stage Two, you can branch out into conservative investments—but not stocks. I recommend investing in stocks only after you have passed the $100,000 plateau. This is the stage where you have built up your investable net worth to between, say, $100,000 and $1 million. You are still actively building wealth, because you have less than you need in order to stop working and live well on your passive income. But you can afford to take a little more risk.

Here's what I think your Stage Three portfolio should look like:

1. *Emergency cash.* Everyone needs some cash hidden away for immediate access. There are different opinions as to what constitutes a safe minimum. Some say as little as one month's pay or expenses. Others argue for six months or more. My suggestion is a little more than three months' worth of expenses. If, for example, you spend about $75,000 after taxes to maintain your lifestyle, you'll want to have about $20,000 in cash somewhere . . . just in case.

2. *Emergency gold.* I'm not a gold nut, but I do like to know that I have a significant amount of gold coins hidden away in case I ever need them. I've accumulated rolls of Krugerrands over the years. They are nice to look at, are easy to hide, and provide a substantial feeling of stability in the face of all sorts of imagined disasters—hurricanes, computer hacking, identity theft, government confiscation, the war on terrorism, or the like.

   I don't think you need to buy into the argument that gold will appreciate in value to appreciate the value of gold. I have about 3 percent of my investable net worth in gold. That's enough to buy a little place somewhere in the tropics and disappear if I ever need to. Not a bad disaster fantasy, I think you'd agree.

3. *Hard assets/collectibles.* You shouldn't view hard assets and collectibles the same way as you view stocks and bonds. Yet if you buy and sell them right, they can give you a consistently much higher rate of return, even over a longer period of time.

   My preference in terms of hard assets is fine art. I'm a collector of early-twentieth-century European masters (Derain, Pascin, Grosz), American folk/naïve art (Edward Larson, Reverend Howard Finster), Cobra art (Appel, Alechinsky, Corneille), and twentieth-century Latin American masters (Rivera, Tamayo, Siqueiros, Orozco, Matta).

I recommend collecting art because it brings with it so many other gifts:

- The pleasure of learning
- The excitement of building a collection
- The stimulation of new friends
- A wider, more sophisticated view of history

If you focus your collection, you can develop a feel for what is good and what is overpriced—and you can develop a pretty fair ability to buy quality, appreciating assets. As with other collectibles, it is usually worthwhile to pay extra for quality and rarity when it comes to buying art. I achieve that dual goal by refusing to buy reproductions of any sort. I'd rather have a simple pencil sketch by Dali or Picasso than one of, say, 200 of their limited-edition prints.

Fine art used to be considered somewhat illiquid—hard to get rid of in an emergency. But because the Internet has now connected art dealers and auction houses worldwide, it's pretty easy to buy and sell art quickly—and without taking a big "haircut."

I have about 5 percent of my wealth tied up in art—and I might actually increase that a bit, because I'm toying with the idea of creating a little side business selling high-end art to a limited number of wealthy collectors. Nowadays, you don't need a retail presence to do that. I'm using fine art as the example here, but you could do the same thing with almost any collectible. In fact, most of the advantages of fine art are also available to collectors of antique furniture, dolls, rare coins, Americana, vintage guns, cameras, and so on. So long as there is an active, interconnected market, you can enjoy yourself and make some decent money—or simply enjoy a reasonable appreciation—by collecting.

4. *Real estate.* I recommend investing in equity-building real estate during your second wealth-building stage. In Stage Three, you should add income-building (rental) real estate to your portfolio.

Real estate is an essential part of my investment program. I have almost half of my investable net worth in real estate. Of that sum, about 25 percent is invested in buy-and-flip proper-

ties—transactions that I used to do myself and now have someone else handle for me. The majority is in rental apartments
and office space. These investments have been relatively easy to
run. (I use professional management companies for all my
properties that are 10 units or larger.) Not only do they provide me with regular income, they have also been appreciating
at an average rate of about 12 percent per year—and over a
period of five years, that amounts to almost 50 percent a year
in real terms, since most of these properties are mortgaged.

5. *Side business(es).* Having a significant (i.e., 25 percent or more)
   share of several small but growing businesses is the single best
   way I know of to get rich. In Stage Three, there are several
   ways to do this. Here are two ideas:
   • Find a small, fast-growing business in your local area and
   buy into it. This is easier to do than it seems. Many entrepreneurs would be happy to trade a little stock for cash if it
   could help them grow faster, reduce risk, and boost their
   confidence. One of the shareholders of a major client of
   mine invested with a young entrepreneur 20 years ago. The
   $25,000 he plunked down is worth between $6 million and
   $10 million today.
   • Identify a smart, hard-working relative or friend and back
   him or her in some small but potentially sizable business
   that doesn't require you to risk a lot of cash.

6. *Bonds.* In my preretirement, active stage of investing, I like to
   have about 15 percent to 20 percent of my investable wealth in
   bonds. I prefer to invest only in top-quality bonds (because I'm
   looking for safety, not yield), and I always stay in my bonds till
   they mature. Again, the idea is not to maximize return—I'm
   getting plenty of maximized returns from my side businesses
   and real estate. My goal with my passive investments is to stay
   passive. Staying passive means staying in for the long haul and
   reducing risk to an absolute minimum.

7. *Stocks and stock funds.* As I said, if you invest in quality real
   estate and develop a side business, it won't be long before you
   have more cash coming in than you can reinvest in those enterprises. You'll put a good deal of that extra cash in bonds
   (because you realize it makes sense to be conservative with this

money), but you'll probably still have plenty left over. That's when you have to consider stocks and stock funds.

Most of the money I put in the stock side of my portfolio is invested in no-load funds that track major markets. But now and again I'll have some fun with an individual stock that is recommended by someone I trust and follow. In either case—stocks or stock funds—I'm not looking to get the best possible return for my money. I'm looking for a better return than bonds, but I'm happy with the return that the market has historically afforded—about 10 percent.

By following the advice of certain conservative investors, I've been able to achieve a slightly higher than average rate of return on stocks. My goal is currently 12 percent, and I'm thinking it might be possible to hit 15 percent. But I am not betting my retirement on that. Of my total investable wealth, less than 10 percent is ever invested in stocks of any sort. With a side business and real estate giving me superhigh, relatively risk-free yields, why would I want to take risks with stocks?

Stage Four: What to Invest in When You
Are Financially Independent

When I first retired, at age 39, I did nothing but paint pictures and write short stories for a year. This was an enjoyable way to pass my time—but my income that year (not counting passive investments) was $600. I realized that would never do. I needed to find some sort of retirement hobby that could make me money. That hobby, as it turned out, transformed into a full-time consulting position, which earned me millions more than I needed and robbed me of a lot of the time I wanted to paint and write stories.

You don't want to make the same mistake. That's why it's so important to come up with your retirement plan now—and stick with it when the moment comes.

How Will You Know When You're
Financially Independent?

When I use the term *financially independent,* I mean that you have at least 10 times the amount of posttax income you need to enjoy the kind of life you want to live. (By now, you should have figured out what that number is.)

If, for example, you are confident you can live well on $80,000, you have to have an income, before taxes, of about $120,000 per year. (I'm using an overall tax rate of 30 percent here, which is probably a fair estimate if you consider that you'll be paying the top tax rate on only a portion of your income—and if you use a personal corporation and enjoy a retirement business, some of your expenses will be tax deductible.)

Ten times $120,000 is $1.2 million—the retirement nest egg you'll need to pay for your lifestyle without ever digging into your principal.

As I explained before, if you're a conservative planner, you might want to budget up on this—making $1.5 million your financial independence target. But don't try to pinpoint the exact amount of savings you'll need. There are too many variables in the economy and in your future to do that accurately anyway. The idea is to realize that you need a sizable chunk of savings—probably millions—and to plan your financial life to achieve that goal.

If and when you do, you'll be able to relax and consider yourself financially independent. And if you are smart, when you hit that number, you'll radically change your life so that you can have more time to enjoy those things that really matter to you.

ONCE YOU REACH THAT POINT, HOW SHOULD YOUR
RETIREMENT PORTFOLIO BE SET UP?

My recommendation is very simple. I suggest you have your wealth invested in a combination of the following:

- Stocks and stock index funds
- Fixed-income instruments
- Managed real estate
- Emergency cash and gold
- "Play" money

Let's take a look at these five investments, one at a time.

1. *Stocks and stock index funds.* As I pointed out before, you won't need much money in stocks if you have a reasonable amount in real estate. Stocks will give you a 10 percent return, on the

average. Real estate should give you more than that, particularly if you are valuing it at cost and you've been holding onto it for 7 to 15 years.

I will probably never have more than 10 percent of my money in equities (of any kind), because I don't get any enjoyment out of equity investing. But if you like watching the stocks you pick go up and down, I believe a 20 percent commitment is reasonable.

I wouldn't recommend more than 20 percent—even for a 50- or 60-year-old retiree. Why? Because the stock market, generally (and individual stocks, especially), is unpredictable in the short term. And when you are living out your golden years, everything is short term.

2. *Fixed-income instruments.* I like bonds—even in today's low-yield environment. Quality bonds give you the peace of mind that you should be looking for in retirement. I like all sorts of bonds, but I'm particularly fond of municipal bonds. They are very safe and offer tax-free income. So a return of 5 percent, for example, would be worth about 7.5 percent if you are in the top tax bracket.

The thing I like best about bonds is how simple they are. If you hold them till they mature, as I do, they are the perfect zero-hassle, zero-worry investment. You know what return you are getting when you buy them . . . and that's the end of it. Bond funds are a good alternative if you want to diversify a bit. Like individual bonds, they can give you a fixed rate of return, simplicity, and peace of mind.

What percentage of your retirement portfolio should be in bonds? If you have enough money to live well off a yield of, say, 4.5 percent or 5 percent after taxes, you can have most of your money in bonds. My closest financial adviser has *all* his retirement funds in bonds.

Chances are, you will need to earn a higher return. If that's the case, I recommend allocating between 40 percent and 50 percent of your funds to bonds.

3. *Managed rental real estate.* Rental real estate can offer some very impressive rates of return—depending on how you measure them. A $75,000 investment in a triplex 10 years ago in my

hometown in South Florida would be worth about $300,000 today. With a net rental yield of about $20,000 a year (after property taxes, upkeep, and management fees), that investment is earning either 27 percent or 7.5 percent, depending on whether you calculate from the original investment or the appreciated value.

In a case like this, you might be better off selling the property and investing the money in bonds. If you could get a 5 percent return and were in the highest tax bracket, your effective yield would be 7.5 percent or better. (These are very rough calculations. I'm not taking into account depreciation, continuing appreciation, other write-offs, etc.) But most of the real estate deals I bought 7 to 15 years ago are producing rental yields of between 10 percent and 15 percent of their current (admittedly conservative) estimated value. That higher yield, combined with the continuing appreciation of the property, is why I recommend a 20 percent to 40 percent commitment to managed rental real estate.

4. *Emergency cash and gold.* As I said earlier, we all need to have some cash tucked away in a safe-deposit box, just in case. I keep a sum that's equal to about three months' worth of spending. I also think it's sensible to have between 2 percent and 5 percent of your investable net worth in gold.

5. *"Play" money.* Retirement is supposed to be fun. And some fun—not the best kind of fun, but some fun—costs money. I'm not talking about money that you spend on golf and vacations. Your general retirement funds are supposed to take care of that. I'm talking about the fun of trying new businesses, converting your passions or hobbies into profit centers, and adding choice pieces to your collections. If you are good (and lucky), you'll have fun *and* make some money with this part of your Stage Four portfolio. But if you don't make money, that's okay.

WHY YOU SHOULDN'T COMPLETELY RETIRE EVEN WHEN YOU CAN AFFORD TO

I belong to a book club with eight other very successful businessmen in their mid-50s. We had just read Viktor Frankl's famous book, *Man's*

Search for Meaning (Washington Square Press, 1971), and at our monthly dinner meeting, were recounting small stories of our own experiences.

In the second half of the book, Frankl said that chasing money and power are deviant aspects of a more important and fundamental yearning: finding meaning in life. Although pursuing money and power could be all-consuming while you are doing it, the moment you experience the achievement of a specific goal (say, financial independence), you are likely to have a feeling of gladness . . . followed by a period of sadness. The sad feeling is the vacuum created between the hope that money and power can provide meaning and the realization, after achieving them, that they can't.

Of course, this doesn't deny the usefulness of money or the practical benefits of financial independence. When you are wealthy, you can

- Wake up when you want to
- Go to bed when you wish
- Live anywhere
- Associate with whom you please
- Work as little or as much as you want to
- Never have to worry about paying bills
- Make modest financial mistakes without suffering

Becoming financially independent is a worthy, sensible goal. But what Viktor Frankl suggested—and what the nine of us were discussing—is that a life of financial independence would be relatively unfulfilling if we didn't also have other, more important, goals.

One of the guys, a recently retired corporate attorney, said that he wants to spend a good part of his future helping people in the Third World develop small businesses. Another one—a wholesale clothing manufacturer—wants to sponsor local theatrical groups. Our sponsor, a direct-mail catalog pro, wants to promote reading through a series of books he is writing on the subject.

"Giving something back" was the most common refrain of our conversation—and I noticed that this idea was coupled with the enthusiasm that is evident anytime people think that what they are doing (or are about to do) has meaning.

I've talked about this important psychological phenomenon many times and in many contexts in *Early to Rise*—that having a purpose in life gives you direction and drive. The purpose you aim for at any given time is a function of everything else that life has provided you with at that moment. As Viktor Frankl said, there is no best purpose in life, just as there is no best way to swing a tennis racket. If you can recognize that you are always free to choose your purpose (even if it is merely to suffer nobly), and if you can devote yourself enthusiastically to that purpose, your life will have meaning, your heart will be full, and your mind will be light and energized.

That's exactly how you imagine financial freedom to be, isn't it?

And that brings us to this apparent contradiction: If you want to enjoy all the best things about retirement (i.e., the best things you imagine retirement to be), you must never do what most of us think we should do when we retire—that is, devote your time to being happy.

The Problem with the Conventional Idea of Retirement

I've said this before, but it bears repeating: You can't find happiness by trying to be happy.

It's one of the wonderful ironies of life. Happiness seldom if ever comes to us when we are trying to please ourselves. Much more often, it arrives while we are focusing on something or someone we care about.

In fact, this experience has been so common in my life that I'd like to suggest it as a sort of life secret: The way to be happy is to focus your time and energy on someone or something you care about.

There are three points to this secret that are worth noting:

1. The already stated irony that happiness comes only when you are not seeking it.
2. And this is certainly related to the first point—that to achieve happiness, your attention must be cast outside of yourself.
3. That you must devote your time, your attention, and your energy to this outside object—in other words, you must *work*.

This last point is difficult for some people to absorb—especially in the context of a discussion about retirement. We've conditioned ourselves to think that happiness in retirement means

- Spending more time trying to be happy
- Paying attention to "number one"
- Doing little or no work whatsoever

In fact, people who do just that usually end up bored, unhappy, and forever trying to fix themselves by spending more of their time pursuing pleasure.

Our book club conversation about *Man's Search for Meaning* illustrates this point. Here we were—nine very successful, reasonably well educated, financially independent men—who, when asked what we intended to do with the rest of our days, had certain very similar perspectives:

- Although we all expressed an interest in playing more golf or spending more time reading, not a single one of us wanted to spend all his time in leisure activities.
- When asked by our host, "How would you like to spend your retirement years?" everyone included some sort of meaningful work in his answer. One, for example, wanted to join the Peace Corps. Another wanted to sell the virtues of reading to more people. Two talked in general terms about doing something that would give back to their communities . . .

We didn't all begin our careers thinking this way. We weren't all and always focused on meaningful work and giving back. For the most part, our working lives were driven by the desire to succeed and even to excel. And in achieving those goals, we may have ignored or lost track of the idea of having meaning in our work—of having a purpose that goes beyond money, beyond power, beyond ourselves.

Whatever we failed to do, we now recognized the value in meaningful work.

And so that's my first early retirement recommendation for you.

Finding a Meaningful Purpose—and Happiness—
in Your Work

You don't have to wait until you are financially independent and actually retire to enjoy an early retirement mind-set. The sooner you can make your business about something other than making money, gaining power, or in some other way enhancing your personal situation, the sooner you'll begin loving your work.

That will happen the moment your work stops being about you.

Here are five ways you can find more personal pleasure in your work.

1. *Make customer satisfaction your number one priority.* Ultimately, business should not be about sales, market share, renewals, repurchases, or even profitability. It should be about leaving the world you inhabit a little bit nicer than it was before you entered it. You can do that only by focusing on customer satisfaction.

   In my many years of starting and running businesses, I've had all sorts of goals. For many years, I was a big advocate of sales. Then, of profitability. Then, of a combination of numbers. By focusing everyone's time and attention on those numbers, I was able to stimulate a lot of growth. But after the initial successes were achieved, I never felt that good about hitting the numbers again. When I changed that policy and made qualitative goals a priority, I noticed that business started feeling more rewarding. I still paid attention to the important numbers, but I didn't make them my primary focus. And an interesting thing happened: Sales and profits continued to increase, but so did product quality and customer satisfaction—two objectives that always eluded me when they were secondary.

2. *Focus on improving your people for their benefit, not yours.* Every time you interact with your employees, you have an opportunity to make them wiser and thus increase their prospects of being successful. If your goal is to create a great business that provides great products and terrific customer service, you will want all employees to be at their best. You won't achieve that by badgering or belittling. Yes, you can browbeat some people into improving themselves—but it's much easier (and better) to inspire them to transform themselves.

3. *Don't do more than you can do well.* There is such a thing as being overly productive. I've been overly productive for many years. By taking on ambitious goals and translating them into demanding monthly, weekly, and daily objectives, you can force yourself into a situation where you have to race through almost everything you do to get it all done.

Rushing through meetings and memos doesn't mean doing a bad job with them. Most meetings and memos I've experienced are not worthy of as much time as they usually get. The problem with rushing is not necessarily quality (because you can learn to rush in an effective way), it's the way rushing makes you feel. As someone who has rushed through 12- and 13-hour days for more than 20 continuous years, I can attest to the wear and tear it causes. If you want to enjoy your job, start doing fewer things and do each of those things at a slower pace. Naturally, you'll have to be selective about what you do and what you delegate, but you'll notice a difference in how you feel almost immediately.

4. *Don't grow your business too fast.* When you are actively growing a company, you are automatically creating a certain amount of chaos. By pushing to create more products, sales, and customers, you inevitably put a strain on your ability to do things well. The product, rushed to market, has some flaws. Yes, you will fix them later. But they are there now and some of your customers notice. Problems are also inescapable in other phases of your business: packaging, product delivery, order taking, and customer service.

   It takes a while to get all the small problems fixed that are caused by growth. If you keep growing, year after year, so will your problems. And if your growth is aggressive, your problems will be significant. Significant problems bring stress—and that's why, if and when you want to enjoy a low-stress life, you are going to have to moderate the growth plans of your business, even if your best employees might prefer to see a more bullish stance and pace.

5. *Don't ever feel sorry for yourself.* You don't always have a choice about the problems you have to deal with in business, but you definitely have a choice about the way you respond to them. When you are feeling beaten up or rundown, the worst thing you can do is to complain about it. Complaining focuses your (and others') attention on you-know-who. And paying attention to yourself is, as I've said, counterproductive.

What Makes for a Perfect Retirement?

I've already made the case that certain commonly held assumptions about retirement are not true. That a good retirement is without work, without care, full of play.

And that begs the question: What would a perfect retirement be?

Gee. Let's see. You certainly want it to be happy. And that means, we've already decided, that it must involve work. The work involved must be focused on something outside of yourself . . . and it must be meaningful. But that's not all. Hmmm. What else? What other things might affect your happiness in retirement?

Four spring quickly to mind:

- Money
- Freedom
- Time
- Purpose

1. *Enough money to support your lifestyle.* Much of this book has been devoted to money—how to get more of it (raising your income) and how to put it to work (developing equity). Our ultimate financial retirement goal is simply to have enough money to live well—without working.

    If you can pay for your lifestyle without working, you don't have to compromise when it comes to work. You can choose the work that is most meaningful to you, even if that work pays very little or nothing for your time.

    My case is a typical example. I'm planning to retire (again) in about eight months. What I intend to spend my work time doing is writing short stories and literary novels. I know, going into it, that I'm highly unlikely to make any money working this way. After all, the last time I did that—during my first retirement—I made $600 in a 12-month period. (It amounted to about a penny an hour.) But I also know, from experience, that writing fiction will improve the quality of my life—that I'll feel good about doing it. This isn't the only thing I'll be doing in my retirement, but it will probably be the most mean-ingful to me.

Happily I can afford to write fiction because I've spent 12 years (since my last retirement) increasing my net worth. You will want to be in the same situation. And you will—if you follow the recommendations about raising your income and developing your net worth.

2. *The freedom to be in charge of your life.* When you are working for a living, you may sometimes feel as if everybody but you is in charge of your life. Your boss dictates when you get to work, when you leave, and what you do in between. Your family—especially if you have a young family—takes up most of the rest of your time. If you can find a half hour a day for yourself, you feel lucky. An indentured servant—even a slave—must have had that much time, you figure.

When you achieve financial independence, you should strive for other forms of independence, too. Retirement is a great time to make changes. And right now—while you are becoming wealthy—is a great time to rethink the major possibilities:

- Where do I want to live?
- With whom do I want to spend my personal time?
- What kind of work do I want to spend my working time doing?
- With whom do I want to work?
- How much time do I want to spend working?
- How do I want to spend my leisure time?

Start by asking yourself if you might want to live somewhere else. In today's world of Internet communications and inexpensive jet travel, there is very little reason to feel locked into any particular geographic location. Draw up a list of the 5 or 10 places you'd most like to live and then spend the next several years visiting them. That way, when the time comes, you will have a good idea of where exactly you'll most want to live.

Now is also the right time to reconsider all your personal relationships. If you've been unhappy in a particular relationship but have been unsuccessful in bringing it to a healthy end, the transition into retirement will give you a good opportunity to do so.

Choosing meaningful work, as I've said, may be the single most important way to create a sense of freedom and power in your life. Promise yourself that you are going to choose work to do in retirement that really excites and motivates you. Forget about how much money you can make. That will no longer count. Pick something that will make you feel good about yourself and stick to it.

In considering the work you'll be doing in retirement consider, too, whom you'll be dealing with—clients, colleagues, consultants. Populate your chosen retirement profession with a network of perfect people. (Again, since you won't need the money, why settle?) Make it clear from the outset that you will be in charge of all your relationships.

3. *Enough time to enjoy yourself.* One of the most important decisions you will have to make in retirement is how much time you want to work. As someone who's used to 60- and 70-hour workweeks, the idea of working just four hours a day seems like nothing. I've noticed, however, that when I'm on vacation, the perfect amount of work each day is just two or three hours.

The good news is that you can run a retirement business/ enterprise by working only 5 to 15 hours a week—so long as you have two things:

- A very good second-in-command
- The determination to not allow your business to grow quickly . . . even if it wants to

Harry Paul, a former protégé and friend of mine, is a good example. After building a successful business with the help of a handful of talented people, he decided to semi-retire at the age of 57. He now works about three hours a day and enjoys a very nice six-figure supplemental income. "I don't really need the income," he told me, "but it doesn't hurt. And I still love the business. I come in about 9:30 in the morning and make some phone calls. Then, I putter around and ask questions until my people tell me to go home. I'm always home by lunchtime."

Another friend, Nathan Jacobs, works about three hours a day lending money to businesses and individuals who can't get conventional financing. He relies on his personal assistant of 20 years to get most of the work done. "She does everything," he told me. "I just come in and sign papers."

Nathan is a very wealthy guy. He could support his lifestyle very well on bond income, but he doesn't want to. "I enjoy the challenge of analyzing deals," he said, "and I feel good about lending money to good causes. If, at the end of the year, I end up making an extra half-million, I can't complain."

Recently, Nathan started another business—a boutique publishing business. "Some of my friends think I'm crazy to get started with another business at my age," he said, "but I enjoy the work . . . so why shouldn't I?"

About three years ago, another friend and colleague, Sam Briant, had an idea about starting a temporary agency specializing in computer workers. He invited me to go in on it with him, but I didn't have a spare moment to lend him and I didn't want to get involved financially with a start-up business I wasn't participating in. So he launched it with his cousin, someone he'd worked with before. His cousin turned out to be a superstar—and today, both cousins are earning six-figure incomes from profit distributions alone.

"At this point, the business is pretty much running itself," Sam told me, "but I'm going to keep on spending a few hours a week fooling around with it. Just for fun."

As I said before, doing what Harry and Sam and Nathan are doing will work only if you have good people working for you and you don't push to make the business grow faster than it wants to. Fast growth in business demands constant innovation. If you are pushing your business to grow as fast as it can, you can also expect to be dragged into the hassles that result from that growth.

But if you have very good people and you stimulate but don't overwhelm them, you will soon find that you can enjoy being involved in the business without having to spend more than a few hours a week working at it.

4. *A purpose that makes you feel good.* If you are smart, you will develop a side business now that is both emotionally fulfilling and financially rewarding. If you do that, you won't have to start over with some new enterprise when it comes time to retire.

My aforementioned friend Sam is a good example. His primary business, financial public relations, is his primary source

MY OWN PERFECT RETIREMENT SCHEDULE

6:00 A.M., wake up, shower, and so on

6:30 A.M., yoga or Pilates

7:00 A.M., write fiction

11:00 A.M., jiujitsu or weightlifting

12:00 noon, lunch meeting with someone

1:00 P.M., work on real estate, side businesses, and so on

4:00 P.M., walk or run along the beach

4:30 P.M., be with family

10:30 P.M., bedtime

This may seem like a somewhat busy day, but it's actually filled with all sorts of recreational activities. Four hours a day of writing fiction is about all a person can do effectively. And after exercising vigorously for an hour, I'll be ready to get to some business for a few hours.

What kind of business can I expect to accomplish in two or three hours a day? Not much, if my job is to actually grow or manage a business. But if I have good people doing that for me, that modest amount of time is plenty.

That's pretty much what I'm doing right now with two businesses I started several years ago. Each one is run by some very capable people. Neither one needs my day-to-day input. I meet with the top people once a month for about two hours. They come prepared with test results, marketing samples, financial summaries, and questions. I give them my best for the time we've allocated and then they go away and do what they think best. The next month, we do it again.

of income. But his side business—which he started with his cousin—inspires and excites him. When Sam is financially independent and ready to retire (which will come well before his 40th birthday), he'll be able to sell his main business but hang onto the side business that he loves. He'll be able to work on it whenever he likes and for as long as he likes. And he'll have a nice supplemental income from it that he won't even need.

I'm hoping to get Dorothy, a relative, into a side business selling pet advice and nutrition on the Internet. She loves pets and knows a great deal about them. The idea of actually earning a living from a pet business thrills her. It's certainly something she'd be happy to do without pay. And as a direct-marketing business with Internet potential, it can be run on a part-time basis from her home. In other words, it has all the prerequisites of a good retirement job. And since Dorothy is on the 7- to 15-year financial independence plan, she'll have adequate time to get this up and running.

What would you like to do in your retirement years? Write screenplays? Teach marketing? Rebuild automobiles? If you spend a little time thinking about it, you'll probably find that it has some sort of low-key, home-based business application to it. I have a friend, for example, who likes to spend his time teaching what he knows about wine to wine novices. In a recent conversation about his upcoming retirement, I told him that he might be able to make a nice supplemental income doing that. He was skeptical of my claim, but when we did a search on the Internet we found dozens and dozens of operating businesses that do exactly that.

"I guess I'm too late," he said when he realized how much commercial activity there already is in the wine education field.

"On the contrary," I told him. "When you are starting a new business—especially one that you are going to launch on a shoestring budget—you want to be sure that there is an active, ready market to sell to. That means plenty of other people doing more or less what you want to do.

"Study these businesses," I said. "They are your future colleagues. See what they are doing and find something you could do better. Find out how they sell their publications and programs. Learn everything you can. Create a little business plan and then begin your test marketing.

"You may not have a success with your first effort, but by controlling your expenses and keeping your promotions close to what is already out there, you will soon find a marketing model (a way to acquire new customers cost efficiently) that you can use as the basis of your new business."

You Can Get Closer to Your Retirement Dream . . .
Starting Right Now

If you fall for the Million-Dollar Lie and convince yourself that you can save yourself into a comfortable retirement, you will wake up one day feeling like you just can't stand to work another day—but when you look at your retirement account, you'll realize you will probably have to keep working for the rest of your life.

If you take my advice seriously, face the future realistically, develop wealth-building habits, get your income up there, and begin to develop equity, you will be able to retire in 7 to 15 years—and that will be early, believe me, compared to most of the rest of the retirement-age population.

But since even seven years may seem too long to wait, I suggest the following nine-point strategy for getting close to retirement much sooner.

1. *Start a side business as soon as possible.* If you select a subject area that you care about, you won't mind the work. In fact, the work will feel good and rewarding—like a hobby. It will relax you. It will amuse you. It will challenge you. And it may enrich you.

2. *Buy at least one rental property.* This will give you a feeling of security, because you'll own something substantial—something with a value that is easy to determine, something with a value that cannot be erased by an Internet malfunction, something that can't be stolen from you, lost, and so on. It may also turn you on to a very effective way to build your net worth on a leverage basis (using bank loans) that could, if you get even a reasonable amount of appreciation on your investments, make you wealthy—not counting any of the other wealth-building ideas I gave you in this book.

3. *Consider buying a second home in a tropical paradise.* This is not a good idea for everyone. But if you've always dreamed of owning a second home on the beach or in the mountains and you'd like to "live like a king" for a fraction of what it costs to live in the United States, a second home in Latin America, say, or the Caribbean might be a very rewarding way to go.

My family and I have a second home in Nicaragua. It's a three-bedroom, ocean-view bit of paradise that we built for $48 a square foot—about one-third of what it costs to build in the U.S. We have a full-time housekeeper and maintenance man, who keep everything up and running, spotless, and safe. We eat fresh fish and lobster pulled from the ocean for pennies a day. We swim in our own pool, play tennis on one of the community's courts, surf and swim at one of four beaches, ride horses, hike, and so on. And it costs us less than $1,500 a month to maintain it all, including fees, salaries, food, and taxes!

The point is, you don't have to spend a fortune to live a life of luxury. Two-bedroom *casitas* in this same development were originally priced at $69,000. If you are interested in affordable, wonderful retirement properties, see International Living at internationalliving.com.

An inexpensive second home can double the fun of retiring. And it can also serve to put you into retirement much earlier than you could do it in the States—if you choose, as you might one day, to make your second home your first.

4. *Relocate to a retirement location early.* If you are dreaming of retiring to the Sun Belt or the mountains but feel that you have to wait till you are 65 to do so, think again. Twenty years ago, on a vacation to Key West, I went on a few job interviews and discovered, quite to my surprise, that I could live in sunny South Florida and still make good money. As it turned out, I acquired equity in the business that hired me—and then the money got better and better.

Because of the way the world works today, there are very few businesses that can't be transported to more favorable climates. Your business might be able to make the move. If not, you may be able to convert yourself into a freelance consultant, make more money than you do now (see Chapter 5), and relocate your headquarters to your dream location.

Living in a retirement destination doesn't mean you are retired. But being able to partake of the activities you enjoy in your spare time will put you in that retirement mood now and then—and that's worth a great deal.

5. *Don't work when you are not working.* This is something you can do right away. Tonight.

   When you leave the office, leave your thoughts about business there, too. Don't spend your evenings—as I did for so many years—pretending to be listening to your family while work worries crowd your head. Force yourself into the here and now of your personal life, even if it feels artificial.

   When people ask you how your day went, be very careful what you say. "Great . . . and how was your day?" is probably the best answer. (The idea is to divert attention away from yourself and your work.) But if you must talk about your day, try to express yourself in terms of short anecdotes—little dramas that are fun to listen to. Your purpose in talking about work is not to unload your emotional burdens by complaining, but to entertain someone you care about with enjoyable stories.

   You'll be able to make this transformation more easily if you end each day by reviewing your task list and planning the next day's tasks before you leave the office. By setting up your next day's agenda and then forgetting about it, you'll activate your subconscious mind to sort out work problems, even while you are keeping the stress away by not actively focusing on them.

   Once made, this change will make you a more entertaining person, lighten up your evenings, and make your weekends feel a little like retirement.

6. *Care about what you do.* You can make your work feel a lot more like a retirement passion or hobby by simply caring more about what you do. That means finding a good, useful purpose in it.

   Forget—for the moment, at least—your own ambitions. Forget—for the moment—about how much extra income you want. Focus, instead, on how you can improve the work lives of everyone around you—your boss, your employees, your colleagues, and your competitors. Not by helping them with their personal problems but by helping them make their work experience better.

   As I suggested earlier, ultimately the purpose of a business should be about providing value to the customer. If you can improve the value your business provides by helping everyone around you do a better job for your customers, the value your business gets back from your customers (in terms of loyalty and long-term profits) will increase radically—and some of that value will be yours.

7. *Interrupt your schedule with regular minivacations.* You can get more fun and energy in your working life by breaking up the year with minivacations. You don't need much time to get away. A three-day weekend is more than enough. The trick, again, is to find something to do that means something to you.

Forget the "I want to just vegetate" vacations. They don't energize. They deplete. Instead, incorporate something that excites you into your little getaways. If, for example, you want to spend your retirement years buying and selling antiques, plan your minivacation around antiquing. Plan your itinerary so that you can have plenty of fun, make contacts for the future, and learn something useful every day. Leave plenty of time to enjoy meals and relax, but make the trip a learning, growing adventure. In addition to rejuvenating you, such vacations will accelerate your progress toward wealth.

8. *Live rich now.* As I explained in Chapter 3, you don't need to be a billionaire to live like one. Most of the luxuries that wealth affords are within reach of anyone who makes a decent living. Slipping your feet into a soft pair of cashmere socks, for example, is a luxury that no one—not even a billionaire—can improve on by spending more than $15. The same—as I said—is true of the mattress you spend seven hours a day on. Spend an extra few hundred dollars to buy the best, and you'll have comfort at night that even Warren Buffett can't top. Get rid of 80 percent of your wardrobe—all the stuff you bought on impulse and secretly despise. Wear fewer things—but make sure everything you wear makes you feel rich and comfortable. Get over the idea that brand names convey value.

Think like a self-confident billionaire and buy only good-quality products that make you feel good. With almost everything, you'll be much richer if you buy a select few items of the very best quality—but without the designer labels. Never buy impulsively. Understand what you are buying. Remember that most purchases make you poorer, not richer . . . so make every purchase count.

9. *Be proud of yourself.* You don't have to wait till you are rich and retired to be proud of what you have accomplished on your way to financial independence. Wealth, as I said at the beginning of this book, is a very relative thing. The moment you have more than you owe, you are becoming wealthy—and so long as you earn more than you spend, you are building more wealth.

These are your first goals: Earn more than you spend and have more than you owe. When you have achieved those goals, you will have earned the right to feel proud. Because you will have taken the most important step toward turning yourself into an automatic wealth builder.

INDEX